I0827210

Contemporary Issues in South African Military Psychology

Published by African Sun Media under the SUN PReSS imprint

This publication was subjected to an independent double-blind peer evaluation by the publisher.

First edition 2020

ISBN 978-1-928480-62-4
ISBN 978-1-928480-63-1 (e-book)
https://doi.org/10.18820/9781928480631

Set in Charter Regular 10/12

Cover design, typesetting and production by African Sun Media

SUN PReSS is an imprint of African Sun Media. Scholarly, professional and reference works are published under this imprint in print and electronic formats.

This publication can be ordered from:
orders@africansunmedia.co.za
Takealot: bit.ly/2monsfl
Google Books: bit.ly/2k1Uilm
africansunmedia.store.it.si *(e-books)*
Amazon Kindle: amzn.to/2ktL.pkL

Visit www.africansunmedia.co.za for more information.

CONTEMPORARY ISSUES IN SOUTH AFRICAN MILITARY PSYCHOLOGY

EDITED BY

N.M. Dodd

P.C. Bester

&

J. van der Merwe

Dedication and Acknowledgements

This book was made possible by the generous support of Stellenbosch University's Faculty of Military Science and sub-committee A.

Special thanks also to the publisher, reviewers, and copy editor for their invaluable feedback.

For Daniella and the serving members of the SANDF.

Table of Contents

About the Edtiors

Nicole Dodd is an extraordinary Associate Professor in the department of Industrial Psychology (Military) at Stellenbosch University. She is a psychometrist in private practice specialising in psycho-educational assessment. Her research spans human, organisational, and national development.

Petrus C. Bester is an industrial psychologist working at the South African Military Health Service as the Senior Staff Officer Psychology Tertiary Military Health Formation. He obtained a D Phil Leadership in Performance and Change from the University of Johannesburg. His research interests include leadership, integrity, performance enhancement, test construction and national security. He is currently attached to the Department of Industrial Psychology (Military) in the Faculty of Military Science at the University of Stellenbosch.

Justin van der Merwe is a research fellow in the Centre for Military Studies in the Faculty of Military Science, University of Stellenbosch. He holds a DPhil in Human Geography from Oxford University. His research centres on the nexus between government, business and the media.

Author details

Major Danille Elize Arendse is a Research Psychologist at the Military Psychology Institute in the South African Military Health Services. She completed her PhD in Psychology at the University of Pretoria in 2018 and is currently a Research Associate in the Department of Psychology at the University of Pretoria. Her research interests include psychometric assessments, cognitive psychology, psycholinguistics, military, wellbeing, gender and sexuality and decolonial research.

Kyle Bester is a psychology lecturer and research psychologist at the University of South Africa (Unisa) and is currently completing his studies at the Military Academy (Stellenbosch University). His doctoral topic titled "Exploring the perceptions and views of cybersecurity among South African military officers". His research interests are student retention, cyber-awareness and open distance learning.

Yolika Kleynhans is an MCom candidate in Industrial Psychology at the University of Stellenbosch. She is pursuing her internship at the Military Psychology Institute. Her research interests include personality, work behaviour and career psychology.

Mandisa Yasmin Mabuza holds an Honours degree in Industrial and Organisational Psychology and a Postgraduate Diploma in Public Management. She is currently serving the SANDF as a commander who strives to bring change to the DoD. Her main inspiration for her research includes bringing change by focusing on military service ethics and its link to social responsibility disclosure.

Tumelo Clement Mahlelehlele is an operational officer at Joint Operational Headquarters in the SANDF. He holds a BMil (Hons) in Industrial Psychology from the University of Stellenbosch. His current research focuses on virtuous leadership, new war practices, and military performance.

Lieutenant Ngoako Japhta Mashatola is an MCom Industrial psychology graduate (Stellenbosch University) He is pursuing his internship at the Military Psychological Institute at Pretoria. His research interest is in Organisational Development and applied positive psychology which includes: posttraumatic growth, work-study-family interface, student academic success, resilience, general work stress, psychometrics, and quantitative psychology.

Lindiwe Masole holds a Master's degree in Industrial Psychology from Stellenbosch University. She currently works as a Lecturer at the Faculty of Military Science, Military Academy. Her research interests include Positive Psychology and Military Psychology.

Edward Mogaladi was an officer in the SANDF. He held a BMil Hons in Industrial Psychology (Military). He passed away in December 2016. In memorium.

Wim Myburgh holds a DPhil (Psychology, NMU). He is an independent assessment practitioner in private practice and has been associated with SUN as Coordinator of the BPsych Eq. Programme for psychometrists since 2010. His research interests include: career failure, career transitions and involuntary job loss.

Zinhle Londiwe Nzimande holds a BMil (Hons) and is an MCom (Industrial Psychology) candidate at the University of Stellenbosch. She is also currently a military officer in the SA Army.

Jan-Louis Werner holds a masters degree in Industrial Psychology from the University of South Africa and is currently a PhD candidate at the University of Johannesburg. He currently works as a Rewards Consultant at EY New Zealand. His research interests include learning agility, psychometric testing, employee development, and organisational culture.

Charles van Wijk holds a masters degree in clinical psychology from Stellenbosch University. He works as a clinician at the Institute for Maritime Medicine, and his current interests include occupational mental health surveillance.

Gerhard van Zyl is a senior lecturer in the School of Human and Organisational Development in the Faculty of Military Science, University of Stellenbosch.

List of Figures and Tables

Figures

Tables

List of Acronyms and Abbreviations

21 SAI BN	21st South African Infantry Battalion
AC	Affective commitment
APA	American Psychological Association
APIL-B	Ability, processing, information and learning battery
BQMA	Biographical questionnaire for the Military Academy
CAR	Central African Republic
DoD	Department of Defence
DRS	Dispositional resilience scale
ECI	Emotional competence inventory
EFA	Exploratory factor analysis
EI	Emotional intelligence
FFM	Five-factor model
FMS	Faculty of Military Science
FSI	Family-study interaction
HCP	Health care practitioner
HR	Human Resources
HRM	Human Resources Management
ICE	Isolated, confined and/or extreme environments
ITE	Interactive telematic education
J Ops HQ	Joint Operational Headquarters
JS	Job satisfaction
JSS	Job Satisfaction Scale
KMO	Kaiser-Meyer-Olkin test
MDT	Multidisciplinary team
MIT	Multi-integrated team
MT	Mental toughness
MTQ	Mental Toughness Questionnaire

PAF	Principal axis factoring
PCA	Principal component analysis
PCB	Psychological contract breach
PCI	Psychological contract inventory
PCV	Psychological contract violation
PD	Psychological debriefing
PERMA	Positive emotion, engagement, relationships, meaning and accomplishment
POB	Positive organisational behaviour
POS	Perceived organisational support
PSO	Peace support operation
PTG	Posttraumatic growth
PTSD	Post-traumatic stress disorder
SA	South Africa
SAAF	South African Airforce
SAMA	South African Military Academy
SAMHS	South African Military Health Service
SANDF	South African National Defence Force
SAQ	Self-assessment questionnaire
SPSS	Statistical Package for the Social Sciences
SSA	Sub-Saharan Africa
TI	Turnover intentions
UWES	Utrecht Work Engagement Scale
WE	Work engagement
WSFC	Work-study-family conflict
WSFF	Work-study-family facilitation
WSFI	Work-study-family interface
WSI	Work-study interaction

1

Military Psychology and the SANDF in a Changing World

Nicole Dodd
Petrus Bester
Justin van der Merwe

Every military initiative or activity involves people, and the nature of soldiering in Africa in the 21st century involves deploying personnel in conventional and unconventional activities, generally under conditions of heightened stress. For these reasons, "the field of psychology has never been more important to the military than it is today" (Van Heerden, 2016a, p.10). It is people who unlock the potential of technology and who must possess wide-ranging competencies to respond to the multiple threats with which the modern military contends. As much as technology may be replacing people, human resources and their mental health remain a source of competitive advantage in battle. Military psychology is thus a crucial support function for the South African National Defence Force (SANDF), as well as an intrinsic factor in the security of South Africans. The focus of this book is to explore the critical issues facing the South African military in terms of psychology and the implications of current psychological research for the military.

THE LOCAL AND GLOBAL CONTEXT OF THE SANDF

The end of apartheid and the Cold War concluded a period of intense regional conflict for southern Africa. It also signalled the end of the South African Defence Force, which re-emerged as the South African National Defence Force. The media sometimes (unfairly) portrays the SANDF as an indolent, somewhat unnecessary expense in the 21st century. This perception could not be further from the truth.

The SANDF's mandate is to "defend and protect the Republic, its territorial integrity and its people" (Constitution of the Republic of South Africa, Act 108 of 1996). The 2015 *South African Defence Review* highlighted that, given the changing global security environment, the SANDF would be expected to participate in wide-ranging operations (conventional and unconventional). These might include disaster relief, support to government departments, counter-terrorism and counterinsurgency, and responding to safety and security threats at many levels (Van Heerden, 2016a, p.10). Recently, the SANDF has had to embark on several domestic operations ranging from improving food and water security to maintaining law and order during elections. Climate change is also expected to present new disasters and creates new scenarios where the SANDF will be expected to defend and protect the Republic and its people.

In terms of the African community at large, South Africa will also be relied upon to provide humanitarian relief to most of its neighbours for the foreseeable future. Further, South Africa's borders will need to be carefully patrolled, given the economic and political realities facing the region.

Although much of the armed conflict has subsided in the Southern African region, it remains a relatively permanent feature on the continent. Because of South Africa's membership in the African Union and United Nations, the SANDF actively participates in joint, combined, national and multinational operations in Africa. In these operations, the SANDF contributes to security through peacekeeping, humanitarian, and disaster-relief activities. Because of the broader African and global security context, the role of the SANDF in the 21st century cannot be precisely delimited, and the organisation must do more with ever-diminishing resources. This reality requires an agile and responsive force capable of redefining 'soldiering' as and when new challenges arise. This places primary responsibility on the SANDF to ensure that it optimises its workforce. In practical terms, it must optimise the recruitment, development, deployment, and maintenance of its human resources.

DEFINING MILITARY PSYCHOLOGY

Military psychology is a behavioural science that combines theory and practical application. In South Africa, military psychology, as applied through the SANDF, should ideally merge theory and practice in a way that also incorporates and formalises indigenous knowledge systems (Van Heerden, 2016a, p.10). Drawing from Bester (2016, p.1), we define military psychology as the use of psychological research methods, principles and practices to address challenges and improve capabilities in the military. Specifically, military psychology applies scientifically proven techniques to enhance the effectiveness of military organisations with an emphasis on mentally equipping and developing people. The aim is to boost mission effectiveness by increasing soldier capability, combat readiness, operational effectiveness and force preservation (Bester, 2016, p.1). In many ways, military psychology could be understood as a hybrid of industrial–organisational psychology and clinical psychology, where we are concerned with the individual as instrumental to organisational effectiveness but, at the same time, still being significant in his or her own right. Soldiers carry a high personal cost for their choice of occupation. Military psychology concerns itself with 'psychological casualties' (as opposed to physical casualties), soldiers who cease to function effectively in an operational context because of their debilitated mental state. Given enough exposure to combat, all soldiers will eventually collapse. In many ways, military psychology aims to defer this state for as long as possible.

The practice of military psychology does not operate in isolation, as holistic interventions are favoured. The military employs multi-professional teams who treat both physical and mental problems. They prepare soldiers physically, mentally and spiritually for deployment, and provide psychological support during and after deployment.

Military psychologists perform many of the same functions performed by civilian organisational psychologists and human resources practitioners, such as attraction, selection, development, motivation, utilisation, release and disciplining. Over and above these functions, they perform others that are specific to the military context (Bester, 2016):

- *Force preparation*: military psychologists provide support during pre-deployment and foster psychological readiness.
- *Force maintenance*: military psychologists aim to reduce attrition by preventative and promotional activities, and by providing support to those in distress. These activities prevent malingering, mental breakdown, desertion, self-harm and maladaptive coping.
- *Force enhancement*: military psychologists must optimise the performance of individuals, teams and units over time.
- *Force transition*: during the post-deployment period, military psychologists help soldiers to reintegrate and to successfully negotiate adjustment challenges such as chronic fatigue and delayed stress.

It is hard to outline one set of standardised military psychology-related practices in the SANDF. As military psychologists operate in large, geographically dispersed units, and this creates the risk of fragmentation and siloed activities with little coordination and synergy. The barriers created by security clearances, confidentiality, and the communication barriers created by rank structures and arms of service further aggravate these issues. In effect, different approaches are used for the same activities depending on whether they are undertaken by human resources or by the various psychological services (e.g. the Military Psychological Institute and the Institute for Maritime Medicine). We hope that shared, peer-reviewed research output, such as some of the material collected in this book, will provide an opportunity for best practices to be disseminated across the units and arms of service, ultimately leading to a comprehensive 'scope of practice' for military psychologists in South Africa.

TOWARDS A SCOPE OF PRACTICE

The Directorate of Psychology of the South African Military Health Service' (SAMHS) represents the ambit of military psychological service (Bester, 2020). The Directorate's vision is "A psychologically healthy and effective military organisation", achieved through the following mission:

> To support the SANDF by providing a quality psychological service for the full range of military deployments and to sustain and promote the health and mental functioning of the organisation, members of the armed forces, and others eligible for care by the SAMHS (Burgess, 2018, p.8).

In achieving the vision, military psychologists undertake activities within the two relatively broad streams of industrial–organisational psychology, and clinical and counselling psychology, both of which are supported by research psychology.

Recruitment and selection and training and development all fall firmly within industrial-organisational psychology (specifically human resources management/ personnel psychology). The military psychologist might also concern him/herself with climate and morale, as well as with motivation. Military psychologists are also involved in organisational development and design. At the group level, they work on improving cohesion within teams and units, while on an individual level, they conduct leadership assessment and development. Military psychologists also focus on human factors and ergonomics, going as far as providing expert assistance during accident investigations.

Besides focusing on organisational effectiveness, military psychologists may offer clinical services, for example, screening candidates for mental fitness for deployment or security clearance. To a limited extent, military psychologists implement performance enhancement at specialist units, such as the special operations forces. They conduct psycho-education and promote mission and combat readiness. Although their work aims to improve the resilience of members, but also extends to working with members' families before deployment. Therapeutic services may involve debriefing, suicide prevention and grief counselling. Military psychologists are, therefore, consultants, clinicians, researchers and trainers.

Research underpins and informs all these activities. In support of the SANDF, the Behavioural Sciences capability of the Council for Scientific and Industrial Research (CSIR), conducts applied military psychological research to predict and understand both individual attributes and other factors determining success in the military, (Van Heerden, 2016a). Van Heerden (2016a, p.14) notes that the CSIR is involved in research that: develops and evaluates South African assessments; enhances selection, training, and development (including leadership and life skills development); supports career development; boosts retention; assists in psychological profiling; promotes positive psychology and resilience; and provides insights into cyber warfare.

Although the SANDF conducts research internally, publications are primarily limited to outputs from a few researchers (Van Dyk and Van Heerden being among the most notable and prolific). The topics are also limited and do not embrace the full scope of practice of the South African military psychologist as described in the preceding pages. The CSIR, South African Military Academy (SAMA), Institute for Maritime Medicine (IMM) and Military Psychological Institute (MPI) (the last two, under the auspices of the Directorate Psychology) have all produced research in the past. A look at recent studies (2013 to date) suggests that the research has focused more on deployment and organisational psychology in the military and less on the clinical aspects of military psychology. For instance, Masole and Van Dyk (2016) and Ditsela (2016), focused on work readiness and career success, while

Shinga (2016) and Kalamdien (2016) focused on combat readiness and deployment. Bester (2016) and Bruwer (2016) explored military psychology in peacekeeping and conventional operations.

Military psychologists make extensive use of psychological assessments and must adapt these to the South African demographics and the unique research 'population' comprehended in this context. There is, therefore, a great need for strengthening research in this area; recent publications include Mlangeni and Van Dyk (2017), who examined the psychometric properties of measures of work engagement and psychological wellbeing in the South African security environment; and De Beer and Van Heerden (2016), who developed a new test of hardiness.

In recent research in the subfield of organisational development, Van't Wout and Van Dyk (2015) focus on morale; Luzipo and Van Dyk (2018), explore the interaction of organisational climate and job satisfaction, including hardiness and self-efficacy; similarly, Makhathini and Van Dyk (2018) explore organisational climate and job satisfaction, but in conjunction with leadership style and organisational commitment. Van Dyk (2016a), Grundlingh (2016), Bester and Du Plessis (2014), and Mphofu and Van Dyk (2016) have all covered aspects of military leadership in the South African context including an overview of the military leadership training landscape in relation to extreme situations by Bester and O'Neil (2017). Kalamdien and Lawrence (2017) addressed one of the darker aspects of military leadership in an innovative take on bullying and provided a typology of the military bully. Along the same lines, Bester and Van't Wout (2016), and Bester and Du Plessis (2015) explored two other issues in the field of military leadership, namely negative leadership and leadership challenges.

The SANDF's selection process deserves significant academic attention. The CSIR's Behavioural Sciences capability, led by Adelai van Heerden has devoted considerable attention to the screening, selection, and development of Special Forces operators. Van Heerden and her team have examined motivation and coping resources (De Beer & Van Heerden, 2014); reasons for voluntary withdrawal from selection (Van Heerden, 2016b); psychological coping, learning potential and career preferences (De Beer & Van Heerden, 2017); and attributes and skills for career success (Rawoot, Van Heerden & Parker, 2017), to mention a few examples of their output. Van Wyk and Du Toit (2018) further contribute to this by outlining the use of behaviour-based assessments in the selection of Special Forces operators.

As mentioned, although little has been written about the more clinical aspects of military psychology in South Africa, issues relating to trauma and post-traumatic stress disorder in the military have been highlighted in recent research (Van Dyk, 2016b, 2018; Loubser, 2016a, 2016b; and Dhladhla & Van Dyk, 2016), and De Beer and Van Heerden (2018) explore coping mechanisms in the Special Forces population. Van Dyk's edited volume (2016) also made some attempts to decolonise military psychology by affording attention to Ubuntu and traditional healing's role in treatment (Lesolang, 2016; Matoane, 2016), with Van Heerden (2017) also incorporating Ubuntu's role in military performance motivation.

Earlier researchers (Martin, Van Wijk, Hans-Arendse & Makhaba, 2013) explored African bereavement rituals in the South African Navy. This book follows on from this research but also seeks to examine potentially under-researched areas.

In Chapter 2, Ngoako Mashatola, Nicole Dodd and Gerhard van Zyl focus on one such under-researched area, the demographic determinants of what they call the work-study-family interface (WSFI) among first-generation university students enrolled at the South African Military Academy (SAMA). Their study analyses these influences using scarcity and role expansion theories. They added the study domain with work and family roles. They found that positive participation in roles such as student and family member can facilitate the work role positively and vice versa.

In Chapter 3, Nicole Dodd, Wim Myburgh, Jan Louis Werner and Ngoako Mashatola go on to identify the psychological determinants of military student success. They go beyond cognitive ability, which is a popular predictor of academic achievement to include personality and resilience. Their research shows that students who are younger and have higher commitment are more likely to pass at the Military Academy. The best predictors for academic success were conscientiousness, commitment and age, and the other predictors were memory and understanding, and extraversion. What is interesting is that they found that older students tended to require more academic support than younger ones, highlighting the importance of academic support at an institution such as the Academy.

In Chapter 4, Danille Arendse proposes a psychosocial wellbeing model for prospective Military Academy students in South Africa. She coined the term "intermittent social stressors" which describes some of the personal and social stressors that are recurring in nature, such as marital status, having children, financial responsibilities, financial stress, cultural responsibilities and a lack of friends. Although based on a modest model, built on psychological wellbeing, psychological capital and intermittent stressors, her most significant finding is that when military students effectively manage intermittent social stressors, their psychological wellbeing and psychological capital are positively affected, and this, in turn, enhances their psychosocial wellbeing. Arendse also highlights the importance of student support at an institution such as SAMA.

Mandisa Mabuza and Nicole Dodd focus on securing and retaining human resources when they investigated the turnover intentions of SAMA, which offers both residential and distance education programmes to students who are officers and candidate officers. They discuss how perceived psychological contract breach, affective organisational commitment and job satisfaction all influence employee turnover intentions. They concluded that soldiers who want to leave the SANDF demonstrate low levels of job satisfaction and limited affective organisational commitment, and they have perceptions of a high level of psychological contract breach.

The issue of the psychological contract is then further explored in Chapter 6 by Zinhle Nzimande, Nicole Dodd and Lindiwe Masole who also focus on SAMA. They look at how perceived organisational support and psychological contract fulfilment affect organisational commitment to the SANDF. They found that employees who perceive their organisation as more supportive reported higher levels of organisational commitment. Their findings furthermore suggest that when employers fulfil their employees' psychological contracts, they give them the confidence to invest their time and effort in reaching organisational goals and objectives in return for job security and career development. The study also found that some people joined the military because they have strong emotional ties with the military, but contrary to expectations, employees actively seek support in the form of empowerment and career mobility.

In Chapter 7, Yolika Kleynhans underscores the importance of evaluating the psychometric properties of test instruments in the military. Her study, undertaken in the military education environment, investigates the validity of the NEO Personality Inventory's six subscales of conscientiousness (competence, order, dutifulness, achievement striving, self-discipline, and deliberation), finding that it can be used when selecting SAMA students.

The importance of studies investigating the psychometric properties of measurement instruments is further emphasised in Chapter 8 by Danille Arendse, Petrus Bester and Charles van Wijk who explored two instruments that measure respectively two subscales of the overarching construct of resilience/hardiness (DRS-15) and mental toughness (MTQ-18). They applied exploratory factor analysis to each of the instruments to compare results across other studies done internationally and in developing countries. Their findings indicate that the language used in the DRS-15 might not be clear to all users and that different language groups might interpret the items differently, which confirms that South Africa, with its 11 official languages, presents challenges to test developers. The utility of the MTQ-18 seems at present to be a bit more promising than that of the DRS-15 but requires further research to validate it for a South African population. This affirms the notion that practitioners should be cautious when applying new instruments before proper research has been completed.

In Chapter 9 Tumelo Mahlelehlele, Nicole Dodd and Lindiwe Masole move into the military operational domain in investigating the nature of the relationship between emotional intelligence, job satisfaction, and work engagement, as observed at the Joint Operations Headquarters (J Ops HQ). In their study, they found that job satisfaction proved to be a better predictor of work engagement of military personnel than emotional intelligence. Their findings support the notion that job satisfaction is an antecedent of work engagement, and they made the remarkable discovery that males at the J Ops HQ who are aged between 18 and 25, or 42 and 49, and who have

Grade 12 or a higher educational level, are more likely to be engaged in their work than other categories of employees. Less-educated individuals were also less engaged than their educated counterparts.

In Chapter 10, Kyle Bester and Edward Mogaladi also focus on work engagement and its impact on employees' intentions to terminate their contract of employment at an Infantry Battalion. From the perspective that the retention of human capital is a strategic issue and that employees are the most valuable asset in any organisation, they look at how employees perceive supervisory support and how it may have an impact on their work effort and morale. They found that an employee's intention to leave the SANDF is likely to depend on the engagement dimensions of vigour (energy level of mental resilience through continuous involvement and despite facing difficulties at work), and absorption (being fully engaged in their work to the degree of finding it difficult to disengage).

In Chapter 11, Ngoako Mashatola and Petrus Bester identified the absence of a positive trauma-survivor-oriented framework in the SANDF. They address the gap by suggesting a conceptual SANDF post-traumatic growth model. Post-traumatic growth (PTG) is a lifelong process extending across a soldier's career from pre-employment selection to retirement, including all the phases of deployment. The model focuses on a system of positive development dealing with primary prevention of post-traumatic stress disorder (PTSD), an interventional system focusing on secondary prevention, and a system of care focusing on tertiary prevention. The growth part of the model deals with fostering and facilitating growth and ultimately affecting positive change in an individual.

Lastly, in Chapter 12, Nicole Dodd, Justin van der Merwe and Petrus Bester conclude the investigations and insights of this book by reviewing some of the critical issues and implications facing military psychology in South Africa. They also put forward some suggestions for future contextual research in the field of military psychology.

A NOTE ON THE SOUTH AFRICAN MILITARY ACADEMY

The largest proportion of research findings reported in this book are drawn from the student population of the South African Military Academy (SAMA, or the Academy), which houses the Faculty of Military Science of Stellenbosch University. Situated at Saldanha in the Western Cape province, SAMA offers military-related education at undergraduate and postgraduate levels to employees of the South African National Defence Force (SANDF), via programmes accredited by Stellenbosch University. Although Stellenbosch University offers the programmes, the Academy operates as a military educational space where officers are provided with both university education and professional military development (Pretorius, 2010). All four arms of service of the SANDF are represented at SAMA: the South African Military Health Service (SAMHS), the South African Air Force (SAAF), the South African Navy (SA Navy) and the South African Army (SA Army). The Academy caters for the higher education needs of both residential and non-residential students (the latter also being referred to as Interactive Telematics Education (ITE) students). However, most SAMA students are full-time boarders during each academic semester and are expected to participate in both academic and military activities during this time. Offering both undergraduate and postgraduate military qualifications, the Academy is the SANDF's flagship of higher education.

CONTEXTUALISING MILITARY PSYCHOLOGY

The underlying narrative emerging from this group of studies is that military psychology is a 'lens' through which to study contemporary issues in the SANDF. These studies commence at SAMA, where future SANDF leaders enter the military. Insight into factors that contribute to academic success and employee retention in their early careers is essential. From there, the focus shifts from the student soldier to the working soldier, who needs to be resilient enough to deploy; needs to remain engaged in his or her work; and needs to build positively on the negative impact of trauma. Although the scope of this book does not allow us to cover every theme in the field of military psychology, we have aimed to provide practical information for practitioners in this field. Whereas the generalisation of the findings of most of the current research is limited to target populations, such as SAMA students or J Ops HQ personnel, it is our overriding intention to offer a stimulus for research efforts that address the needs of the broader military community as well.

It is worth noting that everything discussed in the following chapters links with what the SAMHS's Deputy Surgeon General postulates as the future primary purpose of what he refers to as the 'Military Mental Health Psychological Services' and that is: "...mental and cognitive superiority over our opponents..." (Ndhlovu, 2019, p.19).

REFERENCES

Bester, P. & Du Plessis, A. 2014. Adaptable leaders for the South African Army. In: Lindsay, D. & Woycheshin, D. (eds), *Adaptive leadership in the military context: International perspectives*, pp.127-156. Kingston ON: Canadian Defence Academy Press.

Bester, P. & Du Plessis, A. 2015. When military leaders differ from their political leaders: Overcoming leadership challenges. In: Lindsay, D. & Woycheshin, D. (eds), *Overcoming leadership challenges: International perspectives*, pp.203-226. Kingston ON: Canadian Defence Academy Press.

Bester, P. & Van't Wout, C. 2016. Dealing with military leadership incompetence in the South African National Defence Force. In: Watola, D. & Woycheshin, D. (eds), *Negative leadership: International perspectives*, pp.203-226. Kingston ON: Canadian Defence Academy Press.

Bester, P. 2016. Military psychology for conventional operations in Africa. In: Van Dyk, G.A.J. (ed.), *Military psychology for Africa*, pp.1-37. Stellenbosch: African Sun Media.

Bester, P.C. & O'Neil, J.W. 2017. The military leadership training landscape of the South African National Defence Force as related to extreme situations. In: Holenweger, M.O.; Jager, M.K. & Kernic, F. (eds), *Leadership in extreme situations*. Cham: Springer.

Bester, P.C. 2020. Military psychology and the fourth industrial revolution: Implications for the South African National Defence Force's Directorate Psychology. In: Kumar, U. (ed.), *The Routledge international handbook of military psychology and mental health*, pp.75-88. New York, NY: Routledge.

Bruwer, N. 2016. Military Psychology and peacekeeping operations. In: Van Dyk, G.A.J. (ed.), *Military psychology for Africa*, pp.43-66. Stellenbosch: African Sun Media.

Burgess, W.B.H. 2018. Draft D[irectorate] Psych[ology] statement of intent 2019-2024. 16 July. Unpublished internal document. Directorate Psychology, South African Military Health Services.

De Beer, M. & Van Heerden, A. 2014. Exploring the role of motivational and coping resources in a Special Forces selection process. *South African Journal of Industrial Psychology*, 40(1):1-13. https://doi.org/10.4102/sajip.v40i1.1165

De Beer, M. & Van Heerden, A. 2016. First steps in the development of a resilience measure. Paper presented at the 58th International Military Testing Association (IMTA) Conference, 07-11 November 2016, New Delhi, India. Available at http://bit.ly/39yXBVD

De Beer, M. & Van Heerden, A. 2017. The psychological coping, learning potential and career preferences profiles of operational force military candidates. *Journal of Psychology in Africa*, 27(1):33-40.

De Beer, M. & Van Heerden, A. 2018. An exploration of coping with stress in an operational forces military context. In: Pešić, A. & Marković, D. (eds), *Stress in military profession: Thematic collection of articles*, pp.15-48. Belgrade: Media Center Odbrana.

Dhladhla, T. & Van Dyk, G. 2016. PTSD management in military forces in Africa. In: Van Dyk, G.A.J. (ed.), *Military psychology for Africa*, pp.197-214. Stellenbosch: African Sun Media.

Ditsela, N.J. 2016. Factors involved in subjective career success of soldiers in Africa. In: Van Dyk, G.A.J. (ed.), *Military psychology for Africa*, pp.447-472. Stellenbosch: African Sun Media.

Grundlingh, A. 2016. New military leaders for new wars in Africa. In: Van Dyk, G.A.J. (ed.), *Military psychology for Africa*, pp.323-347. Stellenbosch: African Sun Media.

Kalamdien, D.J. 2016. A psychological model to support military families during deployment. In: Van Dyk, G.A.J. (ed.), *Military psychology for Africa*, pp.289-310. Stellenbosch: African Sun Media.

Kalamdien, D.J. & Lawrence, A. 2017. A proposed typology of the military bully. *Scientia Militaria: South African Journal of Military Studies*, 45(1):122-144.

Lesolang, N. 2016. Traditional healing and mental health of military forces. In: Van Dyk, G.A.J. (ed.), *Military psychology for Africa*, pp.237-260. Stellenbosch: African Sun Media.

Loubser, H. 2016a. Trauma management: The theory of the effect of trauma on the brain and body. In: Van Dyk, G.A.J. (ed.), *Military psychology for Africa*, pp.149-168. Stellenbosch: African Sun Media.

Loubser, H. 2016b. Trauma Management: Body psychotherapies for trauma. In: Van Dyk, G.A.J. (ed.), *Military psychology for Africa*, pp.169-196. Stellenbosch: African Sun Media.

Luzipo, P. & Van Dyk, G.A.J. 2018. Organisation climate mediation of the relationship between hardiness, self-efficacy, and job satisfaction among military followers. *Journal of Psychology in Africa*, 28(3):192-195. https://doi.org/10.1080/14330237.2018.1475461

Makhathini, T.N. & Van Dyk, G.A.J. 2018. Organisational climate, job satisfaction, and leadership style influences on organisational commitment among South African soldiers. *Journal of Psychology in Africa*, 28(1):21-25. https://doi.org/10.1080/14330237.2018.1438834

Martin, J., Van Wijk, C., Hans-Arendse, C. & Makhaba, L. 2013. "Missing in action": The significance of bodies in African bereavement rituals. *Psychology in Society*, 44:42-63.

Masole, L. & Van Dyk, G. 2016. Military work readiness: A theoretical framework In: Van Dyk, G.A.J. (ed.), *Military psychology for Africa*, pp.425-446. Stellenbosch: African Sun Media.

Matoane, M. 2016. HIV/AIDS and Military Personnel with Ubuntu-Oriented Therapy as a Healing Option. In: Van Dyk, G.A.J. (ed.), *Military psychology for Africa*, pp.215-236. Stellenbosch: African Sun Media.

Mlangeni, N. & Van Dyk, G. 2017. Reliability of measures of work engagement and psychological wellbeing among South African state security forces. *Journal of Psychology in Africa*, 27(4):330-333.

Mphofu, R.A. & Van Dyk, G. 2016. Military leadership: Process approach for Africa. In: Van Dyk, G.A.J. (ed.), *Military psychology for Africa*, pp.349-378. Stellenbosch: African Sun Media.

Ndhlovu, N. 2019. Discussion paper on enabling the South African Military Health Service to deliver an affordable and best-quality military healthcare service, 07 January, Pretoria.

Rawoot, I., Van Heerden, A. & Parker, L. 2017. Operational Forces soldiers' perceptions of attributes and skills for career success. *South African Journal of Industrial Psychology*, 43:1-9. https://doi.org/10.4102/sajip.v43i0.1440

Shinga, G.N. 2016. Factors involved in combat readiness in Africa. In: Van Dyk, G.A.J. (ed.), *Military psychology for Africa*, pp.261-288. Stellenbosch: African Sun Media.

Van Dyk, G. 2016a. Personality and war: A Jungian framework. In: Van Dyk, G.A.J. (ed.), *Military psychology for Africa*, pp.311-322. Stellenbosch: African Sun Media.

Van Dyk, G. 2016b. Trauma management: A holistic Approach. In: Van Dyk, G.A.J. (ed.), *Military psychology for Africa*, pp.129-148. Stellenbosch: African Sun Media.

Van Dyk, G. 2018. Stress and post-traumatic stress management and treatment in the military: A holistic approach. In: Pešić, A. & Marković, D. (eds), *Stress in military profession: Thematic collection of articles*, pp.351-378. Belgrade: Media Center Odbrana.

Van Heerden, A. 2016a. A behavioural science approach to strengthen military ranks. *The CSIR Dossier of Science and Technology for Defence and Security*, 1:10-11. Available at http://bit.ly/2wNXJSv

Van Heerden, A. 2016b. Exploring factors contributing to voluntarily withdrawal by candidates during South African operational forces selection. CSIR research paper. Available at http://bit.ly/2VXAwrK

Van Heerden, A. 2017. Exploring military performance motivation from an African Ubuntu perspective. CSIR (DPSS). Available at http://bit.ly/38DqIpF

Van Wyk, S. & Du Toit, R. 2018. Behaviour-based assessments in the special forces environment: A procedural review. *Scientia Militaria: South African Journal of Military Studies*, 46(2):109-126. https://doi.org/10.5787/46-2-1154

Van't Wout, M.C. & Van Dyk, G.A.J. 2015. Managing morale on the battlefield: A psychological perspective. *Scientia Militaria: South African Journal of Military Studies*, 43(1):127-148. https://doi.org/10.5787/42-1-1112

2

Determinants of Work-Study-Family Interface of First-Generation Military Students

Ngoako Japhta Mashatola
Nicole Dodd
Gerhard M. van Zyl

Work, studies and family continue to be the fundamental domains for individuals' psychological wellbeing and related vocational success. Employee self-worth tends to be defined by the type of work, career enhancement pursuits (higher education), and the family structure they embrace. All three of these domains constitute what we term 'work-study-family interface' (WSFI), which, for the purposes of this study, is the degree to which students' work, study, and family involvement impact their ability to meet study-related demands and responsibilities – both positively (work-study-family facilitation) and negatively (work-study-family conflict). This description of WSFI was conceptualised to be consistent with the Work-Study Interface model proposed by Butler (2007).

When students' work and family involvement impact positively on their ability to fulfil study-related demands and responsibilities, work-study-family facilitation (WSFF) ensues. Conversely, where students' involvement in both family and work domains is experienced negatively, their ability to satisfy their study demands is compromised, and work-study-family conflict (WSFC) is likely to occur (Ford, Heinen & Langkamer, 2007). These outcomes may be due to the antecedents of both work-study interface (WSI) and family-study interface (FSI) that determine the degree of WSFI. When resources in each domain are managed effectively, inter-role facilitation will develop and will lead to WSFF. Conversely, when relevant resources are ineffectively managed, inter-role conflict (WSFC) is likely to ensue.

Many first-generation students enrolled at the South African Military Academy (SAMA) simultaneously play three roles – employee, student and parent – motivating a research interest in the tension and synergy between these roles. A high likelihood of conflict (WSFC) was expected to exist because of the way students are required to satisfy work-, study-, and family-related demands. Consequently, a high level of facilitation (WSFF) is demanded of them by their employer (the Department of Defence) and their higher education facilitators.

This study, therefore, aimed to show how role combinations within WSFI are influenced by these three demographic variables (roles) associated with students in military higher education and training. The study may contribute to the achievement of institutional excellence through the accurate management of human capital within military higher education and training. Furthermore, gaining insight into the complexity of multiple-role involvement in respective life domains of students, into their particular demographic variables and the influence of these variables on WSFI, is essential in the pursuit of positive WSFI, i.e. facilitation (WSFF). The results of the study may be useful in explaining how specific demographic variables influence students' experiences of WSFC and WSF, and in turn, assist leadership in devising strategies to help students manage integrated work, study and family demands effectively.

Our study also examined how simultaneously carrying out key roles as an employee, a student and a parent can be inter-augmentative/inter-supportive and result in positive role facilitation (WSFF), rather than in role conflict (WSFC). Much of the existing research into WSFI and associated roles has focused primarily on the negative side of role combination (Voydanoff, 2005). Research has ignored the study domain's *central* role in many adults' wellbeing, a role that is no less significant than the family and work domains. The working-studying-parenting profile does not present itself as a typical student profile in well-resourced contexts. However, in South Africa, with its history of economic oppression and associated broken family structure, students who assume a tripartite role of worker-student-parent. Our study can thus mitigate the gap in research by measuring the WSFI of first-generation Stellenbosch University students at its military faculty at the Academy (SAMA), which offers full-time and part-time higher education to students who are in full-time employment and are, in many cases, parents.

Facilitation – WSFF – is the central construct in research into WSFI. WSFF occurs when students' parallel involvement in work and family impacts positively on their ability to fulfil study-related demands and responsibilities. Conversely, where students' simultaneous involvement in family and work domains negatively impacts their ability to satisfy their study demands, conflict – WSFC – is likely to occur (Ford et al., 2007). We examined the antecedents of both work-study interface (WSI) and family-study interface (FSI), and measured different forms of conflict experienced by respondents, such as time-based, strain-based and behaviour-based WSFC.

Experiencing WSFC can have serious psychological consequences, such as academic burnout and depression (Allen, Herst, Bruck & Sutton, 2000). Allen et al. (2000) gave much attention to probing the questions: Is WSFC all there is to role combination (WSFI); and is non-experience of WSFC the best possible outcome of WSFI?

However, this study focused on facilitation (WSFF), suggest that WSFF is the best outcome to role combination. Through the WSFI model, greater attention was afforded the positive side of role combination. With this focus, we found that individuals can experience role combination positively, and embrace role exchange between work, study and family roles. This finding gives rise to a construct called positive 'work-study-family facilitation' (WSFF) through the attainment of a positive 'work-study-family interface'.

In focusing on the positive facilitation construct (WSFF), we addressed several questions on the work-family interface and work-study-family interface that previous research did not consider. We posed the following questions:

- How do certain demographic variables determine students' experience of WSFI?
- Specifically, how may married, single and cohabitating students differ significantly in their experiences of WSFF and WSFC?
- Do male and female students differ significantly in their experiences of WSFF and WSFC?
- In what ways is the impact of WSFI dependent on the mode of study (non-residential versus residential)?
- How does examining WSFF in relation to WSFC contribute positively to desired organisational and individual outcomes?

In answering these questions, scarcity and role expansion theories were used to assess the influence of three specific demographic variables on WSFI for first-generation university students.

THEORETICAL BACKGROUND

Scarcity theory and work-study-family facilitation

Existing studies on the work-family interface primarily focused on the detrimental effects of participating simultaneously in work and family roles (work-family conflict). However, this study adopted a positive facilitative approach. Relevant to this research, the study domain was added to WSFI. Subsently, the scarcity theory (scarcity of human energy) which assumes that personal resources such as time, energy and attention are finite, has been disputed by this study. According to the scarcity theory, affording attention to one role necessarily depletes resources required to invest in another role (Greenhaus & Beutell, 1985; Marks, 1977). An important assumption of this theory is that "participation in one role tends to have a negative effect on any other role" (Marks, 1977, p.11). Our findings countered these assumptions in suggesting that participation in one role has the potential to facilitate another role.

For this study, the scarcity theory was considered inadequate in that it excluded the study domain. An individual's work, career and family life emerge from their early study life and accomplishments. The study domain plays an essential role in the contemporary workplace, which puts a high premium on continuous knowledge acquisition and life-long learning (Schreuder & Coetzee, 2011). Our integrative and facilitative WSFI approach (combining WSFC and WSFF) thus goes beyond the typical focus on the experience and impact of WFC. Contrary to the theory of Greenhaus and Powell (2006), this integrative and facilitative approach postulates that positive participation in one role can make it worthwhile and even desirable to participate in other roles. The facilitative approach may further be explained by role expansion theory.

Role expansion theory and work-study-family facilitation

According to Marks's role expansion theory (1977), human energy is considered to be abundant and expandable, allowing participation in multiple roles. Similar to Marks (1977), our research led to a positive perspective on role combination, as we found that participation in one role may enhance and facilitate the others: in this case, work, study and family roles (WSFF). In particular, our quantitative study among military university students demonstrated that certain demographic variables have a positive effect on role combination. The main focus of the study was on work-study-family facilitation, as a positive extension of role expansion theory.

In line with the premise of role expansion theory, that combining multiple roles provides a positive energy expansion in the life of the individual, our WSFI study maintained a facilitative approach and examined the construct of facilitation (WSFF) in relation to conflict (WSFC). For this study, the WSFF construct was examined by capturing respondents' experiences of the impact of participation in one role on fulfilling the demands of another. Similar to the research findings of Van Steenbergen and Ellemers (2009), which postulated that facilitation could be bi-directional, our WSFI study proposes the same perspective through the concept of work-study-family facilitation for first-generation military university students, whose work and/or study roles can facilitate the fulfilment of family roles and vice versa.

THE SCOPE OF THIS STUDY

Recently, real and direct efforts to examine the impact of WSFI among first-generation university students and to determine the association between WSFC and WSFF were hindered by the limited availability of theoretical models. Previous studies treated the work, study and family domains as separate entities that result in and contribute to conflict (WSFC) (Byron, 2005; Ford et al., 2007). In this study, we examined the co-existence of facilitation (WSFF) in terms of the impact of particular demographic variables on participants' WSFI experience. The research question this study sought to answer was:

> Q1: Do students' demographic variables determine their experience of WSFI?

Hypotheses

The following hypotheses were formulated for this study and suggested that there is an ancillary or indirect mutual association between respondents' demographic variables and work-study-family interface:

- H1 Gender, marital status and mode of study have a significant effect on students' WSFI experience.
- H2 Students differ significantly in their WSFI experience.

Research method and design

The study adopted a quantitative exploratory approach. The independent demographic variables were gender, marital status, and mode of study. The dependent variable in this study was students' WSFI in relation to WSFC and WSFF. Self-administered questionnaires were used to collect data relating to the research questions and hypotheses. This approach provided descriptive data through deduction of themes arising from quantitative findings, as well as prescriptive findings derived from quantitative data. It comprised the identification of participants' experiences and underlying common issues and concerns.

DESIGN

The study adopted an exploratory quantitative approach. The independent demographic variables were gender, marital status, and mode of study (residential and non-residential). The dependent variable in this study was students' WSFI in relation to WSFC and WSFF.

The organisation in which this study took place

The research findings of this study were qualitatively and quantitatively derived from a unique military university student population. The study took place at the South African Military Academy (SAMA). The population comprised both residential and non-residential students; the latter students are also known as Interactive Telematics Education (ITE) students (see Table 2.1). The main objective of the study, based on the measured impact of WSFC relative to WSFF, was to develop a new body of knowledge on WSFI and to examine specific demographic determinants. Many first-generation students in this institution, especially ITE students, assume three roles namely being an employee, student and parent. An interest in the tension and synergy between these roles motivated the research. A high likelihood of WSFC is expected to exist because of the way they are required to satisfy work, study, and family-related demands. Consequently, a high level of WSFF is demanded of them by their employer and HE facilitators.

A diverse workforce characterises the Academy's student population. The largest proportion of students are single African males whose ages range between the early and late twenties. The largest student complement for this study comprises distance education students (ITE) (N=87). Overall, the first-year residential student cohort is the largest (N=90) of the total population. These students' demographic profile is very relevant to an examination of the impact of WSFI on students in the population for this study.

TABLE 2.1 Demographic Profile of the Sample (N=160)

Variables	*N*	%
Ethnicity		
• African	124	78%
• Coloured	21	13%
• White	15	9%
Gender		
• Female	73	46%
• Male	87	54%
Marital Status		
• Married	31	19%
• Single	124	78%
• Living together (cohabitating)	5	3%
Parental Status		
• Father	49	31%
• Mother	29	18%
• Guardian	15	9%
• None	67	42%
Mode of Study		
• Residential	73	46%
• Distance (ITE)	87	54%
Level of Study		
• First year	90	56%
• Second year	41	26%
• Third year	5	3%
• Postgraduate	24	15%

Note:
This table reflects the demographic profile of the student population of the Faculty of Military Science, referred to as "participants" in the text.

Participants

A sample of 160 was drawn from an age-cohort of 18 to 45-year-old SAMA first-generation students who, in addition to being employed by the Department of Defence (DoD), are single, cohabitating or married; and are either guardian or parent of any number of children (age range: 0-18 years). The judgemental sampling method was used. It is based on the researchers' knowledge about the population and demographics of individuals within it (Black, 2010). The sample size provided a confidence level of 95.5%.

Materials

Quantitative measures were utilised to examine the demographic variables' influence on students' experiences of work-study-family domain variables and to explain some differences between WSFC and WSFF. A WSFI instrument (questionnaire) comprising four subscales was compiled and developed for this study. The reliability and validity of the chosen instruments were qualitatively pilot tested (N=30) for item development that best reflects their lived experiences. Subsequently, the same instrument was quantitatively pilot tested (N=160) for reliability and validity using factor analysis and the Cronbach's coefficient alpha:

Work-family conflict scale (WFCS)

Background: Conflicts between work and family were assessed with scales developed by Netemeyer, Boles and McMurrian (1996).

Purpose: The WFC scale was re-developed by this study measuring the three dimensions of conflict (time, strain and behaviour) in a way that explains the degree of conflict in each domain (work and family).

Items: The scale contains 18 items measuring conflict between work and family, and vice versa.

Scoring: the WFC scale is a self-report instrument consisting of 18 items that take approximately 20 minutes to complete. Items are scored on a seven-point Likert scale ranging from strongly disagree (1) to strongly agree (7).

Reliability and validity: internal consistencies for conflict facets ranged from α=.71 to .87 across the three surveys (Olson, 2014). A pilot study was conducted, results of which indicated a Cronbach alpha of α=.86 for the WFC scale.

Work-study conflict scale (WSCS)

Background: This study assessed conflicts between studies and work through modified versions of the 18-item work-to-family conflict and family-to-work conflict scales developed by Netemeyer et al. (1996).

Purpose: the WSC scale was developed for the study to measure three dimensions of conflict (time, strain and behaviour), in a way that explains the degree of conflict in each of the two domains, study and work.

Items: The scale contains 18 items which measured conflict between studies and work and vice versa.

Scoring: the WSC scale is a self-report instrument consisting of 18 items that take approximately 20 minutes to complete. Items are scored on a 7-point Likert scale ranging from strongly disagree (1) to strongly agree (7).

Reliability and validity: This scale demonstrated an internal consistency that exceeded the conventional level of .70, where internal consistencies ranged from α=.79 to α=.87. A pilot study was conducted, the results of which indicated a Cronbach alpha of α=.90 for the scale.

Family-study conflict scale (FSCS)

Background: This study assessed conflicts between family and studies with modified versions of the 18-item work-to-family conflict scale, and family-to-work conflict scale respectively, developed by Netemeyer et al. (1996).

Purpose: The FSC scale was developed for the study measuring the three dimensions of conflict (time, strain and behaviour) in a way that explains the degree of conflict in each of the two domains, family and study.

Items: The scale contains 18 items which measure conflict between family and studies, and vice versa.

Scoring: The FSC scale is a self-report instrument consisting of 18 items that take approximately 20 minutes to complete. Items were scored on a seven-point Likert scale ranging from strongly disagree (1) to strongly agree (7).

Reliability and validity: The inter-item consistency of the construct was found to be adequate, with Cronbach's alpha coefficients for each factor ranging from α=.86 to α=.95 (Olson, 2014). A pilot study was conducted, the results of which indicated a Cronbach alpha of α=.92 for the FSC scale.

Work-study-family facilitation scale (WSFFS)

Background: The work-study-family facilitation scale was assessed with modified versions of the combination of nine items from the scale developed by Butler (2007) and items from Broadbridge and Swanson's (2006) role congruence scale.

Purpose: The WSFF scale was developed to measure the degree of facilitation between work-study-family domains. The aim was to explain the degree of facilitation by each of three domains, i.e. work, study, and family.

Items: The scale contains nine items measuring the degree of facilitation by the three domains.

Scoring: WSFF is a self-report instrument consisting of nine items that take approximately ten minutes to complete. Items are scored on a seven-point Likert scale ranging from strongly disagree (1) to strongly agree (7).

Reliability and validity: Butler's (2007) scale has shown a coefficient alpha of α=.85. A pilot study was conducted, the results of which indicated a Cronbach's alpha of α=.98 for the WSFF scale.

Factor analysis

Initially, the factorability of the 54 WSFI items (18 items per subscale), and nine WSFF items, was examined. Several well-recognised criteria for the factorability of a correlation were used. The factor labels proposed by Netemeyer et al. (1996) and Olson (2014) suited the extracted factors and were retained.

Internal consistency for WSFC subscales was pilot tested and examined by using Cronbach's alpha (see Table 2.2). The overall scale alpha was revealed as high, i.e. above α=80. A summary of factor analysis for each subscale is outlined next.

Table 2.2 Reliablitiy Statistics of the WSFI Scale (N=160)

	Cronbach's Alpha	*Cronbach's Alpha Based on Standardised Items*	*No. of Items*
• FC Subscale	.86	.855	18
• WSC Subscale	.90	.900	18
• FSC Subscale	.92	.917	18
• WSFF Subscale	.98	1.00	9

Note:
This table demonstrates the reliability coefficients of the various WSFI subscales used for this study and referred to in the text

Factor analysis for WSFI scale was conducted on four subscales: three subscales with 18 items and one with nine items. In all the subscales, the items of the subscales correlated at least .3 with the corresponding item, suggesting reasonable factorability. The Kaiser-Meyer-Olkin measures of sampling adequacy were all above the recommended value of .6 (see Table 2.3). Bartlett's test of sphericity for all subscale items was significant. The communalities were all above .3, which further confirms that each item shared some common variance with other items.

Table 2.3 Factor Analysis for WSFI Subscales (N=160)

Subscales	*No. of Items*	*% Variance Explained*	*KMO*	*Bartlett's Test of Sphericity*
• WFC	18	4/73	.80	840.26
• WSC	18	4/75	.83	2132.94
• FSC	18	5/80	.82	2067.52
• WSFF	9	2/61	.84	569.09

Note:
This table demonstrates factor analysis of the WSFI scale comprising 54 items. The factorability of the 54 WSFI items were briefly discussed in the text.

Convergent validity

This study suggests that strain-based, time-based and behavioural-based conflict and facilitation (WSFF) can be empirically distinguished. The study examined the dimensionality of the scale by conducting confirmatory factor analyses. Correlation for the subscales was conducted to examine convergent validity. According to Carlson and Herdman (2012), convergent validity is sometimes claimed if the correlation coefficient is above .50, although usually recommended at above .70. This study examined whether strain-based, time-based and behaviour-based WSFC and WSFF were statistically distinct or correlated.

As shown in Table 2.4, the developed WSFI items for the facilitation (WSFF) subscale demonstrated a negative correlation of *r*=–.30 whereas items for conflict (WSFC) subscales indicated a positive correlation above *r*=.60. In this case, convergent validity for this study can be claimed based on Carlson and Herdman's (2012) recommendations. Table 2.4 shows only modest (inter) correlations between the WSFC and WSFF subscales. Thus, both factor analytic results and correlations indicated that WSFC and WSFF represent different but related constructs (Carlson, Kacmar & Williams, 2000; Wayne, Musisca & Fleeson, 2004) and support the distinction between the different forms of WSFC and WSFF.

Our study conducted a correlation between subscale totals. Based on Table 2.4, correlation is significant at α=.01 level (2-tailed) (Field, 2000). The correlation results of this study indicated that there is both a significant positive correlation and a significant negative correlation across the WSFI subscales. The data results for the chosen sample (*N*=160) revealed a significant positive correlation for the WSFC subscales, and a positive correlation between WFC and WSC (*r*=.63) and FSC (*r*=.65). However, the WSFF subscale indicated a significant negative correlation with WFC and WSC (*r*=–.28) as well as FSC (*r*=–.23), as shown in Table 2.4. The results indicated that WSFC and WSFF subscales should be seen to measure related but distinct WSFI constructs. The WSFI subscales met the requirements for construct validity, in particular, convergent and discriminant validity.

Table 2.4 Correlations for WSFC and WSFF Items Used in This Study (N=160)

WSFI Subscales	*M*	*SD*	*WFC*	*WSC*	*FSC*
• WFC	68	18	-	-	-
• WSC	67	21	.629a	-	-
• FSC	71	20	.650a	-	-
• WSFF	41	10	-.283a	-.283a	-.232a
a - Correlation is significant at the 0.01 level (2 tailed)					

Procedure

Letters to request institutional permission to administer WSFI questionnaires were submitted to the controlling authority of the host institution of prospective participants in this study, the Commandant of the South African Military Academy. Participants were contacted and gave informed consent to participate in the study. Each consent form contained an assigned identification number. A demographic questionnaire was completed by each participant to collect biographical data. The WSFI questionnaire was administered in a group setting. Between 30 and 45 individuals as per agreed schedule were assessed in group setting conditions, in a well-lit, quiet and ventilated venue.

The instructions for each WSFI questionnaire were read verbatim from the instruction manuals. Once the assessments had been completed, the questionnaires were hand scored and the data captured in MS Excel, then imported into SPSS (Field, 2000). The validity and reliability of the instruments were pilot-tested and assessed using factor analysis and Cronbach's coefficient alpha. Correlation and regression analysis were used to determine whether the demographic variables identified accurately predicted differences in students' WSFI.

Ethical considerations

Participation in this research study was voluntary. Anonymity and confidentiality were upheld. Participants were informed of the reasons for the study and had the option of withdrawing at any point without consequences. The risks, discomforts and benefits of this study were explained to participants. Only participants who consented formed part of this study. The participants were told in advance what data would be shared and how research findings would be disseminated.

All feedback was conducted in a secure, discreet venue where conversations could not be overheard. All ethical requirements as stipulated by the Psychological Society of South Africa and Stellenbosch University Research Ethics Committee were adhered to.

DATA ANALYSIS AND RESULTS

Cronbach alphas for the four subscales of WSFI, inter-correlation between the subscales, bivariate correlation, *t*-test for examining gender and marital status differences, and ANOVA were computed to test the differences in terms of mode of study.

Results

Variance in students' WSFC and WSFF was predicted based on the given demographic variables. The study predicted that inclusion of the WSFF item scale, in addition to the conflict (WSFC) item subscales, would plausibly demonstrate the variance explained in the students' level of WSFC and WSFF. Variance in WSFF and WSFC was explained based on students' demographic variables: gender, marital status, and mode of study (residential/non-residential).

An independent-sample *t*-test was run to determine significant differences in WSFI experiences among participants based on gender, marital status and mode of study. WSFI scores for each subscale and demographics were normally distributed, as assessed by the Shapiro Wilks test ($p>.05$). Homogeneity of variances was violated, as assessed by Levene's test (Field, 2000). These statistical tests were conducted to examine the significant differences between the groups based on the impact of demographic variables on their WSFI experiences, as discussed next.

Gender differences in conflict and facilitation levels

Our study separately examined the conflict models and conflict facilitation models for men and women with the intention of establishing whether male and female employee-student-parents differ in their experiences of WSFF and WSFC. This question aligns with our second hypothesis that students differ significantly in their WSFI experience.

This study reckoned that for both men and women, the inclusion of facilitation (WSFF) would significantly increase the variance explained in terms of conflict (WSFC) experienced. It further reckoned that the examination of facilitation (WSFF) conjointly with conflict (WSFC) would explain more variance for female students than for male students.

An independent-sample *t*-test was conducted to examine the level of variance (Stevens, 2002). In terms of WSC, female students scored higher (M=71, SD=20) than male students (M=67, SD=21), $t(158)$=–1.14, p=.25. For WFC, the results also indicated that female students differed significantly (M=71, SD=18) from male students (M=66, SD=18), $t(158)$=–1.78, p=.07. However, FSC results indicated that female students did not differ significantly (M=71, SD=20) from male students (M=71, SD=20), $t(158)$=–.24, p=.81 (failed to reject the null hypothesis). Moreover, WSFF: results indicated that female students respectively differed (M=41, SD=10) from male students (M=42, SD=11), $t(158)$=.42, p=.68. Overall, the findings indicated no significant gender differences in WSFI experience. In this case the study failed to reject the stated null hypotheses.

The study tested the significance of gender difference in variance explained by the conflict-facilitation subscales by computing the mean statistics for both:

Based on the mean scores, females experienced higher levels of WSFC (M=71, SD=20) than males (M=67, SD=20). Although females differed respectively in their experience of WSFC, males experienced higher levels of WSFF (M=42, SD =11) than females (M=41, SD=10). The study further examined the level of significance. The study conducted a test for homogeneity of variances and one-way ANOVA for males and females to examine consistency with both hypotheses (Field, 2000). Tests for homogeneity and one-way ANOVA were conducted to determine whether female and male students were homogeneous or different in their level of WSFC as well as WSFF. One-way ANOVA results indicated that there were no significant differences (p=.07) in WSFC between the genders. The results indicated no significant differences between the groups (p=.25). For FSC, the results indicated no significant differences between the genders (p=.81). Concerning WSFF, the results indicated no significant differences between the genders (p=.68). These results indicated no significant differences and the study failed to reject the stated null hypotheses (Field, 2000).

Effects of marital status on conflict and facilitation differences

Having established that males and females do not differ in their level of experience of shared role conflict (WSFC) or role facilitation (WSFF), the study further examined such differences based on marital status. Using WSFC subscales and WSFF subscales to explore the differences, our key question was: Does students' marital status impact significantly on their WSFI experience? The study tested the degree of significance in terms of the marital status difference in variance explained by the conflict-facilitation subscales, by computing the statistical mean scores for the groups.

Based on the statistical mean scores for the groups, single (non-married) respondents experienced high levels of WSFC (M=71, SD=21) with reasonable WSFF (M=40, SD=11). Those married and cohabitating experienced slightly different levels of both WSFC and WSFF. Married respondents had a mean score of M=62, SD=14 for WSFC and a mean score of M=44, SD=7 for WSFF. Although those married and cohabiting had different levels of WSFC; they all experienced a level of facilitation (WSFF) relative to their WSFC. These findings supported the null hypothesis. This is because although they differ in their levels of WSFI, the differences are not statistically significant for all groups.

Consistent with H1, marital status has a significant impact on students' WSFI experience, one-way ANOVA results indicated that in terms of FSC, there were highly significant differences (p=.03) among those married, single and cohabiting (hypotheses one and two were supported). However, For WFC, the results of a test for homogeneity of variances were the same (p=.38) for the married, single and cohabitating groups respectively. The level of significance was p=.05, thus indicating significant differences among mean scores of the groups (Field, 2000). Post-hoc testing was conducted, which revealed significant differences in the mean scores among those participants who either were single (p=.004) or married (p=.004), rather than cohabitating (p=.83).

Furthermore, in terms of WSC, the test for homogeneity of variances for the married, single and cohabitating groups was not the same (p=.05). The results indicated significant differences in the mean scores of the groups (p=.014). These results supported hypothesis one and hypothesis two. Post-hoc testing was conducted as recommended by Field (2000), and the results indicated more significant differences in mean scores between those married (p=.012) and single (p=.012) than cohabitating students (p=.58). The study further examined variance in terms of the mode of study.

Differences in the level of conflict (WSFC) and facilitation (WSFF) based on the mode of study

The study examined the conflict models and facilitation models based on the mode of study (residential or non-residential/ITE). The key question was: Does being either a residential or a non-residential (ITE) student impact students' experiences of WSFF and WSFC? The study examined the existence of the significant differences WSFI experience between the groups by initially computing the statistical mean scores and later conducting an independent-sample *t*-test (Stevens, 2002).

Based on the statistical mean scores, non-residential students (ITE) experienced more WSFC (*M*=71, *SD*=19.02) than residential students (*M*=67, *SD*=22). However, in terms of the differences in the level of conflict (WSFC) experienced, these groups experienced near equal levels of facilitation (WSFF). Non-residential students (ITE) experienced WSFF with a mean score of (*M*=42, *SD*=10) and residential students a WSFF score of (*M*=41, *SD*=11).

Consistent with H2, residential and non-residential students differed significantly in their WSFI experience. This study reckoned that for both residential and non-residential (ITE) students, the inclusion of facilitation (WSFF) would significantly increase the variance explained in terms of conflict (WSFC) experienced. However, the study further reckoned that the examination of facilitation (WSFF) conjointly with conflict (WSFC) would explain more variance for non-residential students than for residential students. An independent-sample *t*-test was conducted to examine the differences between these two groups further.

The independent-sample *t*-test found that For WSC, non-residential scored higher (*M*=71, *SD*=20) than residential students (*M*=67, *SD*=22), *t*(158)=–1.24, *p*=.22. However the difference was not statistically significant. For WFC, non-residential students scored higher (*M*=70, *SD*=19) than residential students (*M*=66, *SD*=17), *t*(158)=–1.39, *p*=.17. Once more the result was not statistically significant and the study failed to reject the null hypotheses. For FSC, non-residential students differed significantly (*M*=74, *SD*=18) from residential students (*M*=67, *SD*=22), *t*(158)=–2.21, *p*=.03. There were significant differences and the null hypothesis was rejected (hypotheses one and two were supported). In terms of WSFF, although non-residential students scored higher (*M*=42, *SD*=10) than residential students (*M*=41, *SD*=11), *t*(158)=–.50, *p*=n.s. the difference was insignificant. Overall, the group's differences in their WSFI experience were not statistically significant.

DISCUSSION

The purpose of this study was to determine the impact of the given demographic variables on WSFI among military university students. Our main objective was to gain more insight into the potentially positive experience of individuals having to combine multiple roles (WSFF). This WSFI study addressed different ways in which work, study and family roles can facilitate one another, in addition to examining how they can hinder one another. In so doing, the study aimed to contribute to a more balanced and positive facilitative perspective of the work-study-family interface, thus expanding on Voydanoff's (2005) work-family interface findings. Furthermore, with this in-depth study of work-study-family interface, the focus was on role facilitation rather than role conflict. The study intended to expand the conflict paradigm (WSFC in case of the present study/WFC in case of prior studies) to include facilitation, as suggested by Frone (2003) and Voydanoff (2005).

The stated hypotheses of this study were in line with the premises of the role expansion theory of Marks (1977) and prior theoretical models on facilitation and conflict by Barnett and Hyde (2001) and Carlson et al. (2000). The study postulated that the three domains of WSFI are relevant to understanding the different conflicting and facilitating experiences of military university students. A first qualitative pilot study (N=30), as well as a larger quantitative study (N=160), indicated that the distinction made between strain-based, time-based and behavioural conflict (WSFC) and facilitation (WSFF) is both important and statistically valid.

Our study examined the added value of including a role facilitation (WSFF) subscale in the WSFI scale to predict the various conflicts, frequently represented in the literature on work-family interface, and highlighted by Allen et al. (2000). Consistent with the study's hypotheses, the development of a WSFI scale, and the inclusion of the facilitation (WSFF) subscale items substantially improved the prediction of the impact of the identified demographic variables on WSFI. The WSFI scale may in future be used to predict job performance, academic performance and home performance beyond the effects of WSFC.

In line with previous research by Allen et al. (2000), it was reported that an individual's experience of conflict is highly predictive of the stress-related outcomes. However, the inclusion of the facilitation (WSFF) subscale in the WSFC – or even in the WFC scale – may further enhance the accuracy of predictions. Therefore, the results of this study suggest that the consideration of facilitation (WSFF) experiences, in addition to conflict experiences (WSFC), is of importance to WSFI research. It contributes to the prediction of work, academic and family outcomes. To gain a broader understanding of individuals' attitudes to work, studies, and family responsibilities, it is crucial to examine the positive experiences associated with the combination of multiple roles (WSFF) and not only the negative experiences (WSFC).

Our study identified important demographic differences (gender, marital status, parental status and mode of study), but revealed no significant differences. Female respondents reported higher WSFC than male respondents. However, male respondents experienced only marginally higher facilitation of their work, study and family roles (WSFF). Regarding marital status, single respondents experienced marginally higher WSFC compared to married and cohabitating respondents. Furthermore, in terms of the mode of study, non-residential (ITE) respondents experienced higher WSFC than residential respondents. Interestingly, the level of facilitation (WSFF) experienced across selected demographics is nearly equal for residential and non-residential groups and relative to the level of conflict (WSFC) experienced.

Our findings thus indicate that, regardless of the level of WSFC experienced, both genders also experience WSFF relatively. For this reason, these findings disprove the scarcity theory conclusion where prior research based on this theory have shown that "role-combining is particularly problematic for women" (Behson, 2002, p.20; Greenhaus & Beutell, 1985). However, the results of this WSFI study indicate that this conclusion was based on a view that is negatively inclined (focus on role conflict), rather than positively inclined (focus on role facilitation). Current findings suggest role facilitation in the modern workplace arrangement, value systems, and work-family structure as well as in occupational-study context (e.g. military-academic, military professional-higher-education student context).

Theoretical implications

The results discussed in this study complement and balance the scarcity perspective as well as the spill-over theory that has long prevailed in work-family interface literature. This study has revealed that role combination in terms of work, study and family roles is not inherently difficult, or that participation in one role only negatively impacts another role (WSFC). The scarcity perspective and the spill-over theory have been valuable in identifying the role conflicts that individuals are likely to experience, as well as the associated negative consequences, which are significant phenomena that carry real negative consequences.

This perspective on work-family research has been predominantly one-sided, necessitating the present study, which focused on facilitation (WSFF) of potentially conflicting roles. Our study is supportive and consistent with the role expansion theory of Marks (1977). The present findings have revealed that fulfilling one role could also make people feel revitalised to perform better in other roles (role combination). This study has shown that the experiential domains traditionally seen as the basis of role conflict (Carlson et al., 2000) can also be used to explain individuals' multiple role facilitation (WSFF) relative to multiple role conflicts (WSFC).

Practical implications

The findings derived from our study and discussed in this paper have important implications for organisational practice and academic outcomes, specially academic success. The examination of the interface between first-generation SAMA students' work, study, and family life roles shows that difficulties experienced in role combination (WSFC) can have detrimental consequences for the employee-student as well as the organisation. These consequences include academic burnout, emotional exhaustion, dysfunctional interpersonal family relationships, lower productivity and lower work satisfaction. However, unlike previous work-family studies, the present study has revealed that employees' work, study and family life roles may, in fact, positively affect each other (WSFF). Positive participation in certain life roles such as studies and family can facilitate the work role positively and vice versa. For the study domain, this positive facilitation may result in academic enrichment.

Participation in study and family roles could revitalise an employee-student for their work responsibilities, and make the employee more efficient at work. Studies that support learning as not just knowledge acquisition opportunities but attitude enhancement will verify this claim (graduate attributes are, after all, closely linked with required job attitudes). Studying provides opportunities to acquire new skills and behaviours, relevant not only to studies but as capacitors of performance at work and home. WSFF brings about psychological benefits in terms of a broader frame of reference that helps the employee-student to put work, studies and family matters into perspective.

The role of WSFF becomes more relevant, useful and evident when applied to the SAMA student population, both non-residential (ITE) and residential, who are typically compelled to cope simultaneously with the conflicting demands of their work, their studies and their family responsibilities. A military university environment is a relevant application of the WSFI model (Dodd & Mashatola, 2017).

Significance of the study

The data and scientific findings derived from this study offer new insights. The information generated from the multifaceted environment of the respondents yields crucial information about their academic experience. It could prove valuable to members of similar social settings. A research gap existed on the interface between work, study and family (WSFI) among full-time employed professional soldier-students at the Academy. Our study now contributes to closing this gap by providing insights into events that may impact on essential organisational and individual outcomes in terms of WSFI.

Knowledge of the work-study-family interface and the associated antecedents and correlates of work-study-family conflict may help in the attainment of work-study-family facilitation, and work-life integration for employees and work-study-family enrichment (Butler, 2007). The results of this study allow further research to be conducted into the effects and psychological consequences of WSFC and WSFF in relation to students' academic performance. Findings of this study may be crucial in developing a salutogenic profile for increasing the coping capabilities of full-time employed students who will be determined, thriving, self-actualised individuals who demonstrate a balanced and positive work-study-family interface.

Limitations

There are a few limitations that need to be mentioned. First, in this study, the researchers used their sample as the normative population and therefore used cut-off points based on this sample, as normative values for the entire SAMA population are not yet available. Second, the study was cross-sectional, meaning that no firm conclusions regarding the causality of relationships can be drawn. Again, the study was based on a single institution (SAMA), and the sample size was relatively small.

Finally, as the study group comprised residential students and non-residential students of a unique institution (SAMA), the results might not be generalisable to other settings.

Future research

Given the amount of variance that may not be explained by this study, there is room for other variables in future studies: such as involvement in academic and social activities in the Academy; personality; cultural identity; personal development; and socio-economic background. In future studies, larger sample sizes and additional institutions will increase the power of multiple analysis and generalisability of the results.

CONCLUSION

The results of this study have revealed a practically significant association between participants' demographic variables and WSFI. Although there were no significant differences in students' WSFI experience, the findings indicated that gender, marital status and mode of study do influence students' WSFI experience. These demographic variables are likely to influence students' academic success. The study results partly supported the stated hypotheses, even though there was no significant association between demographic variables and WSFI experience among first-generation military university student participants in this study. Further research still needs to be conducted on personality as a predictor of WSFC or WSFF.

REFERENCES

Allen, T.D., Herst, D.E.L., Bruck, C.S. & Sutton, M. 2000. Consequences associated with work-to-family conflict: A review and agenda for future research. *Journal of Occupational Health Psychology*, 5(2):278-308. https://doi.org/10.1037/1076-8998.5.2.278

Barnett, R.C. & Hyde, J.S. 2001. Women, men, work, and family: An expansionist theory. *American Psychologist*, 56(10):781-796.

Behson, S.J. 2002. Coping with family-to-work conflict: The role of informal work accommodations to family. *Journal of Occupational Health Psychology*, 7(4):324-341.

Black, K. 2010. *Business Statistics for Contemporary Decision Making* (6th Edition). Hoboken NJ: Wiley.

Broadbridge, A. & Swanson, V. 2006. Managing two roles: A theoretical study of students' employment while at university. *Community, Work and Family*, 9(2):159-179.

Butler, A.B. 2007. Job characteristics and college performance and attitudes: A model of work-school conflict and facilitation. *Journal of Applied Psychology*, 92(2):500-510.

Byron, K. 2005. A meta-analytic review of work–family conflict and its antecedents. *Journal of Vocational Behavior*, 67(2):169-198.

Carlson, D.S., Kacmar, K.M. & Williams, L.J. 2000. Construction and initial validation of a multidimensional measure of work-family conflict. *Journal of Vocational Behavior*, 56(2):249-276.

Carlson, K.D. & Herdman, A. 2012. Understanding the impact of convergent validity on research results. *Organizational Research Methods*, 15(1):17-32.

Cronbach, L. 1951. Coefficient alpha and the internal structure of tests. *Psychometrika*, 16(3):297-334.

DeFreitas, S.C. & Rinn, A. 2013. Academic achievement in first generation college students: The role of academic self-concept. *Journal of the Scholarship of Teaching and Learning*, 13(1):57-67.

Dodd, N.M. & Mashatola, N.J. 2017. Resilience: The cornerstone of success in military education in South Africa. Proceedings of the Sixth Asian Psychological Association Convention, 21-23 April, Indonesia.

Field, A.P. 2000. *Discovering statistics using SPSS for Windows: Advanced techniques for the beginner*. London: Sage.

Ford, M.T. Heinen, B.A. & Langkamer, K.L. 2007. Work and family satisfaction and conflict: A meta-analysis of cross-domain relations. *Journal of Applied Psychology*, 92(1):57-80.

Frone, M.R. 2003. Work–family balance. In: Quick, J. C. & Tetrick, L. E. (eds), *Handbook of occupational health psychology*: pp.143-162. Washington DC: American Psychological Association.

Greenhaus, J.H. & Beutell, N.J. 1985. Sources of conflict between work and family roles. *The Academy of Management Review*, 10(1):76-88. https://doi.org/10.2307/258214

Greenhaus, J.H. & Powell, G.N. 2006. When work and family are allies: A theory of work-family enrichment. The Academy of Management Review, 31(1):72-92.

Marks, S.R. 1977. Multiple roles and role strain: Some notes on human energy, time and commitment. *American Sociological Review*, 42(6):921-936.

Netemeyer, R.G., Boles, J. S. & McMurrian, R. 1996. Development and validation of work-family conflict and family-work conflict scales. *The Journal of Applied Psychology*, 81(4):400-410.

Olson, K.J. 2014. Development and initial validation of a measure of work, family, and school conflict. *Journal of Occupational Health Psychology*, 19(1):46-59.

Schreuder, A.M.G. & Coetzee, M. 2011. *Careers: An organisational perspective* (4th Edition). Cape Town: Juta.

Stevens, J.P. 2002. *Applied multivariate statistics for the social sciences* (4th Edition). Mahwah NJ: Erlbaum.

Van Steenbergen, E.F. & Ellemers, N. 2009. Is managing the work-family interface worthwhile? Benefits for employee health and performance. *Journal of Organizational Behavior*, 30(5):617-642. https://doi.org/10.1002/job.v30:510.1002/job.569

Voydanoff, P. 2005. Social integration, work-family conflict and facilitation, and job and marital quality. *Journal of Marriage and Family*, 67(3):666-679. https://doi.org/10.1111/j.1741-3737.2005.00161.x

Wayne, J.H., Musisca, N. & Fleeson, W. 2004. Considering the role of personality in the work-family experience: Relationships of the Big Five to work-family conflict and facilitation. *Journal of Vocational Behavior*, 64(1):108-130. https://doi.org/10.1016/S0001-8791(03)00035-6

3

Psychological Determinants of Success for Military Students

Nicole Dodd
Wim Myburgh
Jan Louis Werner
Ngoako Mashatola

This study aimed to explore psychological determinants of success among South African National Defence Force (SANDF) soldiers enrolled as students at the South African Military Academy (SAMA) at Saldanha. Most SAMA students are full-time boarders during each academic semester and routinely participate in military as well as academic activities during their enrolment at the Academy.

For higher education institutions in South Africa, the national throughput rate (percentage of students who graduate in proportion to the number who enrolled in the first year) is 15%. Stellenbosch University's throughput rate is marginally better than the average and stands at 19% (Department of Higher Education and Training, 2013). In contrast, SAMA's throughput rate is 37%. Although the throughput rate is higher than that seen at other institutions, throughput remains a concern. One reason for this is that they are active members of the SANDF and study at state expense, while also receiving a salary. Therefore, the throughput rate needs to demonstrate return on investment for the state.

DETERMINANTS OF STUDENT SUCCESS

Several factors contribute to student success in higher education. The most notable, and potentially most thoroughly researched, is cognitive ability. Cognitive ability has more to do with the mechanisms of how we learn, remember, solve problems and pay attention than with any actual knowledge. Cognitive abilities are brain-based skills needed to carry out any task from the simplest to the most complex. According to Heckman and Kautz (2014), there is a positive correlation between cognitive ability and learning in educational settings, with cognitive ability predicting academic success.

There is admittedly abundant evidence supporting the validity of cognitive ability measures for predicting work-related criteria in both civilian and military organisations. General intelligence "can be said to be the most powerful predictor of overall job performance" (Gottfredson, 1997, p.83). However, despite its prominence, cognitive ability does not necessarily entirely accurately predict a student's likelihood of succeeding in higher education.

Research suggests that although cognitive ability undoubtedly predicts academic success, it only accounts for between 30% and 50% of the total variance in academic performance at the university level (Chamorro-Premuzic & Furnham, 2008). Although intellect and aptitude are used as admission criteria for university, they do not adequately predict the likelihood of success (Marín, Infante & Troyano, 2001). It follows then that cognitive ability alone may fail to fully predict performance in highly challenging academic environments such as military academies.

The failure of cognitive ability measures to fully predict academic performance may also be because successful academic performance requires individuals to master complex tasks that extend well beyond merely demonstrating cognitive ability. This is evident in the range of academic activities required before finally attaining examination results. Accordingly, it could be argued that focusing purely on cognition presents a misleading picture of the nature of the requirements of academic performance (Kuncel, Hezlett & Ones, 2004).

Kuncel et al. (2004) asserted that academic tasks tend not to be well-defined. Tests, assignments, and examinations, for example, might be complicated, ambiguous, lack a single right answer and often require students to obtain additional information and generate creative solutions, requiring tasks such as analysis and synthesis (Bloom, Hastings & Madaus, 1981). Added to the fact that students are expected to earn good marks, they are subjected to continuous evaluation such as weekly tests and papers, exams and examination results, all of which cause stress for students (Roddenberry & Renk, 2010). Excessive homework, unclear assignments, and time pressures are additional sources of academic stress aside from the challenges inherent in the academic work itself.

It could be argued that failure to acknowledge the complex nature of the demands of academic work may impede accurate identification of individual determinants of success. Ability assessment has always been central to the prediction of academic performance. In combination with other measures, it has proven to provide impressive predictive power. Measures of ability cannot be viewed as the exclusive psychometric correlate of academic performance, given the range of pressures a student faces. Instead, when taking all contextual demands into account, personality traits affecting certain habits should also be considered as they too may influence academic success. Rothstein, Paunonen, Rush and King (1994) argued that "to the extent that evaluations of performance in a programme are influenced by characteristic modes of behaviour such as perseverance, conscientiousness, talkativeness, dominance, and so forth, individual differences in specific personality traits justifiably can be hypothesized to be related to scholastic success" (Rothstein et al., 1994, p.517).

General mental ability is, no doubt, linked to success, but this success depends on the ability to master complex problem-solving and decision-making behaviours and the ability to persevere in the face of adversity. Success in these behaviours will depend not only on general mental ability but also on the ability to work with others (extraversion), the ability to organise one's work diligently (conscientiousness) and being able to manage anxiety (neuroticism). The notion is supported by O'Connor and Paunonen (2007) who reviewed the empirical literature on the relationship between the Big Five personality dimensions and academic achievement and found that conscientiousness, neuroticism, and extraversion (ambition) are important determinants of performance in work and study environments alike. Openness to experience encompasses individual differences in curiosity, creativity and artistic interests and has been found to be significantly positively associated with academic success. This could be because those with higher levels of intelligence are more likely to be curious and to pursue artistic and scientific interests (Chamorro-Premuzic & Furnham, 2008).

Conscientiousness strongly and consistently correlates with academic success. Neuroticism and conscientiousness were found to predict overall final exam marks over and above several academic predictors, accounting for more than ten percent of the unique variance in overall exam scores. Neuroticism may threaten academic performance, while conscientiousness may lead to higher academic achievement. Higher levels of anxiety and neuroticism have been found to have a particularly negative impact on academic success when these levels result in test anxiety (Marín et al., 2001).

Research demonstrates that personality contributes to the prediction of job performance above and beyond that accounted for by other predictors, including general mental ability and biographical data. For example, results from 'Project A' (McHenry et al., 1990) reported that the army could improve the prediction of job performance by adding non-cognitive personality predictors to its present battery of selection tests. This points to the predictive validity of personality measures for long-term educational outcomes, above and beyond general mental ability (Duckworth, Peterson, Matthews & Kelly, 2007). Hence, even modest effects from personality meaningfully contribute to a selection decision, even after one accounts for other significant individual differences.

Individuals respond differently to stress, and these varying responses are partially attributable to personality differences, pointing to stress and anxiety as potential intervening variables in the relationship between cognitive ability and academic success. In an academic environment, the effectiveness of students' response to stress can have an impact on their success.

Accordingly, aside from cognitive ability and other personality attributes, two other factors may have a decisive influence on performance and achievement. The first is hardiness, which was described by Kobasa (1979, p.413), as a "constellation of personality characteristics that function as a resistance resource in the encounter with stressful life events." The second contributing factor is resilience.

Researchers conceptualise resilience in different ways in the research literature, with definitions referring to either the internal capacities of individuals or to the ability of individuals to maintain functioning during adversity. The concept can also be viewed as the growth and positive change that an individual experiences as a result of diversity (Britt et al., 2016). Resilience is multi-faceted and can be defined as "both a process by which individuals use their internal capacities to adapt to significant adversity, as well as the positive adaptation to such diversity which can be represented through aspects such as continued performance, low negative symptoms, high wellbeing, and healthy relationships" (Britt et al., 2016, p.378).

Resilience forms a protective function that enables individuals to remain healthy when exposed to stressors (Bartone, 2001; Bartone, Roland, Picano & Williams, 2008). Hardiness influences performance and achievement through three facets (Bartone, Kelly & Matthews, 2013): commitment, control, and challenge. Commitment refers to an individual's active engagement and involvement with the world, as well as their sense of meaning (Bartone et al., 2013). Control is the individual's belief in their ability to exert influence over events and outcomes through active effort (Bartone et al., 2013). Challenge is the individual's openness to variety and change (Bartone et al., 2013). For this study, we include hardiness traits in the description of resilience.

Cognitive ability, personality, and resilience may, therefore, be hypothesised to play a role in determining the success of students at SAMA. Cognitive ability will most likely convert to academic achievement only when individuals are focused, stable, and able to cope with stress. Consequently, the study aimed to determine whether these predictors do in fact, predict the performance of students at the Academy.

Hypothesis

Our hypothesis for this study was that:

H1 Intelligence (as measured using learning potential, memory, and understanding), personality (neuroticism, extraversion, openness to experience, agreeableness, and conscientiousness), and resilience have a significant combined effect on the likelihood of student success at SAMA.

RESEARCH PROCESS

Method

A cross-sectional, non-experimental research design using self-administered assessments was used to address the research questions and hypotheses. Following the assessments, semi-structured interviews were administered to validate and interpret the quantitative findings and to explore other determinants of military student success qualitatively.

Design

The study adopted a cross-sectional, mixed-methods approach consisting first of a quantitative, and then of a qualitative research stage. The mixed-methods approach to this study supported a complete understanding of the research hypothesis (Cresswell, 2014). The independent variables in the quantitative research design were: age, gender, cognitive ability/aptitude, personality dimensions, and resilience. The dependent variable in this study was the pass rate (the proportion of subjects passed, out of the number of subjects attempted) in the first semester of 2016. The semi-structured interviews further explored the determinants of student success.

Materials

The National Benchmark Tests

Background: The NBT test was implemented in 2008 by Universities South Africa (formerly HESA) to provide a nationally applicable measure of academic readiness for university.

Purpose: The National Benchmark Tests assess student readiness for higher education and comprise three tests. The criterion-referenced tests assess whether the school learner is ready for the demands of higher education, in terms of academic literacy (the critical comprehension and usage of written text), quantitative literacy (the appropriate application of basic mathematical principals and procedures to information), and mathematical ability (the ability to analyse and interpret quantitative data, including spatial and trigonometric analysis) respectively (Centre for Educational Testing for Access and Placement [CETAP], 2016).

Scoring: On each test, student scores may fall into one of four categories (proficient, upper and lower intermediate, and basic). Each category describes the likelihood of success and suggests the level of support that the student may need to succeed in higher education. Proficient students are considered eligible for placement into degree programmes at university. Overall, students in the intermediate category will require academic development support if they are to succeed in higher education. For upper-intermediate students, this may take the form of tutorials, workshops, and language support; lower intermediate students will require extended or augmented study programmes. Students falling into the basic category face severe barriers to success and need extensive academic support, which may take the form of bridging programmes.

Validity and Reliability: A panel of educational experts validated the National Benchmark and it is revised on an annual basis (CETAP, 2016).

Ability, Processing Information, and Learning Battery (APIL-B)

Background: The APIL-B is a measure of learning potential that has been used previously in South African military settings to inform talent decision making. It can be administered in a group setting.

Purpose: By looking only at the potential for development, the APIL-B avoids elements of unfairness associated with 'pre-market discrimination' (the expectation of future discrimination, or a belief among minorities that education will not be recognised.

Scoring: The APIL-B provides a profile of eight scores. These scores are integrated with a learning curve to create a global score.

Validity and reliability: The simplicity of the APIL-B, along with the fact that the assessment is non-verbal, means that the assessment is relatively culture-fair. Predictive validity and reliability have also been found to be acceptable in previous studies (Lopes, Roodt & Mauer, 2001).

The Revised NEO Personality Inventory (NEO-PI-R)

Background: Costa Jr and McCrae (2010) operationalised the measurement of the NEO-PI-R five-factor model of five factors (or domains) of personality, commonly known as the 'Big Five' personality traits: openness, conscientiousness, extraversion, agreeableness, and neuroticism. This measure is widely used and researched and is applicable across different cultures.

Purpose: The NEO-PI-R measures the five factors/domains of the five-factor model in a manner that provides detailed information about key concepts in the domains (Laher & Croxford, 2013).

Scoring: The NEO-PI-R is a self-report instrument consisting of 240 items that take approximately 40 minutes to complete. Items are scored on a five-point Likert-type scale where 0 is strongly disagree and 4 is strongly agree.

Validity and reliability: The reliability and validity of the NEO-PI-R are acceptable both in South Africa and internationally (Laher & Croxford, 2013).

Dispositional Resilience Scale (DRS)

Background: Hardiness and resilience are positively associated with performance across both civilian and military environments and have been found to be highly significant for military selection and training (Hystad et al., 2010). The DRS was developed by Bartone (2001) to produce a brief, psychometrically sound instrument to measure hardiness.

Purpose: The DRS is a self-report measure that seeks to establish current levels of the hardiness of individuals in a military environment.

Items: The scale includes five items for each of the three facets of hardiness, that is 'commitment', 'control', and 'challenge'.

Scoring: Respondents are asked to respond to 15 items on a four-point scale. Six items are negatively keyed. A summated score is then developed.

Validity and reliability: Although it is a valid predictor of academic and military success (Bartone, 2001), there is mixed evidence regarding the reliability of the DRS in cross-cultural environments (Hystad et al., 2010).

Procedure

A stratified random sample of 98 respondents was drawn using a sampling frame that listed residential first-year students, sorted by their academic programmes (providing a 95% confidence level). The researchers contacted each individual and obtained informed consent for their participation in the study. The participants each completed a structured background questionnaire to collect biographical data.

The assessments were administered in a group setting. Between 10 and 30 individuals were assessed at a time in a well-lit, quiet and ventilated venue. The instructions for each assessment were read verbatim from the instruction manuals. Once the assessments had been completed, the instruments were hand scored and the data captured in MS Excel then imported into SPSS (IBM Corp, 2016).

The reliability of the instruments was assessed using Cronbach's coefficient alpha. Correlations and regression analysis were used to determine whether the predictors do indeed predict academic performance and therefore have adequate predictive validity.

Steps to ensure ethical compliance

Regarding informed consent, individuals were voluntary participants who had been apprised of the risks and benefits of participating in the study.

In terms of confidentiality and privacy, this study was no exception to accepted professional psychological practice, which is underpinned by protecting the individual's rights to confidentiality and privacy. Practical security measures were undertaken, and confidential records were stored in a secure area, with all identifying information stripped from the records.

Each participant was assigned a case identifier and the list with full identifying information was stored in a password-protected file. The participants were told in advance what data would be shared and how research findings would be disseminated. All feedback was conducted in a secure, discreet venue where conversations could not be overheard.

RESULTS AND DISCUSSION

Most students in their first year at the Military Academy are in their late twenties (*M*=27.47, *SD*=4.56) (see Table 3.1). The most substantial student complement stems from the South African Air Force (SAAF), and most students are enrolled in programmes in Human and Organisational Development, and Technology and Defence Management.

TABLE 3.1 Demographic Profile of SAMA First Year Students

Variables	*N*	%
Race (*N*=98)		
• Black	87	88.78%
• Asian	1	1.02%
• Coloured	6	6.12%
• Indian	1	1.02%
• White	3	3.06%
Total	**98**	**100.00%**
Gender (*N*=98)		
• Female	24	24.49%
• Male	74	75.51%
Total	**98**	**100.00%**
Arm of Service (*N*=98)		
• Army	10	10.20%
• Navy	30	30.61%
• Air Force	41	41.84%
• Health Services	15	15.31%
• Missing	2	2.04%
Total	**98**	**100.00%**
Study Programme (*N*=98)		
• BMil Human and Organisational Development	35	35.71%
• BMil Organisation and Resource Management	8	8.16%
• BMil Security and Africa Studies	16	16.33%
• BMil Technology and Defence Management	31	31.63%
• BMil Technology	8	8.16%
Total	**98**	**100.00%**

Cognitive results

Pass rate

The overall pass rate for the first-year students was 80.19% (*SD*=19.47). The Technology programme achieved the highest pass rate (*M*=97.92, *SD*=5.89), followed by the Technology and Defence Management programme (*M*=89.06, *SD*=13.12) (Table 3.2). The three largest programmes were selected for further assessment and analysis (*N*=82): Human and Organisational Development; Security and Africa Studies; and Technology and Defence Management.

TABLE 3.2 Pass Rate Per Study Programme (N=98)		
Study Programme	*N*	*M*
• BMil Human and Organisational Development	35	78.38
• BMil Organisation and Resource Management	8	71.88
• BMil Security and Africa Studies	16	64.58
• BMil Technology and Defence Management	31	89.06
• BMil Technology	8	97.92
Total Pass Rate	**98**	**80.61**

Academic literacy

Although the average score for academic literacy for the first-year students was 50.58% (*N*=33, *SD*=9.45), interpretation of the national benchmark tests reveal that only three percent of the students were proficient, 45.50% upper intermediate, 48.50% lower intermediate and three percent demonstrated only a basic level of academic literacy. There was no statistically significant difference with the national norms for academic literacy of (*M*=54.75, *SD*=14.39, *N*=81 669), *t*(81 700)=1.3652, *p*=.172 (CETAP, 2016).

TABLE 3.3 Cognitive Test Results				
Variable	*N*	*Min.*	*Max.*	*M*
National Benchmark Test Results (Sample)				
• Academic Literacy	33	34.00%	71.00%	50.58%
• Quantitative Literacy	33	25.00%	80.00%	41.52%
• Mathematics	19	26.00%	66.00%	40.89%
National Benchmark Test Results (National)				
• Academic Literacy	81 669	14.00%	95.00%	54.75%
• Quantitative Literacy	81 694	5.00%	98.00%	46.29%
• Mathematics	59 644	2.00%	97.00%	40.40%
APIL-B Results				
• Learning Aptitude	53	31.00%	82.00%	54.49%
• Memory and Understanding	54	40.00%	96.00%	74.50%

Quantitative literacy

The average score for quantitative literacy was 41.52 (*SD*=13.89) whereas the national score was 46.29 (*SD*=15.60, *N*=81 669) (CETAP, 2016). There was no statistically significant difference in the quantitative literacy levels of the sample in comparison with the national score *t*(81,700)=1.7562, *p*=.0791. The majority (42.40%) of students demonstrated only basic levels of quantitative literacy, followed by lower intermediate (33.30%), upper-intermediate (18.20%) and proficient (6.10%) respectively. Mathematics results followed a similar trend (*M*=40.98, *SD*=11.83) to the national norm (*M*=40.40, *SD*=16.59, *N*=81 669). No students were found to be proficient. Most students fell in the lower intermediate category (42.10%), followed by basic (31.60%) and upper-intermediate (26.30%).

Academic readiness

Although many of the students demonstrated a deficit in academic readiness as demonstrated by the national benchmark test scores when tested on the APIL-B, the students demonstrated above-average levels of learning aptitude (M=54.49, SD=12) when compared to the norm of M=50 and SD=12, t(2,452) =2.719, p<.01. The students also demonstrated higher levels of memory and understanding (M=74.50, SD=12.58).

Personality

Reliability analysis revealed that neuroticism, extraversion, conscientiousness, commitment, and resilience all demonstrated high enough alpha levels for use for decision-making at group-level (α>.65, Foxcroft & Roodt, 2015). Openness to experience includes the propensity to fantasise, to appreciate the beauty in the world, to experience feelings, prefer variety, demonstrate intellectual curiosity and think independently (Costa Jr & McCrae, 2010). The NEO-PI-R did not demonstrate reliability for this subscale (α=.45). While the validity and reliability of the NEO-PI-R and its dimensions, including openness to experience, have been shown in other studies (McCrae, Costa Jr & Martin, 2005), openness to experience was removed from further analysis in the present study due to the low Cronbach's alpha that was found for this dimension. The low coefficient alpha implies that openness to experience might not be a valid construct for all cultures in South Africa in determining aptitude in the military field.

Neuroticism

Neuroticism relates to the levels of emotional distress experienced by an individual. Those who are low on neuroticism are more likely to be emotionally stable and are calm, capable of experiencing stressful situations without becoming unduly upset (Costa Jr & McCrae, 2010). The sample demonstrated lower levels of neuroticism (M=70.42, SD=23.20, N=57) than the levels found by Laher and Croxford (2013) among undergraduate students at the University of the Witwatersrand (M=82.7, SD=22.3, N=425), t(480)=8.66, p=.001. First-year students at the Academy demonstrate lower levels of anxiety, hostility, depression, self-consciousness, impulsiveness, and vulnerability than the international norm (Costa Jr & McCrae, 2010). The sample demonstrated similar levels of extraversion (M=119.44, SD=20.71, N=57) when compared to the Witwatersrand sample (M=119.4, SD=20.71, N=425). However, the students' levels of extraversion was significantly higher than the international norm (M=110.4, SD=19.3), (Costa Jr & McCrae, 2010) t(692)=3.48, p<.001. It can be concluded that SAMA students tend to demonstrate higher levels of warmth, gregariousness, assertiveness, activity, excitement-seeking and positive emotions than the international norm.

Agreeableness

Agreeable individuals can be described as altruists who are sympathetic to others, want to help and to demonstrate high levels of trust (Costa Jr & McCrae, 2010). The students at the Academy demonstrated higher levels of agreeableness (M=124.23, SD=13.78, N=57) than those surveyed at the University of Witwatersrand (M=115.74, SD=17.81, N=425, $t(480)$=3.46, p=.001 (Laher and Croxford, 2013). They also scored higher levels than the international norm (M=119.1, SD=18.2, N=635, $t(690)$=2.08, p=.05. This finding is in keeping with the role of military personnel in society and the altruistic nature of their work.

Conscientiousness

Conscientiousness broadly encompasses the capacity to control impulses, to manage desires and temptations and to exercise self-control. Conscientiousness enables individuals to complete tasks, empowering them to achieve. This trait has been associated with academic and occupational achievement (Costa Jr & McCrae, 2010). Given the disciplined and structured nature of military work, it is unsurprising then that the Academy's students demonstrated very high levels of this trait (M=133.02, SD=23.96, N=57) when compared with Laher and Croxford's (2013) Witwatersrand sample (M=115.40, SD=21.45, N=425, $t(480)$=5.73, p=.001) and Costa Jr and McCrae's (2010) international norm (M=121.1, SD=19.9, N=635, $t(690)$=4.25, p=.001). There was a significant difference in levels of conscientiousness between the international norm group (Costa Jr & McCrae, 2010), Laher and Croxford's (2013) Witwatersrand sample of students and the SAMA students at the p=.05 level [$F(2,1.114)$=22.34, p=.001].

Hardiness

Hardiness refers to attitudes that influence individual perceptions and sense-making when it comes to experiencing the world. This is very important during stressful times in one's life. The students attained high scores on one of the facets of resilience, namely, commitment. Committed individuals view life as interesting and meaningful (Bartone, 2001).

Resilience

The Academy's students were considerably more resilient (M=32.71, SD=4.36, N=73) than the international norm (M=30.37, SD=5.206, N−7281, $t(7)$=3.829, p=.001), as well as more committed (M=11.89, SD=2.11, N=73) than the international norm (M=10.20, SD=2.48, N=7 281, $t(7\ 352)$=5.801, p=.001).

Correlation of the data

This study sought to investigate whether intelligence, personality, and resilience have a significant effect on the likelihood of student success at SAMA.

TABLE 3.4 Correlation coefficients

	1	2	3	4	5	6
1. Pass Rate	-					
2. Age	−.30[a]	-				
3. Memory and understanding	.28[b]	−.37[a]	-			
4. Extraversion	.24[b]	.02	−.12	-		
5. Conscientiousness	.35[a]	.27[b]	−.03	.31[b]	-	
6. Commitment	.37[a]	.22[b]	−.15	.44[a]	.80[a]	-
7. Resilience	.29[a]	.18	−.10	.41[a]	.70[a]	.77[a]

a - Correlation significant at the 0.01 level
b - Correlation significant at the 0.05 level

The correlation coefficients (Table 3.4) indicated that memory and understanding $r(50).28$, $p=.05$, extraversion $r(55).24$, $p=.05$, conscientiousness $r(55).35$, $p=.01$, commitment $r(68).37$, $p=.01$, and resilience r(68).29, $p=.01$ all correlated significantly with the pass rate of first-year students at SAMA.

Regression analyses were conducted using conscientiousness and commitment as independent variables and pass rate as the dependent variable. These two variables were selected because they demonstrated the highest correlations with the pass rate. Commitment demonstrated predictive validity, $\beta=.36$, $t(68)=3.186$, $p=.001$, indicating a significant relationship with the variance in the pass rate, $R^2=.12$, $F(1, 68)=10.151$, $p=.001$. The students' predicted pass rate is 45.354 plus 3.059 (commitment, where commitment has a maximum score of 15). Student pass rate increased by 3.06% for every one-point increase in commitment.

Conscientiousness also significantly predicted pass rate scores, $\beta=.38$, $t(55)=3.05$, $p=.01$, also explaining a significant proportion of variance in the pass rate, $R^2=.14$, $F(1, 55)=9.3$, $p=.01$. When using conscientiousness to predict pass rate, the predicted pass rate is 40.183 plus 0.30 (commitment, where commitment has a maximum score of 192).

Multiple regression was used to predict pass rate based on conscientiousness and age. A significant regression equation was found, $R^2=.29$, $F(1, 49)=10.104$, $p=.01$. Participants' predicted pass rate is equal to 74.42% plus .396 (conscientiousness), minus 1.72 (age). The higher the conscientiousness of the student and the lower the age, the more likely it is that the student will pass.

Similarly, commitment and age demonstrated a significant relationship with pass rate $R^2=.26$, $F(1, 61)=10.59$, $p=.01$. Highly committed younger students are more likely to pass at the Academy. The student pass rate can also be predicted as 75.90% plus 4.02 (commitment), minus 1.60 (age).

These findings reflect that memory and understanding, extraversion, conscientiousness, and resilience are significantly associated with student success at SAMA. Hypothesis 1 is, therefore supported. The best predictors of student success are conscientiousness, commitment and age. These three factors should, therefore, be added as selection considerations in future.

Insights from semi-structured interviews

Semi-structured interviews were conducted with students (*N*=25) to validate the findings and to explore the determinants of military student success further. These interviews supported more comprehensive insights into the research problem.

The students reported challenges such as family, financial, and time pressures, as well as a lack of adequate sleep. These difficulties support the empirical evidence highlighting the importance of resilience in predicting the academic success of the students – many challenges related to work-family conflict. As already mentioned, the students at the Academy are full-time boarders and participate in both academic and military activities; during their academic recess, they return to their home units to work and to spend time with their families. As a result of the demands of their academic and military training, the students reported experiencing time-, resource- and role-based strain. Time-based strain occurs when the demands of one role begin to interfere with the demands of another (Greenhaus & Beutell, 1985).

The students reported that it was difficult to juggle their military, academic and family demands. Resource-based conflict relates to having enough support from co-workers and the community, as well as financial support (Martins, Eddleston & Veiga, 2002). At times, the students feel that their home units do not provide the support they need to pass, such as time off to study for examinations. They also mentioned that their families do not always understand how stressful it is to balance studying, working and fulfilling family roles. More importantly, many of the students are breadwinners and said that they struggled to pay for study materials (textbooks, internet access and stationery) as well as to support their families.

Role-based conflict occurs when the behaviours required to perform well in one role interfere with performance in another role. During the academic semester, the demands of military and academic commitments sometimes clash. Students feel that they miss out on opportunities for military training and promotion while they are at the Academy. These challenges could be obstacles to student success at the Academy and could cause poor psychosocial outcomes for the affected students.

In the semi-structured interviews, the students indicated that insufficient adaptation to academic activities and not being acquainted with academic workloads and tasks was a challenge to performing academically. This finding may explain the negative correlation between age and the pass rate, as older students may have had a long gap since school or other academic activities and therefore have more difficulties adapting due to a lack of familiarity with the conditions and necessary skills.

Several motivation-related challenges were identified in the interviews, including differences between students' expectations of their programmes and what they experience, especially with regard to expecting a more traditional university experience. Some students also felt that they had been treated like children and had negative perceptions of punishment they had received. Such negative feelings led students to experience a lack of autonomy and control. These motivation-related issues may account for some of the differences in student success, and support the importance of students' commitment, as found in the quantitative findings.

The findings from the semi-structured interviews were consistent with the quantitative findings, which showed the importance of conscientiousness, commitment, and resilience as determinants of student success.

RECOMMENDATIONS

Memory and understanding, extraversion, conscientiousness, commitment and resilience are all positively associated with academic success. These constructs can, therefore, be considered in the selection criteria for students at SAMA. Age was found to be negatively related to academic success; however, discrimination by age could be considered to be unethical. Therefore, the Academy should identify ways to assist older students in succeeding in their studies. This may include providing students with adequate academic and life support structures for managing academic, work and personal pressures.

The descriptive statistics showed that the students had moderate levels of academic success. The semi-structured interviews with the students identified aspects that may be demotivating for students. These included student's expectations being misaligned with their actual experiences, feelings of being treated like children, negative perceptions of punishment, and a lack of autonomy and control. These factors should be addressed to improve levels of motivation among students at SAMA.

It was identified in the semi-structured interviews that some students feel they are forced to study, have miscommunication with their supervisors and that they feel limited in their subject choices. The SAMA should, therefore, work with students to accommodate interests and personal career ambitions. Career managers should aim to achieve realistic recruitment for students so that they know what to expect before commencing their studies. The career managers should also work more closely with the Academy. These strategies can aid in increasing student motivation.

Students should also be assisted with practical issues, such as management of their financial responsibilities, where possible. This may be in the form of offering courses in budgeting or providing more financial resources for textbooks or other study materials.

The Academy should communicate in more detail with students before they begin their studies, ensuring that students have accurate expectations of their study programmes. SAMA can also take significant steps to provide student support, and thereby increase student motivation and resilience. In this respect, support may include giving students a chance to plan their activities, creating support structures, providing facilities for dealing with stress, and providing a greater range of enrichment activities.

The resilience of students can also be increased by assisting them to manage their time, family, and financial pressures better. This could be achieved by providing more resources, such as student counselling or workshops on how to handle these pressures. Students can also be assisted through better integration of their academic and work responsibilities. Also, support structures, such as mentorship programmes, can be implemented as a means to increase student resilience.

LIMITATIONS AND RECOMMENDATIONS FOR FUTURE RESEARCH

The sample size was relatively small, thereby limiting the generalisability of the findings. However, the usefulness of the findings from the tests was increased because they were also validated through semi-structured interviews. Since the research was conducted in the military education context, the applicability of the findings to other contexts is limited. However, the uniqueness of the military education context makes this research relevant and important for this context.

Further research could be useful to determine the differences in determinants of academic success in military education contexts compared to other non-military educational contexts, notably if it replicates the study using larger sample sizes and looking at additional academic and work contexts. Longitudinal research should also be conducted to investigate how the constructs in the study determine academic success over a more extended period, and how changes in these constructs within individuals influence academic success.

CONCLUSION

The findings suggested that age, memory and understanding, extraversion, conscientiousness, commitment, and resilience are all positively associated with academic success. This shows the importance of these constructs as determinants of military student success. Conscientiousness and commitment were found to have predictive validity for the pass rate of the first-year students. Age correlated negatively with the pass rate, with higher conscientiousness and commitment and lower age positively predicting the pass rate.

REFERENCES

Bartone, P.T. 2001. Hardiness, gender, and leader effectiveness in West Point cadets. The International Applied Military Psychology Symposium. http://www.iamps.org/html/body_papers.html [Accessed 02 November 2015]

Bartone, P.T., Roland, R., Picano, J. & Williams, T. 2008. Psychological hardiness predicts success in US Army Special Forces candidates. *International Journal of Selection and Assessment*, 16(1):78-81. https://doi.org/10.1111/j.1468-2389.2008.00412.x

Bartone, P.T., Kelly, D.R. & Matthews, M.D. 2013. Psychological hardiness predicts adaptability in military leaders: A prospective study. *International Journal of Selection and Assessment*, 21(2):200-210.

Bloom, B., Madaus, G. & Hastiings, J. 1981. Evaluation to improve learning. New York: McGraw-Hill.

Britt, T.W., Shen, W., Sinclair, R.R., Grossman, M.R. & Klieger, D.M. 2016. How much do we really know about employee resilience? *Industrial and Organizational Psychology*, 9(2):378-404. https://doi.org/10.1017/iop.2015.107

Chamorro-Premuzic, T. & Furnham, A. 2008. Personality, intelligence and approaches to learning as predictors of academic performance. *Personality and individual differences*, 44(7):1596-1603.

Costa, P.T. Jr & McCrae, R.R. 2010. *NEO Inventories for the NEO Personality Inventory-3 (NEO-PI-3), NEO Five-Factor Inventory-3 (NEO-FFI-3), and NEO Personality Inventory-Revised (NEO-PI-R): Professional manual.* Lutz FL: Psychological Assessment Resources (PAR).

Creswell, J.W. 2014. *A concise introduction to mixed methods research.* Thousand Oaks CA: Sage.

Department of Higher Education and Training. 2013. *Statistics on post-school education and training in South Africa: 2013.* Pretoria: DHET. Available at http://bit.ly/2IF4vNp

Duckworth, A.L., Peterson, C., Matthews, M.D. & Kelly, D.R. 2007. Grit: Perseverance and passion for long-term goals. *Journal of Personality and Social Psychology*, 92(6):1087-1101.

Foxcroft, C. & Roodt, G. 2015. *Introduction to psychological assessment in the South African context* (4th Edition). Cape Town: OUP

Gottfredson, L.S. 1997. Why g matters: The complexity of everyday life. *Intelligence*, 24(1):79-132.

Greenhaus, J.H. & Beutell, N.J. 1985. Sources of conflict between work and family roles. *The Academy of Management Review*, 10(1):76-88. https://doi.org/10.2307/258214

Heckman, J.J. & Kautz, T. 2014. Achievement tests and the role of character in American life. In: J.J. Heckman, J.E. Humphries, and T. Kautz (eds). *The myth of achievement tests: The GED and the role of character in American life*, pp.3-54. Chicago: University of Chicago Press.

Hystad, S.W., Eid, J., Johnsen, B.H., Laberg, J.C. & Bartone, P. 2010. Psychometric properties of the revised Norwegian dispositional resilience (hardiness) scale. *Scandinavian Journal of Psychology*, 51(3):237-245. https://doi.org/10.1111/j.1467-9450.2009.00759.x

IBM Corp. Released 2016. IBM SPSS Statistics for Windows, Version 24.0. Armonk, NY: IBM Corp.

Kobasa, S.C. 1979. Stressful life events, personality, and health: an inquiry into hardiness. *Journal of personality and social psychology*, 37(1):1-11. https://doi.org/10.1037/0022-3514.37.1.1

Kuncel, N.R., Hezlett, S.A. & Ones, D.S. 2004. Academic performance, career potential, creativity, and job performance: Can one construct predict them all? *Journal of Personality and Social Psychology*, 86(1):148-161. https://doi.org/10.1037/0022-3514.86.1.148

Laher, S. & Croxford, S. 2013. Men are from Mars, women are from Venus: Exploring gender differences in personality in the South African context. *SA Journal of Human Resource Management*, 11(1): article 499 (8 pages).

Lopes, A., Roodt, G. & Mauer, R. 2001. The predictive validity of the APIL-B in a financial institution. *SA Journal of Industrial Psychology*, 27(1). http://dx.doi.org/10.4102/sajip.v27i1.777

Marín, M., Infante, E. & Troyano, Y. 2001. Personality and academic productivity in university students. *Social Behavior and Personality: An International Journal*, 29(3):299-306.

Martins, L.L., Eddleston, K.A. & Veiga, J.F. 2002. Moderators of the relationship between work-family conflict and career satisfaction. *Academy of Management Journal*, 45(2):399-409. https://doi.org/10.2307/3069354

McCrae, R.R., Costa Jr, P.T. & Martin, T.A. 2005. The NEO–PI–3: A more readable revised NEO personality inventory. *Journal of Personality Assessment*, 84(3):261-270. https://doi.org/10.1207/s15327752jpa8403_05

McHenry, J.J., Hough, L.M., Toquam, J.L., Hanson, M.A. & Ashworth, S. 1990. Project A validity results: The relationship between predictor and criterion domains. *Personnel Psychology*, 43(2):335-354.

National Benchmark Tests Project. 2016. *NBT national report: 2016 intake cycle.* Cape Town: Centre for Educational Testing for Access and Placement (CETAP), UCT.

O'Connor, M.C. & Paunonen, S.V. 2007. Big Five personality predictors of post-secondary academic performance. *Personality and Individual Differences*, 43(5):971-990. https://doi.org/10.1016/j.paid.2007.03.017

Roddenberry, A. & Renk, K. 2010. Locus of control and self-efficacy: Potential mediators of stress, illness, and utilization of health services in college students. *Child Psychiatry & Human Development*, 41(4):353-370.

Rothstein, M.G., Paunonen, S.V., Rush, J.C. & King, G.A. 1994. Personality and cognitive ability predictors of performance in graduate business school. *Journal of educational psychology*, 86(4):516-530.

Tuckman, B. & Monetti, D. 2012. *Educational psychology with virtual psychology labs*. Belmont CA: Wadsworth (Cengage Learning.)

4

A Psychosocial Wellbeing Model for South African Military Students

Danille Arendse

The purpose of the current study is to examine factors that promote the psychosocial wellbeing of military students. This chapter is an extended exploration of a biographical questionnaire, known as the Biographical Questionnaire for the Military Academy (BQMA). The purpose of the questionnaire was to collect information from prospective students that would assist in improving the selection process for the South African Military Academy (SAMA). 'The Academy provides both university education and professional military development to SANDF officers (Pretorius, 2010). The BQMA developed by the Military Psychological Institute emerged from earlier research into the assessments used for selection of students for admission to SAMA, which indicated that selection procedures had become obsolete and were not capable of accurately predicting academic success.

The new version of the questionnaire (BQMA 1.3) was introduced into the selection process in 2011 and, based on the suggestions from the 2011 and 2012 reports on the findings of the biographical questionnaire', further changes were made to it and implemented in 2013, and in the same process again modified in 2014. This study explores the 2014 version of the BQMA to distill further insights into the 'circumstances that may affect the academic achievement of students at the Academy.

The BQMA was never used in the actual selection process, but only for research purposes. Its function was to identify problems that students were likely to encounter during their studies. In 2016, the Military Psychological Institute ceased to be involved in SAMA student selection, and for this reason, the research project was discontinued. Nevertheless, the wellbeing of prospective students is an enduring topic that merits research. The BQMA thus remains an important and valuable source of information, obtained as it was over six years of successive intakes. Although the biographical questionnaire was not explicitly developed for assessing wellbeing, ultimately, through the extended research, it did assess aspects of wellbeing. Significantly for the present study, this aligns with research on mental health and wellbeing in which demographic factors are considered to play a vital role (Bazazan et al., 2014; Kim & Kim, 2017).

THE CONTRIBUTIONS OF EARLIER RESEARCH

A limited number of studies in the South African context have looked at the psychosocial aspects affecting psychological wellbeing within the contemporary South African military environment (Ditsela, 2012; Grundlingh, 2012; Kgosana, 2010; Mashigo, 2014; Mlangeni, 2017; and Nkewu, 2014). None of these studies has explored the subject in the context of defence force members applying to study at SAMA. For this reason, it is imperative to scrutinise the extended data of the BQMA, as it has specific application to military students, who are unique in having both military and academic responsibilities, as well as other responsibilities common to a student population.

When considering international studies on wellbeing within an academic military context, a study on military cadets' at West Point Military Academy, New York, was relevant to this study. Myers and Bechtel's (2004) research into military cadets' wellbeing during their first semester at West Point found that the students who obtained high scores in their studies also scored high for factors such as social support (friendship and love), physical wellness (exercise), and sense of humour. However, scores also revealed a relationship between perceived stress/wellbeing and work, realistic beliefs (e.g. "I must be liked") and stress management. Low scores recorded for work were related to job satisfaction, as well as to perceptions of efforts not being appreciated by others, and of not receiving enough compensation. The cadets also perceived their lives to be more stressful when compared to their civilian undergraduate counterparts (Myers & Bechtel, 2004). Psychological factors such as grit, effort and hardiness (which may be summed up as commitment) were found to predict academic and military performance success for cadets at West Point (Kelly, Bartone & Matthews, 2014). Similarly, in studies focused on veterans who become students in the United States of America, it was found that academic support and mental wellbeing are factors that need to be considered for students in the military (Falkey, 2016; Jenner, 2017; Norman et al., 2015). These studies on military academy students all highlight the importance of psychological wellbeing within a military student environment, indicating that it is not an issue unique to SAMA students.

Positive psychology

To more accurately contextualise the study, it is positioned within the overarching discipline of positive psychology. The positive psychology paradigm provides the best-suited framework for understanding the data, placing a specific focus on psychological wellbeing and psychological capital (Grundlingh, 2012; Mashigo, 2014; Mlangeni, 2017; Nkewu, 2014). The reason for not considering other common paradigms, such as the medical model, is that this study does not seek to medicalise the experiences of prospective students, and also because the nature of the information available within the biographical questionnaire falls within the themes of positive psychology. Positive psychology differentiates itself as a discipline that is focused on strengths rather than weaknesses. Thus it studies what factors allow individuals to perform better and how negative influences are minimised (Kim, Doiron, Warren & Donaldson, 2018). The range of studies conducted under positive psychology includes wellbeing and happiness; virtue; meaning; gratitude; positive emotions; resilience; positive relationships; positive youth development; and positive organisations. These studies involve focusing on both positive and negative aspects in relation to understanding wellbeing and its expression in different populations (Kim et al., 2018).

Positive psychology can be identified as a shifting focus on factors that can positively affect the individual and group. In terms of the individual, a subjective level of analysis was applied, and this involved exploring concepts such as joy; happiness; wellness; satisfaction and other similar emotions. In terms of the group level of analysis, the focus was on how the military supports individuals to improve themselves (Luthans & Youssef-Morgan, 2017; Seligman & Csikszentmihalyi, 2000). In this study, both the subjective and group levels were regarded as important for consideration.

The focus on positive psychology, therefore, allowed for a shift in thinking about students who struggle to succeed not merely as 'damaged' and requiring therapy, but rather as people who have strengths and virtues, without detracting from or ignoring their human turmoil (Luthans & Youssef-Morgan, 2017; Snyder & Lopez, 2006). We considered this perspective as essential in understanding prospective military students, as it was considered desirable to approach the findings from a constructive position with regard to wellbeing.

PSYCHOLOGICAL WELLBEING

In the initial creation of the BQMA, the concepts of 'psychological wellbeing' and 'barriers to wellbeing' were prioritised. Psychological wellbeing can best be understood in terms of a multidimensional model, as described by Ryff and Keyes (1995), which consists of the following elements: self-acceptance; positive relations with others; personal growth; purpose in life; environmental mastery; and autonomy. These elements contribute in various ways to an individual's psychological wellbeing. Thus, psychological wellbeing involves an evaluation of one's life and whether one is experiencing satisfaction with life (Ryff & Keyes, 1995). This links to 'eudaimonic identity theory' as developed by Waterman (2011), in which self-motivation, meaning and purpose in life are identified as positively influencing individuals, thus encouraging psychological wellbeing (Kalamdien, 2016; Mlangeni, 2017; Waterman, 2011). In a study on the psychological wellbeing of South African soldiers, a significantly positive relationship emerged between psychological wellbeing and willingness to deploy, to the extent that psychological wellbeing was regarded as a reliable predictor of soldiers' willingness to deploy (Nkewu, 2014).

In a recent study by Mlangeni (2017), it was found that positive job attitudes led to increased levels of psychological wellbeing among South African soldiers and police officers (employees of the SANDF and the SAPS). Her study identified that the greatest threats to workplace wellbeing of individuals in this community include occupational stressors from such sources as general stress; role ambiguity; relationships; tools and equipment; workload; autonomy; work-home interface; career advancement and job security. These factors also negatively affect their psychological wellbeing (Mlangeni, 2017). Such factors are key to this study, as they relate to all military personnel and may have a great impact on military personnel who commit to studying, which can heighten stressors.

Seligman's model initially proposed in 2011 (Seligman, 2018), theorised that positive emotion, engagement, relationships, meaning, and accomplishment (abbreviated as PERMA) are the components that comprise wellbeing. He indicated that an overall sense of wellbeing could be equated with the notion of happiness. Although the elements of PERMA are not thought to encompass wellbeing comprehensively, it attempts to measure those elements of wellbeing that are supported by psychometric measurement and theory (Seligman, 2018).

Some information reported in the BQMA positively contributed to their wellbeing. It included factors such as: having support systems; having their families' support for their studies; and whether they felt valued and appreciated in general. The responses across the six years were consistent, as most of the candidates indicated that they had sound support systems and that their families supported their studies. The overwhelming majority of the candidates reviewed stated that they generally felt valued and appreciated (Arendse, 2012, 2014, 2016). This points to specific factors that positively influence students' psychological wellbeing, and which may serve as means of support during the period of enrolment at SAMA.

PSYCHOLOGICAL CAPITAL

Within the realm of psychological wellbeing, the notion of psychological capital has become a significant construct. Recent studies such as Mlangeni's in 2017 emphasised the need to explore this construct in contexts such as the South African military. Current research demonstrates that an individual who is high in psychological capital has the mental ability to cope with the demands of a job, and has self-confidence when faced with challenges. Such individuals are also capable of persevering during challenges and are positively motivated towards success. They are resilient and channel their efforts where required while also dealing with stress effectively (Luthans, Youssef & Avolio, 2007; Luthans & Youssef-Morgan, 2017). Psychological capital, therefore, focuses on the individual's positive psychological state of development, which exhibits characteristics such as hope, efficacy, resilience and optimism (Luthans et al., 2007; Luthans & Youssef-Morgan, 2017).

In a review of the effectiveness of psychological capital in different contexts (Bhat, 2017), psychological capital was found to correlate significantly with wellbeing and mental health. It was also shown to be negatively influenced by depression. Psychological capital predicts employee wellbeing and satisfaction with life and, when combined with functional social support, reduces depressive and anxiety symptoms among those living with HIV/AIDS, as well as mitigating the effect of bullying. Possession of psychological capital also mitigates the effects of stress on aspects of psychological and physical wellbeing.

Mashigo (2014) conducted a study on the work-readiness of African university students, drawing samples from Makerere University in Uganda and the University of Venda in South Africa. She identified optimism, a facet of psychological capital, as a predictor of organisational acumen (which is one of the components in the Work Readiness Scale), while efficacy, another facet of psychological capital, was identified as a predictor of work competence and social intelligence, thus demonstrating that psychological capital contributes significantly to work readiness in an African context. Grundlingh (2012), in a study on junior leaders in the South African military, found that leadership success was significantly predicted by psychological capital and emotional intelligence. Furthermore, psychological capital was found to be an important factor within her South African military sample, and indicated a need for further studies on this construct, specifically within a South African military context (Mlangeni, 2017).

In a study on coping with stress in an organisational setting (Rabenu, Yaniv & Elizur, 2017), a significantly strong relationship emerged between psychological capital and coping skills. Moreover, psychological capital had a strong relationship with wellbeing and performance: coping strategies mediated between psychological capital and wellbeing and performance. Interestingly, 'wellbeing was not shown to contribute to performance, but psychological capital appeared to be a substantial contributor to wellbeing, performance and coping (Rabenu et al., 2017).

The BQMA did not explicitly test for psychological capital but, based on the studies referenced above, some of the information derived from the BQMA can be interpreted as contributing to psychological capital. Subsequently, the research question posed in this study was: can the BQMA measure aspects of wellbeing? This study aimed to explore those aspects of the biographical questionnaire that can be linked to psychological capital.

STRUCTURE OF THIS STUDY

Method

A mixed-methods survey design was employed. The study was both quantitative and qualitative as the questionnaire gathered information via open-ended and fixed-response items (Creswell & Plano Clark, 2011). This design allowed for a comprehensive exploration of both the research question (What factors promote the psychosocial wellbeing of military students?) and the subsequent aim of the study, to establish whether the BQMA can measure aspects of wellbeing.

Participants

The sample size for this study comprised 1,021 individuals who had been assessed by the BQMA over the period 2011-2016. The gender distribution of candidates who attended the SAMA selection process varied from year to year (see Table 4.1 in the Appendix to Chapter 4, at the end of this chapter). The distribution of ages ranged from 18 to 52 years, with most participants aged 27. The racial distribution indicated that Black candidates formed the majority, while Indian candidates were the smallest racial grouping (see the Appendix to Chapter 4, Table 4.2). All 11 official languages (Afrikaans, English, isiNdebele, isiXhosa, isiZulu, Sepedi, Sesotho, Setswana, Siswati, Tshivenda, and Xitsonga) and nine provinces of South Africa were represented in the sample. All participants had completed Grade 12 (the highest grade of secondary schooling). Over the six years, most of the candidates were from the Gauteng, North-West and Limpopo provinces, while the Northern Cape, Mpumalanga and Kwa-Zulu Natal were represented by the smallest percentages of candidates (Arendse, 2012, 2014, 2016) (for further details see the Appendix to Chapter 4, Table 4.3).

The distribution of candidates across arms of service in the period showed that the South African Army (SA Army) consistently formed the bulk of the sample, while the other divisions (South African Navy, South African Military Health Service and South African Air Force) varied in representation over the period. This distribution is proportionately consistent with the size of the SA Army relative to the other arms of service in the SANDF.

Individual biographical characteristics such as age, language, and provincial origin, can either hinder or motivate prospective students to succeed at university. It is significant that, of the full sample of candidates, some were older than the norm, some had matriculated many years before seeking enrolment, most did not speak English as their first language, and most were usually resident far from SAMA (which is in the Western Cape province). Thus, exploration of the psychological and social impact of unchanging factors such as these was pertinent to this study.

Instrument

The BQMA is a self-report questionnaire which includes open-ended and fixed-response questions, under three headings: personal information, social information, and academic information. The core function of the BQMA was to identify problems that might influence the wellbeing of SAMA students in the course of their studies. Following the changes made to the BQMA 1.3 in 2013, most items remained the same, some questionable items were edited to improve understanding, and a few new items were added to elicit more information.

Data collection procedure

The research carried out between 2011 and 2016 employed convenience sampling, as participants attending the SAMA selections were available after their assessments were completed.

Ethical considerations

The ethical considerations considered for this study were anonymity and confidentiality: no identifying information was required for the BQMA, and demographic variables were treated as confidential. Participants were informed that the completion of the BQMA was for research purposes and gave written consent to participate. The safeguarding of information is important, and thus only relevant project members can access the research. The actual data is stored in a locked and secure facility. Official clearance was obtained for the publishing of these results from Counterintelligence. Participants completed the BQMA, which took about 15 minutes, after completing the selection assessments: in this way, the BQMA process had no risk of impacting on their performance during the selection assessment.

Data analysis

Both quantitative and qualitative methods of analysis were applied. The quantitative data analysis was executed by using the Statistical Package for the Social Sciences (SPSS) in which frequencies were generated for responses to the different fixed-response questions of the BQMA (IBM Corp, 2015). The qualitative data analysis involved exploring the open-ended questions for themes. The mutual themes emerging from the quantitative and qualitative data analysis were interpreted to achieve the aim of the study. Since most of the content of the BQMA was consistently similar throughout the six years, the data were not compromised, and only the relevant sections of the questionnaire were interpreted to address the aim of the study.

RESULTS

The quantitative and qualitative data were distilled into dominant themes: motivation for studying at the SAMA; and productivity and confidence as reflected in the form of the reading habits of individuals; and intermittent social stressors.

Motivation for studying at SAMA

A significant indicator for students embarking on tertiary education is the level of motivation to engage with and succeed in their studies (Vero & Puka, 2017). Motivation for studying was one of the factors captured by the BQMA to assess respondents and yielded responses such as:

> "as valuable as I am I need to acquire more knowledge and skills to apply them in the army as part of the rejuvenation of this organisation"
>
> "the course I want to study is only at the Military Academy"

> "I want to be qualified so that I can be promoted and support my family"
>
> "to be the best academic student and develop myself"
>
> "always wanted to study further, have a qualification"
>
> "because [SAMA] is one of the best institutions in South Africa"
>
> "my dream and goal is to be given a chance to study full time and to be the first person in my family to get a tertiary qualification"
>
> "so that I can get my 120 credits and therefore be promoted to the rank of Lieutenant as well as to be [academically] qualified"
>
> "opportunity is available to me with no financial burden"
>
> "because I want to be a qualified military personnel [member]"
>
> "I want to earn a better career for me and my family"
>
> "I will be able to reach my goal because they will pay my fee"
>
> *Arendse, 2012, 2014, 2016.*

These responses demonstrate that some candidates were motivated by a desire to study and to advance academically. A substantial number demonstrated strong motivations to get promoted and to improve their current circumstances – in other words, they were motivated by organisational factors not directly related to academic achievement. It can also be inferred that candidates perceived that academic advancement would create better career opportunities. Moreover, there was evidence of motivation due to the removal of the financial burden of study.

Productivity and confidence as reflected in reading habits

Academic readiness can be ascertained to some degree by observing students' reading habits (Nazarova & Umurova, 2016), in terms of factors such as: how frequently they read, the types of materials they read, and the language of the materials they tend to read. The value of assessing their reading habits lies in the fact that many of the candidates are not first-language English speakers, and since the language of instruction is English, this can be considered a factor which may affect their confidence (Nazarova & Umurova, 2016).

Candidates' reported reading frequency from 2011 to 2016 showed that a majority appeared to read every day, with a large number reporting only occasional reading. While several of the prospective students would appear to be avid readers, one must keep in mind that they may have answered according to perceptions of what is socially desirable. Furthermore, frequently read materials included fiction, magazines and newspapers. Most candidates also reported reading these materials in English, with very few reading in other (African) languages as well (Arendse, 2012, 2014, 2016).

Intermittent social stressors

The term 'intermittent social stressors' was adopted for this study to describe some of the personal and social information that emerged from the biographical questionnaire as causes of social stress. These intermittent stressors include marital status, dependants, financial responsibilities, financial pressures, cultural responsibilities, and having friends. See the Appendix to Chapter 4, at the end of this chapter, Tables 4.4, 4.5 and 4.6, for statistics on these stressors. Most of the candidates assessed over the period were in relationships, and quite a few had children. A large percentage indicated that they had financial responsibilities in terms of a concerning number of dependants for whom they cared. Several of them indicated that they did not have friends at the SAMA, which could make it a lonely experience without social support from their peers (Arendse, 2012, 2014, 2016).

The inclusion of cultural responsibilities

South Africa is unique in terms of its diversity of cultures, and the recognition of cultural responsibilities is intrinsic to the African way of life. These take the form of communal spiritual or culturally based rituals and traditions. It was essential to explore this dynamic within the biographical questionnaire as being a potential source of stress, or potentially having an impact on candidates' performance in their studies.

Very few applicants indicated that they had cultural responsibilities; however, some of the cultural responsibilities that were mentioned included:

> "Cultural marriages and traditions, Muslim festivities, Ramadan, Eid";
>
> "I am the oldest male at home anything cultural or traditional need my approval";
>
> "Time to time I must thank my ancestors by slaughtering (livestock)";
>
> "cleansing ceremonies";
>
> "cultural dance of the rural kingdom";
>
> "ensure that my three boys go through manhood, circumcision passage";
>
> "funerals and unveilings"; and
>
> "I am required to fast a month in our culture"
>
> *Arendse, 2012, 2014, 2016.*

Relocation: Impact on family and dependants

Full-time study at SAMA implies that the student will relocate to the campus at Saldanha (Western Cape). This requires serious consideration for candidates who have dependants, including children, siblings and parents. Thus, it was relevant to ask who would look after the candidates' dependants if the prospective student were to relocate to Saldanha while studying. A few candidates reported being emotionally responsible for siblings and parents. A larger percentage reported being financially responsible for siblings and parents. Concerning their children, most candidates reported that their children would be cared for by their partners, extended family or siblings (Arendse, 2014, 2016). The need for financial and affective arrangements would have to be considered in such cases before candidates could embark on their studies. This can be a stressful experience: making such arrangements could hinder optimal performance at times, or even result in candidates not embarking on study due to the anticipated complications.

Another noteworthy factor reported in the biographical questionnaire was that of social relationships and friendships. Several candidates indicated that they did not have friends at SAMA, with a likely consequence of loneliness, especially for the introverted, although there would always be a possibility of friendships developing during their residence at SAMA (Arendse, 2014, 2016). Full-time residence is likely to have an impact on peer support systems, and thus on student performance.

The implications of dependants

A critical issue emerging from the findings of the biographical questionnaire was the number of dependants for whom a candidate may be responsible, as this entails financial responsibility and may cause financial pressure. The incidence of this potentially severe stressor appears to be increasing: whereas it used to be the exception, it has progressively become the norm. In such circumstances, individuals experience both financial and emotional stress. In the context of intermittent social stressors, the factor of dependants is, therefore, very relevant to our study.

Over the six years, prospective candidates reported having between one and as many as 12 dependants (see the Appendix to Chapter 4, Table 4.7).

The number of dependants and responsibility for them was reported as a stressor by most of the candidates, whose responses regarding the associated financial stress included the following:

> "Because when I give them the little I have they get angry"
>
> "I am responsible for their livelihood"
>
> "I am sole breadwinner"
>
> "My two younger brothers are at tertiary and I must pay for them"
>
> "Sometimes I can't afford to pay school fees"
>
> "Sometimes the money I send home is being misused"
>
> "Because I am not earning enough"
>
> "Because my younger sisters are about to go to college/university next year. So saving money for the three of them it does (stress the respondent out) sometimes"
>
> "Both my parents are pensioners and I have to support them and my brothers who are not working"
>
> "I am not able to do some things for myself"; and "I can't afford to give them everything they need"

> "I have been getting paid almost the same salary for seven years"
>
> "Sometimes because I can't always meet my needs"
>
> *Arendse, 2012, 2014, 2016.*

These responses depict the pressure that dependants place on candidates' finances and the stress it causes them. The strain of supporting dependents can effectively hinder candidates in completing their education.

DISCUSSION

The study aimed to explore aspects of the BQMA findings that could be linked to psychological capital. These included motivations for studying at the SAMA, career and academic advancement, productivity and confidence (deduced from their reported reading habits in English) are discussed here to assess whether the BQMA could be used to measure wellbeing.

Motivations for studying at SAMA

Some candidates were motivated to study by academic achievement and ambition. The possibility of promotion and career advancement through studying was an even greater motivator for some candidates. The unique opportunity for members of the SANDF to pursue studies at SAMA without financial burden was also acknowledged. These motivations are mostly linked to individuals and their aspirations.

For this reason, some of these factors can be connected to psychological capital, as the motivations observed contained hope, optimism and indications of resilience (Bhat, 2017; Luthans, Youssef-Morgan & Avolio, 2007; Luthans & Youssef-Morgan, 2017). Hopes are expressed that studying will enable promotion, allow for academic advancement and improve students' circumstances. Optimism is expressed in their eagerness to study and in having the opportunity to study despite difficulties such as financial liabilities stemming from dependents, the suspending of medium-term career advancement opportunities, and the way study contracts are structured. There is a resilient undertone in the responses, as they assume that they will be able to use the opportunity to study as a privilege and to persevere in achieving their academic and career goals.

Proficiency in English

Productivity and confidence are indicated by the candidates' 'reported reading habits, which suggest that, as English second or third language speakers, they were deliberately making an effort to improve their reading in English. From this can be inferred that on average, they read in English, they read a variety of materials, and they tend to read at least occasionally. These characteristics relate to their productivity and possible confidence in English, which can be associated with the efficacy component of psychological capital (Luthans et al., 2007; Luthans & Youssef-Morgan,

2017; Nazarova & Umurova, 2016). These self-reported responses could have been answered according to perceptions of what is socially desirable, and thus do not offer unequivocal evidence.

The inclusion of cultural responsibilities

A small proportion of candidates have additional responsibilities within their families which relate to cultural practices. These cultural and spiritual activities could positively affect the individuals in that it would serve to keep them motivated (Kim et al., 2018), but could prove to be a hindrance to study. When they commence tertiary education, the level of strain may change, and this can, therefore, be considered a potential stressor.

The impact of relocation on dependants

The social themes indicated over the six years of the study are consistent in that the same pattern of social obligations is observed in each year's cohort. The relationship status of candidates is important and may impact on their psychological wellbeing as a stressor, especially if they are in committed relationships or married (Kgosana, 2010). Relocation may impact on their children and other relationships as well, as caregivers must be arranged for dependants (parents, siblings and children). In addition to this, financial responsibilities and the number of dependants can significantly impact on both their psychological wellbeing and psychological capital. Some cultural activities could, at times, be a hindrance to their studies. The absence of friends at SAMA could limit the social support structures available to them during stressful periods, specifically for residential students. These are thus substantial factors that can affect both psychological wellbeing and psychological capital for the duration of studies. Moreover, these factors could be associated with the PERMA factors of wellbeing (Seligman, 2018).

The implications of dependants

The emotional and financial challenges that candidates already experience before the commencement of studies are alarming. The consequence of not having enough money affects both the candidate and their dependants and becomes a severe social stressor. The effects of having multiple dependants and the responsibilities associated with this are not only financial but also emotional. For this reason, the implications for the student of financial pressures and having several dependants' need to be considered, as these factors may obstruct the psychological wellbeing, and impact on the psychological capital, of the prospective SAMA student. In line with this insight, research conducted on aspiring operational force members found that access to more money was the only extrinsic factor indicated by military members as a motivation for wanting to be part of the operational forces (Rawoot, Van Heerden & Parker, 2017).

Summary of the findings

Overall, the information obtained over the six biographical questionnaires between 2011 and 2016 is consistent. This indicates that there is a definite saturation in the information received. In other words, recurrent patterns could be observed across the six years in terms of the themes that emerged, suggesting the need for a model that can frame the findings more succinctly. Biographical information demonstrated that candidates represent a wide range in terms of age, race, language, provincial origin and arms of service. This indicates the commonality of themes regardless of such biographical characteristics.

The findings of the BQMA were contextualised within the paradigm of positive psychology, with specific reference to psychological wellbeing and psychological capital. When considering the influence of positive psychology on the findings indicated in the above sections, it is evident that the focus should be on locating sources of strength and weakness in order for individuals to reach their potential as optimistic and confident military students. The findings were divided into psychological wellbeing issues, psychological capital influences and intermittent social stressors, and suggest that intermittent social stressors act as a barrier to both psychological wellbeing and the psychological capital of the individual.

The psychological wellbeing of the applicants was characterised by the following: an indication of sound support systems; recognition of family' support for their studies; and the expression of feeling valued and appreciated.

The psychological capital of the applicants was characterised by the following: having no difficulty in using the medium of English, which may contribute to confidence; being motivated to prioritise study to further their education; identifying promotion as a motivator for study; and regularly reading a variety of reading materials, often in English, which can be viewed as productively directing efforts. The intermittent social stressors were characterised by the following: being married or in a relationship; having children; having financial dependants; having financial stress; having cultural responsibilities; and having very few friends at the Academy.

When evaluating the findings and factors that were established under the constructs (psychological wellbeing, psychological capital, and intermittent social stressors) explored in this study, it becomes apparent that these constructs can form a model which could explain psychosocial wellbeing for prospective students at SAMA. This model would, however, only be theoretical, as it was not tested and functions only to explain the findings more efficiently.

A PSYCHOSOCIAL WELLBEING MODEL FOR PROSPECTIVE STUDENTS

There are already models for examining wellness among military personnel (Myers & Bechtel, 2004), such as 'The indivisible self: An evidence-based model of wellness' (Myers & Sweeney, 2004). However, the model derived from this study is based on the biographical findings and does not claim comprehensively encompass wellbeing. It should also be noted that this model has not been tested and is comprised of the information obtained by the biographical questionnaire over the period under review.

The information obtained from the BQMA over six years allows for the creation of a tentative model of psychosocial wellbeing for students at a tertiary military institution. According to the model that was constructed, military students aim to be psychosocially well, which implies that they can handle both psychological and social demands within their environment. An important factor was identified in terms of intermittent social stressors, which influence both psychological wellbeing and psychological capital. If military students can effectively manage such intermittent social stressors, it will positively affect their psychological wellbeing and psychological capital, which in turn ensures their psychosocial wellbeing. The opposite is, however, also possible if they do not effectively manage the intermittent social stressors. This will likely harm both their psychological wellbeing and psychological capital, which becomes a significant threat to their psychosocial wellbeing. Several studies (Bhat, 2017; Rabenu et al., 2017; Mlangeni, 2017) have found that psychological capital and psychological wellbeing were related. For this reason, in the model constructed, these aspects are indicated to be related and as influencing each other.

This model explains the relationship between the factors that impact on the psychosocial wellbeing of prospective military students. It should also be noted that these are not the only factors that may affect the prospective military student, but rather a model depicting the aspects that the biographical questionnaire was able to highlight as having a possible effect. Since this model is untested, it is a hypothetical model based on the findings obtained. It is a modest model in its early stages of development that still requires further research and refinement.

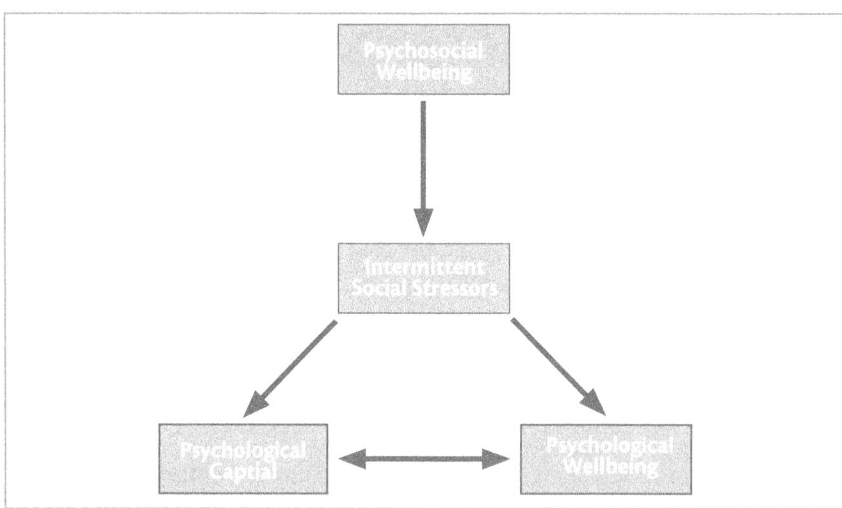

Figure 4.1 Psychosocial wellbeing model for prospective South African Military Academy students

RECOMMENDATIONS AND LIMITATIONS

Several recommendations can be noted based on the findings. First, an Academic Support Programme may serve to assist all students with any difficulty they may have academically. All students need support structures to excel, as they all juggle personal, social and academic responsibilities.

Second, a foundation course is another important consideration. This course could last between three to six months, depending on the amount of subject matter to be covered. Such a course would typically entail basic English skills, relevant skills in practical mathematics, computer skills, and analytical thinking skills. It should be noted that formerly (in 1992) there was a six-week 'bridging course' at SAMA to prepare prospective students before commencement of the academic year. SAMA was the first to offer such a bridging course for tertiary university studies in South Africa. The course was follow up with an academic support programme offered during the first academic year (Smith, 1992). The bridging and academic support programmes were discontinued several years later for reasons unknown, but it may have been due to staffing shortages. As academic preparation is crucial in bridging the gap from school to university, an academic support course should be compulsory for all first-years entering SAMA, as although this would prolong the duration of their studies, it would be likely to alleviate many academic difficulties experienced during the critical first year.

Third, based on the influence of positive psychology, various support structures can be put in place to develop the individual's efficacy, optimism and emotional state of mind. This could take the form of wellbeing initiatives, team building, and classes focused on developing specific strengths. An additional area of research should involve further refinement of the BQMA in order to explore the dimensions identified in the proposed model empirically. This would involve the observation of relationships between the identified dimensions of the BQMA and other resilience measures to confirm the constructs under investigation. Since the BQMA was used only on *prospective* students for SAMA, further studies should include the student population at SAMA to confirm the findings of this study.

A limitation of this present study is that all the information obtained was from candidates attending the selection and therefore did not focus on students who eventually did study at SAMA. Future studies on the BQMA may endeavour to research the opinions of current SAMA students and compare their responses to those of the prospective SAMA students. This will allow for the applicability of the proposed psychosocial model to be evaluated.

Further, no academic performance measures were included in this study, and this may be a limitation as students' academic aptitude was not considered. Another limitation may be the use of psychological wellbeing and psychological capital to understand the findings of the biographical information without the use of specific measures designed to measure these constructs. This limits the inferences that could be made, as the model remains hypothetical. The use of the biographical questionnaire as a self-report instrument requires one to consider the fact that some individuals may have answered according to perceptions of what is socially desirable.

Limitations aside, the exploratory nature of this study allowed for the creation of a psychosocial model of wellbeing – the first of its kind for SAMA students. The specific aspects that were prominent in the BQMA suggest that it has the potential to measure aspects of wellbeing.

CONCLUSION

Historically, the BQMA was an instrument used for research purposes by the Military Psychological Institute in the selections for SAMA over six years. This study sought to explore whether the BQMA potentially measured wellbeing. In doing so, it has been shown that the quantitative and qualitative data distilled from the questionnaire identified common themes, which were used to construct a proposed model of wellbeing for prospective SAMA students based on the extended data of the BQMA.

This proposed model identifies wellbeing as being affected by intermittent social stressors, which influence both the psychological wellbeing and psychological capital of SAMA students. It is, however, only a proposed model based on the data obtained and on linkages to the existing literature on wellbeing. The testing of this model would provide for interesting future research. Moreover, the BQMA was argued to be a potential measure of wellbeing. This research aimed to advance the literature on psychological wellbeing, specifically within a South African military student context.

APPENDIX TO CHAPTER 4: SUPPLEMENTARY TABLES

TABLE 4.1 Gender Distribution of SAMA Intakes Across the Period 2011–2016 (*N*=1 021)

Year	*Males*	*Females*
2011	37%	63%
2012	71%	29%
2013	37%	63%
2014	66%	34%
2015	37%	63%
2016	64%	36%

TABLE 4.2 Race Distribution of SAMA Intakes Across the Period 2011–2016 (*N*=1 021)

Year	*Black*	*Coloured*	*White*	*Indian*
2011	76%	15%	8%	1%
2012	86%	9%	5%	0.5%
2013	82%	13%	5%	0%
2014	79%	17%	3%	1%
2015	80%	10%	9%	1%
2016	90%	8%	2%	0%

TABLE 4.3 Provincial Representation of SAMA Intakes Across the Period 2011–2016 (*N*=1 021)

Provinces	*2011*	*2012*	*2013*	*2014*	*2015*	*2016*
• Eastern Cape	8%	16%	9%	12%	9%	12%
• Free State	12%	7%	22%	14%	7%	7%
• Gauteng	17%	16%	14%	23%	48%	33%
• KwaZulu-Natal	9%	10%	7%	5%	8%	3%
• Limpopo	17%	17%	9%	10%	11%	18%
• Mpumalanga	5%	4%	5%	6%	3%	8%
• Northern Cape	4%	7%	7%	5%	1%	2%
• North-West	15%	14%	21%	11%	5%	8%
• Western Cape	12%	9%	7%	14%	8%	10%

TABLE 4.4 Intermittent Social Stressors for Students, 2011 and 2012

Themes	*2011*		*2012*	
Marital Status	8%	Married	29%	Married
	47%	In a relationship	44%	In a relationship
	45%	Single	25%	Single
Children	22%	Had children	57%	Had children
Financial Stress	76%	Had stress	90%	Had stress
Number of Dependants	1–8	Dependants	1–14	Dependants
Cultural Responsibilities	4%	Had responsibilities	9%	Had responsibilities
Friends at SAMA	87%	No friends	87%	No friends

TABLE 4.5 Intermittent Social Stressors for Students, 2013 and 2014

Themes	*2013*		*2014*	
Marital status	17%	Married	15%	Married
	58%	In a relationship	54%	In a relationship
	25%	Single	31%	Single
Children	52%	Had children	51%	Had children
Financial stress	90%	Had stress	85%	Had stress
Number of dependants	1–9	Dependants	1–12	Dependants
Cultural responsibilities	8%	Had responsibilities	2%	Had responsibilities
Friends at SAMA	88%	No friends	75%	No friends

TABLE 4.6 Intermittent Social Stressors for Students, 2015 and 2016

Themes	*2015*		*2016*	
Marital status	23%	Married	18%	Married
	37%	In a relationship	27%	In a relationship
	41%	Single	54%	Single
Children	50%	Had children	46%	Had children
Financial stress	77%	Had stress	79%	Had stress
Number of dependants	1–8	Dependants	1–9	Dependants
Cultural responsibilities	4%	Had responsibilities	2%	Had responsibilities
Friends at SAMA	82%	No friends	77%	No friends

TABLE 4.7 Distribution of Dependants of SAMA Students Across the Period 2011–2016 (N=1 021)

Year	*Number of Dependants*
2011	0–8
2012	0–14
2013	0–9
2014	0–12
2015	0–8
2016	0–9

REFERENCES

Arendse, D.E. 2012. Exploration of the biographical questionnaire for the Military Academy for 2011–2012. Unpublished report. Military Psychological Institute, Department of Defence: South Africa.

Arendse, D.E. 2014. Exploration of the biographical questionnaire for the Military Academy for 2013–2014. Unpublished report. Military Psychological Institute, Department of Defence: South Africa.

Arendse, D.E. 2016. Exploration of the biographical questionnaire for the Military Academy for 2015–2016. Unpublished report. Military Psychological Institute, Department of Defence: South Africa.

Bazazan, A., Rasoulzadeh, Y., Dianat, I., Safaiyan, A., Mombeini, Z. & Shiravand, E. 2014. Demographic factors and their relation to fatigue and mental disorders in 12-hour petrochemical shift workers. *Health Promotion Perspectives*, 4(2):165-172.

Bhat, S.A. 2017. Psychological capital: A review of literature. National Journal of Multidisciplinary *Research and Development*, 2(2):230-232.

Creswell, J.W. & Plano Clark, V.L. 2011. *Designing and conducting mixed methods research* (2nd Edition). Thousand Oaks CA: Sage.

Ditsela, N.J. 2012. Factors involved in subjective career success of soldiers in the South African National Defence Force: An exploratory study. Unpublished Master's thesis, Stellenbosch University, South Africa.

Etikan, I., Musa, S.A. & Alkassim R.S. 2016. Comparison of convenience sampling and purposive sampling. *American Journal of Theoretical and Applied Statistics*, 5(1):1-4.

Falkey, M.E. 2016. An emerging population: Student veterans in higher education in the 21st century. *Journal of Academic Administration in Higher Education*, 12(1):27-39.

Grundlingh, A. 2012. Intrapersonal and interpersonal predictors of leader success in the military: An exploratory study. Unpublished Master's thesis. Stellenbosch University, Stellenbosch. Available at https://scholar.sun.ac.za/handle/10019.1/71688

IBM Corp. Released 2015. IBM SPSS Statistics for Windows, Version 23.0. Armonk, NY: IBM Corp.

Jenner, B.M. 2017. Student veterans and the transition to higher education: Integrating existing literatures. *Journal of Veteran Studies*, 2(2):26-44.

Kalamdien, D.J. 2016. A psychological model to support military families during deployment. In: van Dyk, G.A.J. (ed.), *Military psychology for Africa*, pp.289-310. Stellenbosch: African Sun Media.

Kelly, D.R, Bartone, P.T. & Matthews, M.D. 2014. Grit and hardiness as predictors of performance among West Point cadets. *Military Psychology*, 26(4):327-342.

Kgosana, M.C. 2010. An explanatory study of family stability under conditions of deployment. Master's thesis, University of Stellenbosch, Stellenbosch. Available at https://scholar.sun.ac.za/handle/10019.1/4183

Kim, J. & Kim, H. 2017. Demographic and environmental factors associated with mental health: A cross-sectional study. *International Journal of Environmental Research and Public Health*, 14(4): article 431 (15 pages). https://doi.org/10.3390/ijerph14040431

Kim, H., Doiron, K., Warren, M.A. & Donaldson, S.I. 2018. The international landscape of positive psychology research: A systematic review. *International Journal of Wellbeing*, 8(1):50-70.

Luthans, F. & Youssef-Morgan, C.M. 2017. Psychological capital: An evidence-based positive approach. *Annual Review of Organizational Psychology and Organizational Behavior*, 4:339-366. https://doi.org/10.1146/annurev-orgpsych-032516-113324

Luthans, F., Youssef, C.M. & Avolio, B.J. 2007. *Psychological capital: Developing the human competitive edge*. New York: Oxford Scholarship Online.

Mashigo, A.C.L. 2014. Factors influencing work readiness of graduates: An exploratory study. Master's thesis, Stellenbosch University, Stellenbosch. Available at https://scholar.sun.ac.za/handle/10019.1/95884

Mlangeni, N. G. 2017. Psychosocial factors influencing psychological wellbeing of South African state security forces: An exploratory study. Master's thesis, Stellenbosch University, Stellenbosch. Available at https://scholar.sun.ac.za/handle/10019.1/101333

Myers, J.E. & Bechtel, A. 2004. Stress, wellness and mattering among cadets at West Point: Factors affecting a fit and healthy force. *Military Medicine*, 169(6):475-482.

Myers, J.E. & Sweeney, T.J. 2004. The indivisible self: An evidence-based model of wellness. *Journal of Individual Psychology*, 60(3):234-245.

Nazarova, G.P. & Umurova, K.H. 2016. Self-confidence and its importance in learning languages. *International Scientific Journal*, 4(2):47-49.

Nkewu, Z. 2014. Impact of psychological wellbeing and perceived combat readiness on willingness to deploy in the SANDF: An exploratory study. Master's thesis, Stellenbosch University, Stellenbosch. Available at https://scholar.sun.ac.za/handle/10019.1/86413

Norman, S.B., Rosen, J., Himmerich, S., Myers, U.S., Davis, B., Browne, K.C. & Piland, N. 2015. Student veterans perceptions of facilitators and barriers to achieving academic goals. *The Journal of Rehabilitation Research and Development*, 52(6):701-712.

Pretorius, M. 2010. Validation of a selection battery used by the South African Military Academy. Master's thesis, Stellenbosch University, Stellenbosch.

Rabenu, E., Yaniv, E. & Elizur, D. 2017. The relationship between psychological capital, coping with stress, wellbeing, and performance. *Current Psychology: A Journal for Diverse Perspectives on Diverse Psychological Issues*, 36(4):875-887.

Rawoot, I., Van Heerden, A. & Parker, L. 2017. Operational forces soldiers' perceptions of attributes and skills for career success. *South African Journal of Industrial Psychology*, 43:1-9. https://doi.org/10.4102/sajip.v43i0.1440

Ryff, D.L. & Keyes, C.L.M. 1995. The structure of psychological wellbeing revised. *Journal of Personality and Social Psychology*, 69(4):719-727.

Seligman, M.E.P. & Csikszentmihalyi, M. 2000. Positive psychology: An introduction. *American Psychologist*, 55(1):5-14. https://doi.org/10.1037/0003-066X.55.1.5

Seligman, M. 2018. PERMA and the building blocks of wellbeing. *The Journal of Positive Psychology*, 13(4):333-335. https://doi.org/10.1080/17439760.2018.1437466

Smith, L.M. 1992. Akademiese steun by die Militêre Akademie: Die aanspreek van andershede in die SA Weermag [Academic support at the Military Academy: Addressing differences in the SA Defence Force]. *Scientia Militaria: South African Journal of Military Studies*, 22(2):12-16. https://doi.org/10.5787/22-2-327

Snyder, C.R. & Lopez, S.J. 2006. *Positive psychology: The scientific and practical exploration of human strengths*. Thousand Oaks CA: Sage.

Vero, E. & Puka, E. 2017. The importance of motivation in an educational environment. *Formazione & Insegnamento*, 15(1):57-66.

Waterman, A.S. 2011. Eudaimonic identity theory: Identity as self-discovery. In: Schwartz, S.J., Luyckx, K. & Vignoles, V.L. (eds), *Handbook of Identity theory and research*, pp.357-379. New York: Springer. Available at https://doi.org/10.1007/978-1-4419-7988-9_16

5

Factors Affecting Turnover Intentions at the Military Academy

Mandisa Mabuza
Nicole Dodd

This chapter considers the impact of three psychological factors on employee turnover intentions: perceived psychological contract violation, or breach; affective organisational commitment; and job satisfaction. Attracting and retaining human resources, crucial to the success of any organisation (Cohen, 2012), requires a climate in which employees feel that the organisation is concerned about their wellbeing. The organisation demonstrates such concern by facilitating their employees' work performance and providing for a work experience that is pleasant and satisfying. Botha and Moalusi (2010) observe that employers typically value employee dedication and loyalty because employees who are emotionally committed to the organisation show heightened performance, reduced absenteeism, and a lessened likelihood of quitting. By contrast, employees are more concerned with the organisation's commitment to them and demonstrate positive work behaviours when they feel valued by the organisation.

As an academic institution, the South African Military Academy (SAMA) provides a student experience characterised by long teaching hours, and limited access to information – about career progression and advancement; opportunities for military development; and proper channels of command and grievance procedure. As a result, psychological contract violation (PCV) is not uncommon: many soldiers have left – and it would seem that many more intend to leave the organisation – because of perceived failure by the South African National Defence Force (SANDF) to fulfil their needs and expectations. The first year of study at the Academy is especially testing as students must adapt to military university life and being in full-time residence at the Academy, and are often far from home.

It would seem reasonable to surmise that employees do not all place the same level of importance on each facet of job satisfaction, or the extent of the breach of contract, or level of organisational commitment. Instead, the importance ascribed to these factors varies among individuals, who have different perceptions and needs. This study aims to investigate the relationship of turnover intentions, PCV and the three-factor bundle of perceived breach, affective organisational commitment, and job satisfaction, among SAMA students, who are both SANDF employees (soldiers) and students.

THE PSYCHOLOGICAL CONTRACT

The notion of the psychological contract has steadily gained popularity since Argyris first introduced the concept (Argyris, 1960). The organisational psychologist, Schein, described the psychological contract as an agreement between individuals and organisations that shapes organisational behaviour, but which, although reciprocal, is unwritten and dynamic (Schein, 1980, quoted in Rousseau, 1989). Between the years 1980 and 1990, as a result of the scale of corporate downsizing, mergers and acquisitions in that period; the construct was deeply explored as a means to explain the resulting employee turnover behaviour, notably by Rousseau (1989, 1990). One of the factors that affect employees' positive attitudes and behaviours within any organisation is their perception of whether their psychological contracts are fulfilled (or breached) at work (Cohen, 2012). The unwritten, informal 'contract' comprises the overall support expected from colleagues – co-workers, supervisors, and the organisation as a whole – and the overall psychological and physical wellbeing of employees.

The psychological contract, from the employee's point of view, centres on the "belief that a promise is being made and consideration is offered in exchange for it" (Rousseau, 1989, p.125). Rousseau later described psychological contracts as "the beliefs individuals hold regarding the terms and conditions of the exchange agreement between themselves and their organisations" (Rousseau, 1995, p.125).

Although little research has been done into specific psychological contracts formed by soldiers in the SANDF, the above definition of the psychological contract could also account for SANDF soldiers' expectations and their general perceptions of their obligations to the organisation. In the past, typical conditions in the military encouraged the development of a 'traditional' psychological contract: it was simple and straightforward, combining the notion of long-term job security in return for hard work, loyalty and obedience. A principal function of the psychological contract for any individual is the reduction of uncertainty. Although the Department of Defence (DoD) provides a measure of security for its soldiers (in terms of a legal contract, insurance, and set disciplines and routines), some aspects of the contract of employment cannot be addressed in a formal written manner, and consequently, a psychological contract forms in the daily experience of the individual soldier to fill the gaps in the felt needs and expectations of the relationship.

Just as in other organisations, the psychological contract shapes the behaviour of soldiers. Like employees in other contexts, soldiers weigh their obligations towards their employer (the DoD) against what the employer holds towards them and adjust their behaviour based on the outcomes they view as valuable. The existence of the psychological contract gives employees a sense of control and influence over what happens to them in the organisation (McFarlane, Shore & Tetrick, 1994, as cited in Ahmed, 2016). The few studies conducted in the military field demonstrate how junior officers of the military, such as candidate officers, lieutenants, and captains, expand their understanding and knowledge about leader behaviours in combat situations (Wilcove, Burch, Conroy & Bruce, 1991).

Hakanen and Conway (2004) suggested that if the human resource department of an organisation adopts HR practices that consider both employee and organisational characteristics, employees will perform better and show positive behaviour. On the other hand, the state of the psychological contract will be visible in how employees experience fairness and trust, and whether they believe that the employer will be able to fulfil their obligations. A positive psychological contract will lead to higher employee commitment and job satisfaction.

In a study conducted by Levinson, as cited in Chi-jung and Chin-i (2014), more emphasis was placed on the functionality of the role of a reciprocal relationship and the effect that anticipated satisfaction might have on both the employer's and employees' expectations.

Concerning the psychological contract, studies by Akin (2008) have established and confirmed some direct effects of the Big Five personality dimensions on psychological contract breach. However, limited research has focused attention on the strength of the relationship between psychological contract breach and work-related outcomes, to check if perceptions of breach will be different due to differences in employees' personality dimensions (Fein, Tziner, Lusky & Palachy, 2013).

The norm of reciprocity states that "fulfilment of employee obligations is conditional on the organisation fulfilling what employees perceive the organisation to owe them" (Liyas, 2013, p. 322). Sometimes these perceptions are ambiguous. Upon enlistment in the SANDF, many contracts are signed, with the recruit and the SANDF each developing mutual expectations. What employees and employers miss is that they also agree to another unwritten and unspoken contract – the psychological contract. The uniqueness of the SANDF sets it apart from the civilian sector concerning its function, structure, and place in the society; it plays a vital role in the protection and security of the country (Smith et al., 1987).

Breach and violation

Psychological contract breach (PCB) is "the cognition that one's organisation has failed to meet one or more obligations within one's psychological contract in a manner commensurate with one's contributions and has deleterious effects on employee motivation" (Jafri, 2014, p.173). When soldiers experience violations regarding the organisation failing to do its part, and their overall expectations are violated, then – as employees – their attitudes, behaviour and health are affected (Tomprou & Nikolaou, 2011).

When breach or violation occurs, then soldiers too as human beings will experience feelings of psychological distress, irritation, poorer general health, broken trust, betrayal, deception, injustice, resentment, anger and frustration as well as a decline in life satisfaction, motivation, job satisfaction, organisational commitment, acts of good citizenship behaviour and loyalty (Rousseau, as cited in Ilyas, 2013). Soldiers will feel that the acts of good faith in the employment relationship are damaged (Ilyas, 2013). Violation of the psychological contract eventually impacts on organisational performance. Organisations may experience lower performance (Robbins, 1996), increased turnover, lower levels of job satisfaction (Van den Tooren, De Jonge & Dormann, 2012), absenteeism, and accidents (Ilyas, 2013).

Previous research by Saeed, Waseem, Sikander and Rizwan (2014) has shown that breach is the norm and not an exception. However, given that PCB is a normal organisational challenge, and thus would affect the SANDF as much as other organisations, it is concerning that not much effort has been made to evaluate the effects of PCB on critical behaviours resulting from soldiers' job satisfaction and affective organisational commitment. Furthermore, existing research on the psychological contract has primarily tended to adopt the 'main effects' approach in examining the psychological contract-outcome relationship and has not addressed various individual and situational variables which can alleviate or aggravate employee reactions, and there is lack of such data concerning soldiers in particular.

Acts of good faith and commitment to the SANDF depend on how well the military employee believes their psychological needs are met, respected and recognised by the organisation (Chernyak-Hai & Tziner, 2012) and, their career or rank progression at a specific time in the organisation. For example, a soldier may exhibit signs of depression, hurt and anger after a breach (Conway & Briner, 2005). They might also experience emotional exhaustion (Van den Tooren et al., 2012); reduced organisational commitment (Cole, 2014; Turnley & Feldman as cited in Saeed et al., 2014); reduced job satisfaction (Bakker, 2011); and increased cynical attitudes toward the organisation (Johnson & O'Leary-Kelly, as cited in Griffith, 2005). These effects are detrimental in the private sector, but potentially devastating in a military context.

In a meta-analysis conducted by Zhao, Wayne, Glibkowski, and Bravo (2007), the results showed that the PCV was very effective in eliciting affective reactions. Such reactions lead to the development and maintenance of less favourable attitudes and behaviours. These affective reactions will then be conveyed by dissatisfied soldiers via increased turnover and decreased worker engagement. Research in the military domain has shown that the differing types of working conditions influence soldiers' overall health. Specifically, for peacekeeping missions, Nkewu (2014) and Fisk (2002) highlighted particular demands that explain the strain on soldiers such as isolation, the absence of tasks considered to be vital, monotony, and family problems. Promoting healthy psychological contracts becomes even more critical in the face of these challenges.

Arguing from evidence evaluated by Chambel (2014), it can also be argued that the psychological contract affects military members' fulfilment, leading to affective organisational commitment on the one hand, or a breach on the other. A breach manifests when a party to the employment relationship perceives the other to have failed to fulfil their promised obligations. A majority of researchers caution against the negative consequences of a breach, more especially for military personnel. The argument is that soldiers need to remain combat-ready and effective in their work. Therefore, positive psychology in the form of fulfilled psychological contracts should be promoted.

The risks are profound, as dissatisfied soldiers tend to be aggressive and violent towards the organisation and management. Poor and negligent performance in operations can lead to a severe breach of state security; such soldiers may also sabotage missions to steal from the organisation for personal benefit and finally quit their work (Nkewu, 2014). According to McCabe and Sambrook, as cited in Ahmed and Muchiri (2014), an employee's response regarding their views about whether the organisation is or is not fulfilling its obligations as per psychological contract is very dependent on whether the perceived breach involves professional or administrative obligations.

Perceived administrative breaches are closely related to job dissatisfaction and high employee turnover, whereas perceived breaches of professional role obligations are most strongly associated with lower organisational commitment, reduced job performance, and higher turnover. Ahmed (2016) has shown that when employees perceive a breach, their emotions are heightened and triggered, resulting in inferior performance, demotivation, lower commitment, absenteeism and turnover. If in the SANDF-soldier relationship, the SANDF's expectations are aligned closely with an individual soldier's beliefs, then the psychological contract would have produced a positive outcome, such as job satisfaction and organisational loyalty.

The SANDF's leadership and its human resource practices determine the quality of the psychological contract, not the workforce. It is employers rather than employees who are in the dominant and advantageous position, as they control the working conditions and employment relationships. In the SANDF, a psychological contract is a silent contract because of a lack of understanding of the relevant management systems and because of its individuality and subjectivity (Ahmed, 2016).

Research conducted by Botha and Moalusi (2010) using a sample drawn from the South African Police Services revealed that breach of the psychological contract is, among a wide variety of causes, related to an unwillingness to exert more effort than the minimum required, low job satisfaction, decreased motivation, decreased organisational commitment, increased turnover and increased absenteeism. This highlights the urgency of exploring the relationship between the psychological contract, job satisfaction and organisational commitment within the similar military context. Fisk (2002) demonstrated that employees might exhibit low levels of commitment and lowered job performance if their psychological contract is violated.

JOB SATISFACTION

Job satisfaction is "a pleasurable or positive emotional state that results from the appraisal of one's job or job experiences" (Locke, in Cole, 2014, p.130). This contemporary understanding of 'job satisfaction' aligns with by the contemporary issues the military faces. These issues place pressure on military personnel to adapt quickly to different roles in order to stay effective. Baruch and Holbeche as cited in Cole (2014) argued that these changes are reflected in the changing definitions of work, resulting in more soldiers being area-bound, not volunteering for missions and studying towards another career beyond the context of the parade ground, diesel, dust, and guns. Job satisfaction has frequently been used in many cases as a critical predictor of turnover intention (Ahmed, 2016), and it has been pointed out that as job satisfaction decreases, turnover intentions will rise. According to Ballou (2013), an employee's intention to leave their current occupation is determined by their commitment to the organisation, job satisfaction, and work-related attitudes.

Viewed by many as a vital work attitude, job satisfaction has been linked to psychological contract breach (Zhao et al., 2007). The basic work attitudes of job satisfaction, organisational commitment, and turnover intentions have shown impressive relations to psychological contract violation (Zhao et al., 2007). In the meta-analysis conducted by Zhao et al. (2007), evidence from 28 studies showed that there is a strong negative relationship between job satisfaction and PCB. Here the concept of job satisfaction involves the evaluation of a soldier's job context, a comparison between the desired and the actual benefits is then made that positively affects the satisfaction of important needs (Cooper-Hakim & Viswesvaran, 2005). Based on this evidence, this study regards job satisfaction as one of the variables associated with psychological contract breach.

Civilian and military literature has portrayed job satisfaction as having a consistent relationship with retention (Nkewu, 2014). Especially important has been the contribution of challenge and autonomy. Other elements of job satisfaction have been associated with the supervisor's style and satisfaction with co-workers (Ahmed, 2016). Job satisfaction or dissatisfaction occurs when an individual (soldier) compares their job (and life) expectations with those provided by the employer (DoD). In practice, such comparisons are performed regularly and at specific points during one's career such as when there is a promotion, selection for an assignment with a service obligation, and so on. This comparison may later lead to a decision regarding career pathing, job satisfaction and commitment.

ORGANISATIONAL COMMITMENT

In the context of this study, Meyer and Allen (1997) emphasised that organisational commitment is defined as a psychological connection that individuals have with their organisation, characterised by strong recognition within the organisation and a strong desire to contribute towards the accomplishment of organisational goals.

Affective commitment, or an employee's emotional attachment and involvement with their work, might be viewed as a subset of the psychological contract (Chernyak-Hai & Tziner, 2012). This form of commitment remains an important consideration for organisational leaders to foster (Coyle-Shapiro & Parzefall, 2008), particularly in light of its role in reducing employee turnover (Ballou, 2013).

Employees with strong affective organisational commitment remain in their jobs and the profession, because they want to and not because they must. For example, service members with a strong sense of affective commitment to their military calling will keep up with developments in their profession such as new wars and new technology in weapons, improve on their skills and knowledge, attend parades, and participate well in their military missions.

Employees who are affectively committed to the organisation will carry on working for it because they want to (Meyer & Allen, 1997) and are happy and satisfied with their occupations. This may also prove true for military personnel, as Conway and Briner (2005) mentioned that soldiers with fulfilled contracts have high levels of commitment towards the organisation. They are also better at task performance, possess a high level of attachment to their supervisor, in this case, military commanders, and they also have a lower level of turnover intentions. Thus, soldiers who are dedicated at an emotional level will usually remain with the organisation because their employment relationship is harmonious with the goals and values of the SANDF where they are currently employed.

TURNOVER INTENTIONS

One obvious response to dissatisfaction is to leave one's job, and it is, therefore, reasonable to expect that when an employee or a group of employees experience dissatisfaction, it can be associated with stronger turnover intentions (Straker, Abbott, Heiden, Mathiassen & Toomingas, 2013). Affective organisational commitment has to do with the psychological connection soldiers experience with the SANDF and is characterised by a strong identification with the organisation and a strong motivation to contribute towards the accomplishment of organisational goals. Commitment to the SANDF is associated directly with how well military employees observe their psychological contract as being met, respected and recognised by the organisation (Chernyak-Hai & Tziner, 2012), as well as their career or rank progression potential at a specific time in the organisation.

The SANDF may be unable to meet all the promises conveyed either explicitly or implicitly to its servicemen and women. Therefore, it sometimes happens that soldiers in the SANDF do not receive equitable recognition, such as promotions for the same kind of work and while having the same qualifications. The intention to quit can be defined in the words of Robinson (1996, p.372), as an "employee's plan or intention to leave the present job and look forward to finding another job in the near future". According to Tomprou and Nikalaou (2011), an employee's intention to leave the organisation is determined by the commitment to work, job satisfaction, and work-related stance.

Alhough intention to quit has been researched extensively because of its importance, little research exists in the military context. When soldiers are dissatisfied, and there is mutual mistrust between them and their employers, there will be higher turnover intentions and the overall security of the nation is jeopardised (Cole, 2014).

Tallman and Bruning (2008) pointed out that when employees perceive a breach, their emotions are heightened and triggered, resulting in inferior performance, demotivation, lower commitment, absenteeism, and turnover. Therefore, if the behaviour is influenced and attitudes formed from these experiences, then employees' level of engagement can be changed for the better or worse by the organisation's actions (Fisk, 2002). Conway and Briner (2005) also mentioned that employees with fulfilled contracts have high levels of commitment towards their organisation, are better at task performance and possess a high level of attachment to their supervisor and a lower level of turnover intentions.

Social exchange theory holds that if employees believe that their employer has fulfilled their expectations and has treated them fairly, they are more likely to perform their jobs better (Adams, in Van den Tooren et al., 2012). Much research (see Robinson, 1996; Zhao et al., 2007) acknowledges that if the contract is fulfilled, employees will have a positive attitude which will include better task performance, and less intention to leave. As the progression theory states, the extent to which people respond to dissatisfaction differs in intensity and employees progress from less to more intense responses as dissatisfaction intensifies.

As a result of intense dissatisfaction, employees may variously end up either leaving the organisation, voicing their dissatisfaction, remaining loyal, or being negligent in their duties (Rusbolt et al., in Saeed et al., 2014). Quitting a job is a painful decision which may require actions by the employee who wholeheartedly believes that things will only get worse going forward. Most of the SANDF soldiers are from social backgrounds dominated by poverty and low-quality education; this makes leaving the SANDF a less viable option (Nkewu, 2014). Loyalty may thus entail passively but optimistically waiting for conditions to improve (Ahmed & Muchiri, 2014).

Employee turnover is costly to the organisation (Cole, 2014). From the organisation's perspective, it takes substantial time, money and effort to recruit new employees, and such loss often disrupts the regular operations of the military as well as fosters low workforce morale. Research indicates that a psychological contract breach is directly related to increased turnover intentions (Paille, 2015, as cited in Ahmed, 2016). Past analytic efforts regarding retention in the SANDF have primarily related to economic considerations and family outcomes (Nkewu, 2014). While there have been many surveys and studies regarding job satisfaction, organisational culture, and family issues, there have been limited efforts to integrate these factors.

Based on the literature surveyed, the following hypothesis was formulated:

H1 Psychological contract breach and violation, job satisfaction and affective commitment have a significant combined effect on turnover intentions of students at the South African Military Academy (SAMA).

RESEARCH METHOD

Participants

Data were collected from a population of 100 first-year students at SAMA. A random sample of 80 SAMA students currently studying on a full-time basis was selected. At the time of the study, participants were employed by the SANDF in professional positions, including both administrative and operational roles and positions, or were soon to occupy leadership positions (some were already in leadership positions). This juncture in their careers is particularly interesting because of the challenges associated with being resident at the Academy and both working and studying full-time. Of the sample of 80 respondents, 58 (72.5%) were male, and 22 (27.5%) were female. The sample was ethnically diverse, and the ethnicities included 73 (91.3%) Black, with the remainder being White (3.8%), Coloured (2.5%), and Asian (2.5%) people. The study had 36 (45%) respondents between the ages of 18 and 24, 37 (46.3%) were between 25 and 30 years of age, and seven (8.8%) were between 31 and 40 years old.

Materials

Robinson and Morrison (2000) developed a scale (α=.92) called the psychological contract breach (PCB) scale. The measure consists of five items and assesses an employee's global perception of psychological contract breach. Some of the items were reverse coded, for example: "I have not received everything promised to me in exchange for my contributions".

The choice of a global instead of a specific measure for perceived PCB was justified by Zhao et al. (2007), who found strong relationships between perceived psychological contract breach and several work-related outcomes. Robinson and Morrison's (2000) PCV scale containing four items (α=.92) was used. One such global item was: "I feel extremely frustrated by how I have been treated by my organisation".

The instrument used to assess job satisfaction comprised five items. One of the items included in the questionnaire was "I enjoy the work that I do". The items were based on the questionnaire of Randsley et al. (2009). All items were indicative of job satisfaction. Randsley et al. (2009) reported a Cronbach's alpha of .90 for the instrument.

Meyer and Allen's (1997) revised six-item scale for affective organisational commitment and loyalty, with a Cronbach's α=.85, was used to measure affective commitment. An example item was: "I really feel as if this organisation's problems are my own". All the items were reverse-coded.

Based on the study of Chiu and Francesco (2003), the scale to measure turnover intentions included three items: "In the last few months, I have seriously thought about looking for a new job" (Chui & Francesco, 2003); "Presently, I am actively searching for another job" (Jenkins, 1993); and "I intend to leave my organisation in the near future" (Krausz, Koslowsky, Shalom & Elyakim, 1995). Chiu and Francesco (2003) reported a Cronbach's α of .93 for these three items.

Data collection methods

Data were collected using self-report questionnaires. For all the scales, the Cronbach alphas were compared using the original questionnaire and the current findings (Table 5.1). A seven-point Likert-scale ranging from one (strongly disagree) to seven (strongly agree) was used in this questionnaire. After a comparison of the alpha coefficients, the scales showed some differences in their scores with all the scales proving to be reliable and above the acceptable α=.70.

TABLE 5.1 List of Measures Used in the Study and their Cronbach Alphas (α)

Measure	*No. Items*	*Original α=*	*Reported α=*
• Psychological contract breach (PCB)a	5	.92	.70
• Psychological contract violation (PCV)b	4	.92	.86
• Job satisfaction (JS)c	5	.90	.94
• Affective commitment (AC)d	4	.85	.76
• Turnover intentions (TI)e	3	.93	.89

Sources:
a - Robinson & Morrison (2000)
b - Robinson & Morrison (2000)
c - Randsley et al. (2009)
d - Meyer & Allen (1997)
e - Chiu & Francesco (2003)

All alpha coefficients were above α=.70, indicating acceptable internal reliability of the scales. Listwise deletion based on all variables in the procedure resulted in two items being deleted on the affective organisational commitment scale, as the α level was below the required estimates for reliability after reverse coding the items.

Ethical considerations

The participants in the study received full disclosure of the nature of the study, the risks, benefits and alternatives, with an extended opportunity to ask questions. This was done in person by the researcher before handing out the questionnaires. The main aim of this study was to maximise benefits while minimising possible harm to the respondents. Fairness in distribution was another consideration as justice occurs when some benefit to which a person is entitled is not denied without good reason or when some burden is not imposed unduly. Information was distributed fairly, as it reached all the participants at the same time and in the same manner.

Methods of data analysis

Correlation between psychological contract violation (PCV), job satisfaction (JS), affective organisational commitment (AC) and turnover intentions (TI) was statistically calculated using SPSS version 23 (IBM Corp, 2015). Multiple regression analysis tested the combined effects of the variables (PCV, PCB, JS and AC) on turnover intentions.

DISCUSSION OF THE RESULTS

The descriptive results, including the minimum, maximum, mean and standard deviation of the scales, are provided in Table 5.2. The high mean value of M=4.70 for AC shows that most of the respondents agreed that their emotional attachment and investment in the SANDF is high. The respondents also reported relatively high levels of job satisfaction. The PCV shows a low mean of M=2.52, suggesting a limited perception of PCV. The respondents also showed a low level of TI. On the other hand, the mean score of M=4.26 for PCB indicates that the respondents experience a sense of psychological contract breach.

Multiple linear regression was calculated to predict the influence of PCB, AC, PCV and JS on TI. A significant regression equation was found (F(4,73) =21.293, p<.001), with an adjusted R^2 of .513. JS and PCV were both significant predictors of TI.

TABLE 5.2 Correlations Among and descriptive statistics for key study variables (N=78)

Variable	*M (SD)*	1	2	3
• Affective commitment	4.71 (1.35)			
• Job satisfaction	4.89 (1.56)	.661 a		
• Psychological contract violation	2.53 (1.47)	−.68 a	−.533 a	
• Psychological contract breach	4.26 (1.15)	−.145 a	−.427 a	.20 a
• Turnover intentions	2.91 (1.83)	−.629 a	−.631 a	.628 a

a - Correlation is significant at the 0.05 level (2-tailed).

In keeping with the literature and based on the correlations demonstrated in Table 5.2 above, those who have higher AC and JS are less likely to want to leave the SANDF. Those who experience higher levels of PCB and PCV are more likely to want to leave the organisation. This means that soldiers who want to leave the SANDF demonstrate low levels of job satisfaction, limited affective organisational commitment, and perceive high levels of psychological contract violation and breach.

After a comparison of the alpha coefficients, the scales proved to be reliable and above the acceptable α=.70. With affective organisational commitment, two items were removed as the α level was below the required estimates for reliability after reverse coding the items. When turnover intentions were used as a dependent variable for affective organisational commitment (AC), job satisfaction (JS), psychological contract violation (PCV) and psychological contract breach (PCB), AC, JS and PCV were significantly related to TI. The relationship between TI and PCV was moderate, meaning that PCB does not have much effect on soldiers' intentions to quit the SANDF.

CONCLUSION AND RECOMMENDATIONS

Psychological contracts, for the purposes of this study, are the beliefs that soldiers at the Academy have regarding the terms and conditions of the exchange relationship between themselves and the SANDF. By closing the missing link between formal contracts and all that applies to the working relationship, positive psychological contracts reduce uncertainty, shape behaviour, and give people a feeling of control over what happens to them in the organisation. This can be seen at the initiation of the agreement when soldiers are still being recruited and will continue to be developed further during their first few months in the SANDF.

If the military manages to succeed in providing for the beliefs soldiers hold regarding the employment relationship, the psychological contract can be said to be in a good state and can be expected to lead to job satisfaction, higher levels of commitment and intention to remain. Conversely, if an individual soldier perceives that the SANDF has failed to meet one or more obligations affecting the psychological contract, a breach occurs. Many studies have revealed the relationships between breaches and lower job satisfaction, trust, commitment, organisational citizenship behaviour (OCB), emotional exhaustion, higher turnover intentions, and turnover.

The psychological contract has shown its contribution in civilian settings, especially concerning the retention of personnel. Implementing the concept into military settings will help explain why capable soldiers leave without completing their service in the DoD, and why satisfaction and commitment levels drop, and intentions of turnover increase.

Military leadership of necessity requires demanding and striving towards building a professional military corps. The military profession and the task endowed on the SANDF in the broader continent impose certain demands on the soldier. However, the deterministic nature of environmental factors has far-reaching implications for employee engagement, thus obliging leadership to evaluate its stance. The advent of the all-volunteer force made it apparent that the values and priorities of soldiers will vary significantly from what the organisational leadership expects. This paper makes recommendations to the SANDF leadership to put more focus on the causes of turnover in the military and take steps to reverse them. The identification of the causes will need to be supplemented with responsive leadership that is attuned to the needs of soldiers. The rigid chain of command must be seen to be approachable and supportive.

Since the psychological contract is dynamic and evolving, organisations like the SANDF need to invest effort into understanding the changes, and at various times and when needed renegotiate the contract (Gotz & McCall, 1980). Salgado and Lester as cited in Chi-jung and Chin-i (2014) suggested that a proactive approach (as opposed to a reactive approach) to the psychological contract has a greater likelihood of reducing employees' intentions to leave, since the organisation will become more likely to meet their needs. Therefore, it should be noted that when open-book management techniques are taken literally, they can form a framework for providing effective communication between the organisation and the employee.

For the SANDF to be successful, it is suggested that management of the psychological contract must begin even before the recruitment and hiring of a soldier, meaning that hindrances must be prevented or dealt with at the stage of attraction of potential personnel (as described in Cohen, 2012, and Fein et al., 2013). Hassan (2014) also emphasised that an organisation's publications or advertisements, the interview process followed, contract negotiation and the orientation process of new employees all contribute towards the initial formation of the employee's psychological contract with the organisation. The argument is that media outreach creates the first impression of the values espoused by the employer. The interview process will then establish the image of the organisation for potential employees (Niehoff & Paul, as cited in Mustosmaki, Anttila & Oinas, 2013).

This approach will help promote expectations ranging from the tangibles, such as pay and benefits, to the intangibles, such as the treatment of employees or degree of empowerment given to an employee (Cole, 2014). Aligning all of these, both with each other and with the DoD's expectations will allow the SANDF to form contracts that are understood by both parties and are less likely to be violated.

Most of the literature surveyed focuses on relatively large organisations with a set number of managers and workforce, thus neglecting educational institutions, and more especially SAMA. Examining the literature in relation to educational institutions such as SAMA will be very helpful in expanding the SANDF's knowledge regarding this area of expertise. Despite the lack of existing research that brings together the construct of the psychological contract and the needs of soldiers engaged in higher education, there should be an abundance of research on a substantial qualitative basis that may warrant further investigation. Essentially, significant room exists to try and test the hypotheses of the various schools of thought on the psychological contract.

However, there will also be certain constraints that must be considered carefully before engaging in such research, such as the availability of the respondents and ethical restrictions. As the theory suggests, numerous complexities differentiate various tertiary institutions, which also vary from country to country (Cole, 2014). This may be a limitation to the formulation of generalised conclusions even for the SANDF. Nevertheless, despite the constraints imposed by the complexity of the SANDF, it is possible to undertake research using a combination of qualitative and quantitative criteria to produce comparative studies that will surpass the differences between contexts.

In any event, the level of difficulty in research further accentuates the need for additional endeavours to enrich these specific parts of the human resource management literature while opening new opportunities for future directions in research involving the SANDF. A potential challenge may exist in forecasting actual turnover intention, but in a future study, it would be useful to measure actual turnover among soldiers to gain a deeper understanding. Another limitation is that this study only included one SANDF academic university rather than a comparison of several units and/or arms of service (army, air force, navy and SAMHS). It would be interesting to see whether a comparison of these would yield similar or different results. Some factors to be considered for future research would be the type of unit (infantry, logistics), type of command, and the specific profiles of soldiers in the unit. For example, some units may consist of soldiers who stay in the service to achieve civilian education/ career goals rather than serving for the love of military career goals and way of life. Further research could also include testing soldiers upon enlistment and tracking their progress longitudinally to determine whether measures of engagement can be accurate measures of retention.

REFERENCES

Ahmed, E. 2016. Psychological contract breach: Consequences of unkept promises of permanent employment. *Contemporary Management Research*, 12(2). https://doi.org/10.7903/cmr.13914

Ahmed, E. & Muchiri, M. 2014. Effects of psychological contract breach, ethical leadership and supervisors' fairness on employees' performance and wellbeing. *World Journal of Management*, 5(2):1-13.

Akin, A. 2008. The scales of psychological wellbeing: A study of validity and reliability. Educational Sciences: *Theory & Practice*, 8(3):741-750.

Allen, N.J. & Meyer, J.P. 1990. The measurement and antecedents of affective, continuance and normative commitment to the organisation. *Journal of Occupational Psychology*, 63(1):1-18.

Argyris, C. 1960. *Understanding organisational behavior*. Homewood IL: Dorsey Press.

Bakker, A.B. 2011. An evidence-based model of work engagement. *Current Directions in Psychological Science*, 20(4):265-269.

Ballou, N.S. 2013. The effects of psychological contract breach on job outcomes. Master's thesis, Paper 4327, San Jose State University, San Jose, California.

Botha, L. & Moalusi, K.P. 2010. Values underlying perceptions of breach of the psychological contract. *SA Journal of Industrial Psychology/SA Tydskrif vir Bedryfsielkunde*, 36(1):1-12. https://doi.org/10.4102/sajip.v36i1.817

Chambel, M.J. 2014. Does the fulfillment of supervisor psychological contract make a difference? Attitudes of in-house and temporary agency workers. *Leadership & Organization Development Journal*, 35(1):20-37. http://dx.doi.org/10.1108/LODJ-03-2012-0031

Chernyak-Hai, L. & Tziner, A. 2012. Organisational citizenship behaviors: Socio-psychological antecedents and consequences. *International Review of Social Psychology*, 25(3/4):53-92.

Chi-jung, F. & Chin-i, C. 2014. Unfulfilled expectations and promises, and behavioral outcomes. *International Journal of Organizational Analysis*, 22(1):61-75. https://doi.org/10.1108/IJOA-08-2011-0505

Chiu, R.K. & Francesco, A.M. 2003. Dispositional traits and turnover intention: Examining the mediating role of job satisfaction and affective commitment. *International Journal of Manpower*, 24(3):284-298.

Cohen, A. 2012. The relationship between individual values and psychological contracts. *Journal of Managerial Psychology*, 27(3):283-301

Cole, B. 2014. The relationship between job demands, job resources, engagement, burnout and intention to quit. Master's thesis, Stellenbosch University, Stellenbosch, South Africa.

Conway N. & Briner R.B. 2005. *Understanding psychological contracts at work: A critical evaluation of theory and research.* Oxford: Oxford University Press.

Cooper-Hakim, A. & Viswesvaran, C. 2005. The construct of work commitment: Testing an integrative framework. *Psychological Bulletin,* 131(2):241-259.

Coyle-Shapiro, J.A.M. & Parzefall, M. 2008. Psychological contracts. In: J. Barling & C.L. Cooper (eds), *The SAGE Handbook of organisational behaviour,* pp.17-34. London: Sage

Fein, E.C., Tziner, A., Lusky, L. & Palachy, O. 2013. Relationships between ethical climate, justice perceptions, and LMX. *Leadership & Organization Development Journal,* 34(2):147-163.

Fisk, C. 2002. Reflections on the new psychological contract and the ownership of human capital. *Connecticut Law Review,* 34:765-785.

Gotz, G.A. & McCall, J.J., 1980. *Estimating military personnel retention rates: Theory and statistical method.* Santa Monica CA: Rand Corporation.

Griffith, J. 2005. Will citizens be soldiers? Examining retention of reserve component soldiers. *Armed Forces and Society,* 31(3):353-383.

Hakanen, D. & Conway, N. 2004. *Employee wellbeing and the psychological contract: A report for the CIPD. Research report.* London: Chartered Institute of Personnel and Development.

IBM Corp. Released 2015. IBM SPSS Statistics for Windows, Version 23.0. Armonk, NY: IBM Corp.

Ilyas, S. 2013. Combined effects of person job fit and organisation commitment on attitudinal outcomes such as job satisfaction and intention to quit. In: *Proceedings of the 2013 Istanbul Eurasian Academic Conference,* 16-19 June 2013, Istanbul, Turkey, pp.81-87. West Chester PA: West East Institute. Available at http://bit.ly/33sXsks

Jafri, H. 2014. Influence of personality on perception of psychological contract breach. *Psychological Thought,* 7(2):168-178.

Jenkins, J.M. 1993. Self-monitoring and turnover: The impact of personality on intent to leave. *Journal of Organizational Behavior,* 14(1):83-91.

Krausz, M., Koslowsky, M., Shalom, N. & Elyakim, N. 1995. Predictors of intentions to leave the ward, the hospital, and the nursing profession: A longitudinal study. *Journal of Organizational Behavior.* 16(3):277-288. https://doi.org/10.1002/job.4030160308

Meyer, J.P. & Allen, N.J. 1997. *Commitment in the workplace: Theory, research and application.* Thousand Oaks CA: Sage.

Mustosmaki, A., Anttila, T.A. & Oinas, T. 2013. Engaged or not? A comparative study on factors inducing engagement. *Nordic Journal of working life studies,* 3(1):49-67.

Nkewu, Z. 2014. Impact of psychological wellbeing and perceived combat readiness on willingness to deploy in the SANDF: An exploratory study. Master's thesis, Stellenbosch University, Stellenbosch. Available at https://scholar.sun.ac.za/handle/10019.1/86413

Randsley de Moura, G., Abrams, D., Retter, C., Gunnarsdottir, S. & Ando, K. 2009. Identification as an organisational anchor: How identification and job satisfaction combine to predict turnover intention. *European Journal of Social Psychology*, 39:540-557. https://doi.org/10.1002/ejsp.553

Robinson, S.L. 1996. Trust and breach of the psychological contract. *Administrative Science Quarterly*, 41(4):574-599.

Robinson, S.L. & Morrison, E.W. 2000. The development of psychological contract breach and violation: a longitudinal study. *Journal of Organizational Behavior*, 21(5):525-546.

Rousseau D.M. 1989. Psychological and implied contracts in organisations. *Employee Responsibilities and Rights Journal*, 2(2):121-139. https://doi.org/10.1007/BF01384942

Rousseau, D.M. 1995. *Psychological contracts in organisations. Understanding written and unwritten agreements*. Thousand Oaks CA: Sage.

Saeed, I., Waseem, M., Sikander, S. & Rizwan, M. 2014. The relationship of turnover intention with job satisfaction, job performance, leader member exchange, emotional intelligence and organizational commitment. *International Journal of Learning & Development*, 4(2):242-256. https://doi.org/10.5296/ijld.v4i2.6100

Smith, P.C., Balzer, W.K., Brannick, M., Chia, W., Eggleston, S. & Gibson, W. 1987. The revised JDI: A facelift for an old friend. *The Industrial-Organizational Psychologist*, 24(4):31-33. Available at https://www.siop.org/Research-Publications/TIP/TIP-Back-Issues

Straker, L., Abbott, R.A., Heiden, M., Mathiassen, S.E. & Toomingas, A. 2013. Sit-stand desks in call centres: Associations of use and ergonomics awareness with sedentary behaviour. *Applied Ergonomics*, 44(4):517-522.

Tallman, R.R.J. & Bruning, N.S. 2008. Relating employees' psychological contracts to their personality. *Journal of Managerial Psychology*. 23(6):688-712. https://doi.org/10.1108/02683940810894756

Tomprou, M. & Nikolaou, I. 2011. A model of psychological contract creation upon organisational entry. *Career Development International*, 16(4):342-363. https://doi.org/10.1108/13620431111158779

Van den Tooren, M., De Jonge, J. & Dormann, C. 2012. A matter of match? An experiment on choosing specific job resources in different demanding work situations. *International Journal of Stress Management*, 19(4):311-332. https://doi.org/10.1037/a0030110

Wilcove, G.L., Burch, R.L., Conroy, A.M. & Bruce, R.A. 1991. *Officer career development: A review of the civilian and military research literature on turnover and retention*. San Diego CA: Navy Personnel Research and Development Centre.

Zhao, H., Wayne, S. J., Glibkowski, B.C. & Bravo, J. 2007. The impact of psychological contract breach on work-related outcomes: A meta-analysis. *Personnel Psychology*, 60(3):647-680. https://doi.org/10.1111/j.1744-6570.2007.00087.x

6

Military Students' Perceptions of Support and Psychological Contract Fulfilment

Zinhle Nzimande
Nicole Dodd
Lindiwe Masole

The primary responsibility of the South African National Defence Force (SANDF) is to secure and protect the borders of the republic against internal and external threats. Besides this, the SANDF plays a critical role in contributing to peace and stability efforts throughout the African continent (Neethling, 2011). However, the numerous challenges facing the SANDF, such as the declining budget and ageing equipment, pose a threat to delivery on this mandate (Neethling, 2011).

During the 2019/2020 annual budget vote, the Minister of Defence highlighted several key challenges facing the SANDF. One of the challenges related to insufficient funds to cover expenditures related to the compensation of employees (Mapisa-Nqakula, 2019). The compensation of employees in the SANDF accounts for more than 50% of the department's expenditure (Martin, 2016). Yet even with this astounding allocation of resources towards employee compensation, the SANDF is still not regarded as offering competitive salary packages. As a result, the SANDF is losing high volumes of members with critical skills to private companies that offer higher salaries (Martin, 2012).

Considering the Department of Defence (DoD) from a more general perspective as an organisation, it is clear that low salaries are not the only reason why organisations find it challenging to retain personnel: factors such as a lack of organisational support, unfair management practices, and poor leadership also contribute toward lower levels of employee commitment (Luddy, 2005). One of the undesirable outcomes of lower organisational commitment is that it may lead to valuable employees seeking alternative employment. Masibigiri and Nienaber (2011), looking at the loss of experienced, skilled public servants to private organisations, concluded that it affects most government organisations in South Africa. The South African National Defence Force (SANDF) is not immune to this situation. Over the years, experienced, qualified and skilled employees have left the SANDF for greener pastures. As a result, the South African Defence Review (Department of Defence, 2014) has highlighted concerns regarding the retention of professionals and specialised skilled employees within the SANDF.

Organisational support forms one of the most critical aspects of the employment relationship and is considered essential to keeping employees attached to the organisation. Therefore, it is essential to examine the effect of organisational support on employee outcomes. A body of literature reflects investigation into the relationship between social exchange and employee outcomes (Aselage & Eisenberger, 2003; Meyer & Allen, 1991; Serfontein, 2014; Van der Nest, 2014), and demonstrates that there is a positive relationship between social exchange and employee outcomes (Van der Nest, 2014).

According to Arshadi (2011), exchange relationships are based on the notion that organisations and employees engage in a reasonably predictable give-and-take relationship with each other. The match between their expectations determines the satisfaction of both. Although previous studies have established an association between exchange relationships and employee outcomes, i.e. job satisfaction, organisation citizenship behaviour, organisational commitment, and work engagement (Meyer & Allen, 1991; Aselage & Eisenberger, 2003; Serfontein, 2014; Van der Nest, 2014), very little research has been done to investigate exchange relationships within the SANDF. The limited research in the military context does not necessarily mean that employer-employee relationships are not functional in the SANDF; it merely shows the need to engage in empirical research to examine exchange relationships in this context. Therefore, this study examined the effect of perceived organisational support (POS) and psychological contract fulfilment on organisational commitment in the SANDF.

PROBLEM STATEMENT AND SIGNIFICANCE OF THE STUDY

The mission of the SANDF is to provide, manage, prepare and employ defence capabilities commensurate with the needs of South Africa, as regulated by the Constitution (Act 108 of 1996), national legislation, and parliamentary and executive direction. The SANDF's capacity to achieve its mission depends mainly on the effective utilisation of its resources (Department of Defence, 2014) and this involves the engagement of the individual soldier as well as the organisation: they need to work together. The expectation mutually assumed in this employee-employer relationship is that soldiers will dedicate their time, effort, and skills in exchange for job security and support from the organisation (Maslach, Schaufeli & Leiter, 2001). It is in this context that scholars are interested in studying relationships between the employee and the organisation.

The SANDF has been subjected to much pressure over the years – in the form of budget cuts, loss of valuable talent, and obsolescent equipment, to mention a few (Department of Defence, 2015). These issues have challenged the nature of the employment relationship within the SANDF. There is continual pressure on the SANDF to perform better with limited resources; and as a result, essential employee values such as job security, pay increases and promotions have been threatened (Department of Defence, 2015). Despite these challenges, the SANDF is still required to support its members in terms of offering career development, job security and competitive salaries.

The defence force invests much money in its members' education and training (Department of Defence, 2014), particularly in military officers, and other members studying at the Academy (SAMA). Since higher education is provided at considerable expense, it is, therefore, reasonable for the organisation (SANDF) to expect soldiers who studied at state expense to feel a moral obligation to remain with the organisation, despite attractive salary packages offered by other organisations. This study contributes to the body of literature by investigating the extent to which military members feel a sense of attachment to the SANDF as a result of perceived support and fulfilment of a psychological contract.

Perceived organisational support

Eisenberger, Huntington, Hutchison and Sowa (1986, p.500) were the first to conceptualise perceived organisational support (POS) and defined it as "employees' perceptions concerning the extent to which the organisation values their contribution and cares about their wellbeing." Based on the norm of reciprocity, when employees perceive their organisation to be supportive, they feel obliged to return the favour and help the organisation to reach its objectives. POS acts as a driving force encouraging employees to feel that their contributions will be rewarded in the future.

POS is rooted in a social exchange relationship. According to social exchange theory, employees expect employers to fulfil financial and social obligations (Cheung & Chiu, 2005). The perception of such obligations emphasises the reciprocity of the employment relationship. As such, employees evaluate treatment received from the organisation in return for their contributions (Mowday, Porter & Steers, 1982). Therefore, it is important to note that POS centres on the employee's perception of how much support they believe an organisation provides them.

Antecedents of POS

Rhoades and Eisenberger (2002) investigated the theoretical framework of POS to identify the antecedents of POS. They reviewed several studies concerning the employees' general beliefs that their organisation values their contribution and cares about their wellbeing. The outcomes of the study indicated the following as the primary antecedents of POS: fairness or organisational justice; supervisor support; as well as favourable rewards and job conditions (Rhoades & Eisenberger, 2002).

Fairness/organisational justice

According to Moideenkutty, Blau, Kumar and Nalakath (2001), employees' evaluation of discretionary actions taken by management has a strong effect on POS. Moorman (1991) explained organisational justice as employees' feelings regarding how well their organisation treats them. The literature distinguishes between the three main types of organisational justice: procedural justice, distributive justice, and interactional justice. Distributive and procedural justice is the focus of this study.

Distributive justice is concerned with the fair allocation of resources (Coetzee & Schreuder, 2010). In an attempt to examine the effect of distributive justice on POS, Moideenkutty et al. (2001) found that distributive justice has a strong positive correlation with POS. To explain this relationship, they added that employees tend to make favourable inferences regarding the organisation's ability to fairly reward their employees' efforts.

Procedural justice is concerned with the process by which outcomes are determined. James (2011) revealed that employers who demonstrate procedural fairness in decision-making have a positive influence on POS. Therefore, Moideenkutty et al. (2001) argued that perceptions of fairness result in employees making favourable inferences regarding the organisation's willingness to recognise and reward extra effort and such inferences make employees feel that the organisation values their contributions.

Supervisor support

The second factor that contributes to POS is supervisor support. Because supervisors act as agents of their organisations, they embody organisational support (Du Plessis, Barkhuizen, Stanz & Schutte, 2015). It can be argued that supervisors who show concern for the welfare of their subordinates contribute to the subordinates' positive evaluation of organisational support. Moreover, involving employees in decision-making that has a direct impact on them and recognising their contributions has a positive effect on POS (Mullen, Kroustalis, Meade & Surface, 2006).

Rewards and job conditions

Rhoades and Eisenberger (2002) suggested several rewards and job conditions that are related to POS, which include pay, opportunities for development, autonomy, job security, recognition and promotion. Also, Mullen et al. (2006) believe that providing employees with developmental opportunities, and a supportive environment that encourages individual development, is key to gaining commitment. Research suggests that providing opportunities for employee development serves as a strong indicator that the organisation cares for its employees (Mullen et al., 2006). It is, therefore, not unreasonable to expect a clear perception of organisational support among students studying at the Academy because their education is paid for by the SANDF.

Consequences of POS

Cheung and Chiu (2005) argued that a variety of rewards and favourable job conditions are associated with POS: factors such as allowing employees an opportunity to develop their skills, providing autonomy in the execution of their jobs, and improving working conditions, result in a positive perception of how the organisation values its personnel. Eisenberger, Fasolo and Davis-La Mastro (1990) and Shore and Wayne (1993) also found that employees tend to display certain attitudes and behaviours when they perceive their organisation to be supportive. Therefore, POS reflects the quality of the employment relationship (Rhoades & Eisenberger, 2002). High levels of POS can be reciprocated in various ways. LaMastro (1999, p.3) stated that "employees who experience a strong level of POS theoretically feel the need to reciprocate favourable organizational treatment with attitudes and behaviours that in turn benefit the organization."

Numerous studies have identified that certain attitudes are associated with POS – such as commitment (Bishop, Scott & Burroughs, 2000); job satisfaction; the desire to remain with the organisation; positive mood at work (LaMastro, 1999); and lower turnover intentions (Rhoades & Eisenberger, 2002). Our study, however, examined organisational commitment as a consequence of POS. Previous studies that extensively investigated the relationship between POS and employee organisational commitment (Satardien 2014; Scott, 2014; Rhoades & Eisenberger, 2002) suggest that POS is important for organisations because it is linked to higher levels of employee commitment. In other words, supported employees are likely to increase their effort, demonstrate organisational citizenship behaviours, and identify with the organisation's goals and objectives (Scott, 2014; Tumwesigye, 2010).

Mullen et al. (2006) believe that organisational commitment is enhanced by providing employees with developmental opportunities, so it can be anticipated that members studying at SAMA at state expense will have high levels of commitment. Panaccio and Vandenberghe (2009) and LaMastro (1999) further examined the relationship between POS and all dimensions of organisational commitment and found that POS is positively related to affective, normative and continuance commitment. Rhoades and Eisenberger (2002) arrived at similar conclusions.

In the wake of so much consensus, Agarwal and Gupta (2016) criticised existing literature on the effect of POS on employee outcomes. They argued that previous studies had focused on the consequences of POS while neglecting the processes through which POS influences work outcomes. Their research thus focused on the effect of POS on employment relationship outcomes. Guchait, Cho and Meurs (2015) claimed that the key contributing factor of POS is when employees feel that an organisation gives them favourable treatment. Aselage and Eisenberger (2003) added that POS and the psychological contract are interrelated because POS leads to employees' perceptions that the company has fulfilled its obligations, and that it is therefore reasonable to expect that POS will lead to organisational commitment. The current study thus contributes to the existing literature in testing the effect of POS on psychological contract fulfilment and organisational commitment. Its outcomes suggest that POS will positively predict organisational commitment.

Psychological contracts

The psychological contract has mainly been studied in labour relations and business contracts and to a lesser extent, in the field of psychology (Sonnenberg, Koene & Paauwe, 2011). Industrial and organisational researchers adopted the concept of the psychological contract and went on to establish links between this concept and various employee outcomes (Coetzee & Schreuder, 2010). However, little to no research exists on the concept of psychological contracts within the South African military context. This study intends to close the existing gap with research into the extent to which psychological contract fulfilment leads to organisational commitment in the SANDF.

The psychological contract is generally used to understand the relationship between the employer and employee in the employment contract (Coetzee & Schreuder, 2010). Rousseau (1989) defined a psychological contract as an individual's belief about the terms and conditions of employment. It involves promises and obligations that both parties make, but that are not explicitly included in the written employment contract. Psychological contracts thus emphasise the reciprocity of the employment relationship. McDonald and Makin (2000) stressed that these obligations and promises are a result of an employee's subjective perceptions about the actions of the organisation. In other words, psychological contracts are implicit and reflect an employee's perception that promises have been made, and obligations offered, which bind the employee and the organisation to a set of reciprocal obligations (O'Donohue, Donohue & Grimmer, 2007).

According to Freese and Schalk (2008), a psychological contract is a multi-dimensional construct. Robinson (1996) and Rousseau (2000) categorised psychological contracts into transactional contracts (dealing with short-term economic benefits) and relational contracts (involving long-term relationships between the employer and the employee). The relational psychological contract is based on the socio-emotional aspects of the employment relationship while transactional contracts are concerned with the employee's material interests (Pohl, Bertrand & Ergen, 2016). Employees whose psychological contracts are relational strive to perform beyond the expected performance standards and therefore expect recognition from the employer for their efforts (Conway & Briner, 2005). Notably, Rousseau (2004), and Zagenczyk, Gibney, Few and Scott (2011) argue that this type of psychological contract leads to increased levels of employee commitment towards an organisation.

Harman and Doherty (2014) claim that employees whose psychological contracts are mainly transactional expect rewards for reaching performance standards at work. Conway and Briner (2005) noted that when an employee's transactional contracts are violated, they tend to show withdrawal work behaviours and start searching for alternative employment.

Rousseau (1995) extended the typologies of understanding psychological contracts by adding a further two kinds of psychological contracts (balanced and transitional contracts). Balanced psychological contracts are "open-ended arrangements with both parties contributing to each other's learning and development, conditioned on the economic success of the employer" (Wöcke & Sutherland, 2008, p.5). Both the employer and the employee benefit from the psychological contract, and therefore it is suggested that this type of psychological contract may lead to a positive employment relationship.

Various researchers studied the relationship between the employee's psychological contract and job outcomes (Cheung & Chiu, 2005; Coetzee & Schreuder, 2010; McDonald & Makin, 2000; Coyle-Shapiro & Conway, 2005; O'Donohue et al., 2007). The focus was mainly on understanding the consequences of psychological contract violation (McDonald & Makin, 2000). These researchers argue that when employees feel that the organisation has not met the expected obligations, the psychological contract becomes damaged and employees will be less committed to the organisation.

According to Gurerrero and Herrbach (2008), researchers are beginning to give attention to the positive outcomes of the psychological contract. They reviewed several studies on the consequences of the psychological contract and found that only a few studies focused on the positive impact of psychological contracts. Nevertheless, researchers continue to demonstrate that employers who fulfil their unformalised promises promote their employees' perceptions that the organisation cares for their welfare (Coyle-Shapiro & Kessler, 2000; Gurerrero & Herrbach, 2008). Therefore, employees may interpret the employer's actions of fulfilling its promises as a sign of commitment to them.

Organisational commitment

Judge and Kammeyer-Mueller (2012, p.243) defined organisational commitment as "an individual's psychological bond with the organisation, as represented by an affective attachment to the organisation, a feeling of loyalty toward it and an intention to remain as part of it". Organisational commitment is a multi-dimensional concept (Meyer & Allen, 1991) that refers to an individual's attachment to the organisation for which they work. The three dimensions of organisational commitment (affective, continuance and normative) conceptualised by Meyer and Allen (1991) are a crucial point of discussion in this paper.

Affective commitment

Affective commitment reflects an employee's emotional connection to an organisation, as well as their identification with and involvement in the organisation. As noted above, affective commitment is associated with POS and relational psychological contracts (Bishop et al., 2000). To explain this relationship, Raina (2013) postulated that the quality of the employment relationship influences an individual's level of organisational commitment. This means that affective commitment is a result of the favourable treatment that employees receive from the organisation. It is, therefore, reasonable to expect that SAMA students with high levels of affective commitment will identify with the goals and objective of the SANDF.

Continuance commitment

Continuance commitment is defined as the "extent to which employees remain in the organisation due to the recognition of the cost associated with quitting, the lack of an alternative job, or the feeling that the personal sacrifices generated by quitting will be considerably high" (Balassiano & Salles, 2012, p.274). Continuance commitment, therefore, represents the soldier's continued need to serve in the military (Gade, 2003). In most cases, employees who are unable to transfer their skills and education are forced to continue working for their employer despite their dissatisfaction (Coetzee & Schreuder, 2010). However, given the rate of employee turnover among soldiers who obtained their qualifications at the Academy, it is argued that the education provided at SAMA is highly transferrable to outside organisations (Department of Defence, 2014). From the above, it could be expected that SANDF members at the Academy will show low levels of continuance commitment (Van der Vaart, Linde, De Beer & Cockeran, 2015).

Normative commitment

Normative commitment is concerned with employees' feelings of being obliged to remain with the organisation because it is a moral duty to stay (Coetzee & Schreuder, 2010). Soldiers who joined the military because they regard it as a calling are more likely to have high levels of normative commitment (Gade, 2003).

McDonald and Makin (2000) argue that individuals show commitment to organisations that meet their expectations. However, the nature of the psychological contract will determine the degree of commitment individuals will have. Individuals whose psychological contracts are predominantly relational will have higher levels of organisational commitment than those with transactional contracts (Meyer & Allen, 1991; Theron & Dodd, 2011). This means that, to some extent, employees may value trusting relationships and loyalty more than the economic benefits offered by the employer.

Most research on the effect of the psychological contract has focused on affective commitment as a consequence of the social exchange relationship (Millward & Hopkins, 1998; Raja, Johns & Ntalianis, 2004). However, this research brings a different approach as it has investigated the effect of the different types of psychological contracts on different dimensions of organisational commitment. It is suggested that the nature of a psychological contract will have differential effects on the different aspects of organisational commitment.

McDonald and Makin (2000) conducted a similar study by investigating the extent to which the various psychological contracts relate to different dimensions of organisational commitment. They suggested that temporary staff have different psychological contracts compared to permanent employees and that this determined the impact on employee commitment. The results showed that relational contracts lead to affective commitment, while transactional contracts lead to both normative and continuance commitment (McDonald & Makin, 2000).

McDonald and Makin's (2000) study did not, however, examine the effect of balanced contracts relative to the dimensions of organisational commitment. Therefore, this study aimed to determine the impact of balanced, relational and transactional psychological contracts on different dimensions of organisational commitment, respectively, within the South African military context.

RESEARCH OBJECTIVES AND HYPOTHESES

The main objective of this study was to examine the effect of perceived organisational support and psychological contracts fulfilment on the organisational commitment of soldiers studying at SAMA. This can be broken into two main components:

Objectives:

To analyse the effect of perceived organisational support and psychological contract fulfilment on organisational commitment.

To analyse the relationship between different types of psychological contract and dimensions of organisational commitment.

Our research was based on the following hypotheses:

H1 POS affects employees' organisational commitment.

H2 Psychological contract fulfilment affects employees' organisational commitment

H3a Relational contracts affect employees' affective commitment.

H3b Transactional contracts have an effect on employees' continuance commitment.

H3c Balanced contracts affect employees' normative commitment.

METHODS

Research design

This study applied a quantitative approach to gather and analyse data. POS and psychological contract were identified as independent variables for the study because they influence the type of organisational commitment employees have towards an organisation (dependent variable). The research design applied to this research question is the descriptive type as it is aimed at describing the relationship that exists between variables (Bless, Higson-Smith & Sithole, 2013).

Sampling design

The population of this study comprised students studying at SAMA: both those enrolled for distance education, and residential uniformed students of various ranks, and from all arms of service. A convenience sampling method was used to collect data from participants (N=211). This sampling method allowed easy access to the participants (Bless et al., 2013), of relevance because distance education SAMA students, particularly, are located in remote areas and could only be reached at certain times. The sample size provided a confidence level of 95%. Therefore, the chosen sample was a fair representation of the population as it comprised individuals from different arms of service, ranks and years of service.

Most of the participants were from the SA Army (N=125), with others from the South African Air Force (SAAF) (N=30), the SA Navy (N=28) and the South African Military Health Service (SAMHS) (N=28). Most of the participants had between six and ten years of service (N=102), followed by 11-20 years of service (N=61), 0-5 years of service (N=37). Only 11 participants had 21 or more years of service. Respondents were also grouped according to their study type, with a large group representing residential students (N=116) and a slightly lower response rate from distance education students (N=95).

Instruments

Data were collected using existing questionnaires that have been widely researched to measure the constructs. To measure POS, an eight-item shorter version of the original 36-item Survey of Perceived Organisational Support (SPOS) by Eisenberger et al. (1986) was used. This instrument measures the extent to which employees feel valued by their organisation on a five-point Likert scale (where one=strongly disagree and five=strongly agree). Higher scores indicate a high perception of organisational support. This version has been used with success in previous studies with a Cronbach's coefficient alpha of α=.886, which indicates that the SPOS is highly reliable (Du Plessis, 2010).

Psychological contract was measured using Rousseau's (2000) Psychological Contract Inventory (PCI). The scale consists of 32 items measuring psychological contract fulfilment as well as identifying the types of psychological contracts of employees. PCI measures psychological contract in terms of several factors, namely internal and external career development, performance-related outcomes, loyalty, job security, and narrow and short-term contracts. According to Rousseau (2000), the scores of the subscales are used to determine the type of psychological contract (balanced, relational or transactional). In this study, a five-point Likert scale which ranges from one (not at all) to five (to a very large extent) was used. The PCI was evaluated against other psychological contract measures and is recommended because it assesses the type of contract and provides an evaluation of the psychological contract (Freese

& Schalk, 2008). Previous studies reported an acceptable reliability co-efficient of α=.70 for the scale (Rousseau, 2000).

A 24-item Organisational Commitment Scale measuring the extent to which employees are committed to an organisation was used (Meyer & Allen, 1991). This scale measures three dimensions of organisation commitment: affective, normative and continuance commitment, each of which consists of eight items. The scale is measured on a five-point Likert-type scale. Theron and Dodd (2011) established a reliability coefficient of α=.90 for the instrument.

DATA COLLECTION AND PROCEDURE

Ethical considerations

Upon obtaining permission to conduct the study from the SANDF authorities, Stellenbosch University granted ethical clearance. A consent form explaining the purpose of the study, and inviting students to participate in the study, was distributed. Voluntary respondents who agreed to participate were then invited to complete a questionnaire at the Academy during a contact session. Completing the questionnaire took between 25 and 35 minutes. A total of 350 questionnaires were distributed, and 211 were usable, representing a 60% response rate.

Data analysis

Data were captured and analysed using the Statistical Package for Social Sciences (SPSS) program (Muijs, 2010; Verma, 2013). The first step in data analysis was to ascertain the validity and reliability of the scales. A principal component analysis (PCA) was conducted to determine the factor loadings of the scales. Reliability was measured using Cronbach's coefficient alpha. A Cronbach's alpha level above α=.70 was considered acceptable for this research. Lastly, correlation and regression analysis were performed to test the hypotheses.

Reliability and validity of the scales

The researcher adopted a factor analysis technique to determine whether the sets of variables could be grouped to form a distinct construct (Muijs, 2010; Verma, 2013). The PCA with varimax rotation was performed to determine the construct validity of all items in the scales. To determine the suitability of factor analysis, Yong and Pearce (2013) suggested that the following requirements must be met: on a correlation matrix all items should be above .30, Bartlett's test of sphericity should be significant ($p<.05$) and the Kaiser-Meyer-Olkin measure (KMO) of sampling adequacy should be above .60. A sample of more than 200 requires a factor loading of .40 to assess statistical significance, and thus low factor loadings and cross-loadings were deleted (Verma, 2013). The Appendix at the end of this chapter provides the summary tables of the factor structure of all the scales.

Perceived organisational support

First, the factorability of all eight items of the scale was examined. Seven of the eight items correlated above .30 with each item. The Bartlett's test was significant ($\chi2(21)=388.63$, $p<.0001$) and the KMO was greater than .60 (.845). Therefore, the scale is suitable for factor analysis. The results of the varimax rotation revealed the presence of one component with eigenvalues above 1, which explained 61.01% of the total variance (see Table 6.6, in the Appendix to Chapter 6, at the end of this chapter). The reliability of the scale was determined using Cronbach's alpha. Cronbach's alpha of POS is acceptable at $\alpha=.81$.

Organisational commitment scale

The correlation matrix shows that the correlation between items is above .30. The Bartlett's test is significant ($\chi2(66)=759.256$, $p<.0001$) and the KMO is greater than .60 (.744), indicating that the scale is suitable for factor analysis. In all, 11 items were deleted from the analysis due to low factor loadings and cross-loadings. The PCA revealed the presence of three factors with eigenvalues above one, explaining 57.75% of the total variance. The first factor (affective commitment) explained 29.68% of the variance, the second factor (continuance commitment) explained 17.54%, and the last factor (normative commitment) explained 10.53% of the variance (see Table 6.7 in the Appendix to Chapter 6). The reliability of all the subscales or factors was determined using the Cronbach's coefficient alpha. The alpha for the overall organisational commitment scale was acceptable, and all the factors also had acceptable Cronbach's alphas of $\alpha=.742$ for affective commitment, $\alpha=.700$ for continuance commitment, and $\alpha=.695$ for normative commitment.

Psychological contract

The correlation matrix between items on this scale indicated that the correlation between items was above .30. Once more, Bartlett's test is significant ($\chi2(378)=3621.852$, $p<.0001$) and the KMO is greater than .60 (.824) which shows that the scale is suitable for factor analysis. Consistent with the studies by Rousseau (2000), and Scheepers and Shuping (2011), this study identified six factors with eigenvalues greater than one, explaining 70.10% of the total variance (see Table 6.8 in the Appendix to Chapter 6). These factors were identified as internal career prospects; external career prospects; performance-related outcomes; loyalty; job security; and narrow and short-term contracts (Rousseau, 2000). The reliability coefficients of the six factors were acceptable and ranged from $\alpha=.82$ to $\alpha=.89$.

RESULTS

Correlation results

Before testing the hypotheses, the researchers measured the association between variables in the study. Table 6.1 represents the means (*M*) and standard deviations

(*SD*) as well as the correlation matrix between the dependent and independent variables. The results of a Pearson product-moment correlation revealed a low positive correlation ($r(209)=.35$, $p<.001$) between psychological contract fulfilment and organisational commitment. A moderate positive relationship was found between POS and organisational commitment ($r(209)=.41$, $p<.001$). It was hypothesised that a relationship exists between the types of psychological contract and different dimensions of organisational commitment.

The results revealed a moderate correlation ($r(209)=.45$, $p<.001$) between the relational psychological contract and affective commitment. No correlation was found between balanced psychological contract and normative commitment. When looking at the relationship between transactional psychological contracts and continuance commitment, a low negative correlation was found between these variables ($r(209)=-.22$, $p<.002$).

TABLE 6.1 The Correlations Matrix of the Study Variables (*N*=211)

M	*SD*	1	2	3	4	5	6	7	8
• 3.29	.71								
• 3.74	.66	.449[a]							
• 3.32	.59	.409[a]	.348[a]						
• 3.03	.83	.437[a]	.398[a]	.824[a]					
• 3.61	.94	.532[a]	.412[a]	.542[a]	.479[a]				
• 3.44	.87	−.077	−.027	.539[a]	.071	−.089			
• 3.53	.85	.250[a]	.276[a]	.074	.051	.205[a]	.017		
• 3.80	.95	.292[a]	.415[a]	.476[a]	.447[a]	.287[a]	.163[b]	.268[a]	
• 2.54	.98	−.343[a]	−.242[a]	−.342[a]	−.397[a]	−.215[a]	−.029	.065	−.378[a]

Variables:
1 - POS perceived organizational support
2 - PCF psychological contract fulfilment
3 - OC organisational commitment
4 - AC affective commitment
5 - CC continuance commitment
6 - NC normative commitment
7 - BC balanced contracts
8 - RC relational contracts
9 - TC transactional contracts

Notes:
a - Correlation is significant at the 0.01 level
b - Correlation is significant at the 0.05 level

Hypothesis results

A total of six hypotheses were tested using simple linear regression analysis. Hypothesis one (perceived organizational support [POS] affects employees' organisational commitment) was tested to determine whether POS predicts organisational commitment. The results indicate that POS explains 26% of the variance of organisational commitment (see Table 6.2). The regression coefficients of POS were statistically significant ($\beta=.340$, $t=6.473$, $p<.001$). Therefore hypothesis one is accepted; that is, employees who believe the organisation values their contribution and cares for their wellbeing will be committed to the organisation.

Hypothesis 2 stated that psychological contract fulfilment (PCF) positively predicts employee organisational commitment. Table 6.2 illustrates that the regression analysis found that 18% of organisational commitment is explained by psychological contract fulfilment. More specifically, psychological contract fulfilment significantly (β=.311, t=5.36, p<.001) predicts organisational commitment and therefore hypothesis 2 was supported.

TABLE 6.2 Regression Analysis Predicting Organisational Commitment

Predictor variable	*B*	*Std. Error*	*Beta*	*t*	*Sig.*
• POS	.263	.058	.340	6.473	.000
• Psychological contract	.184	.062	.311	5.36	.003
R^2=.448					

Hypothesis 3(a) stated that relational psychological contracts (RCs) would predict affective commitment of the participants. The results presented in Table 6.3 support the hypothesis and relational psychological contracts explain 20% of the variance of affective commitment. A significant regression coefficient (β=.388, t=7.227, p<.001) was found.

TABLE 6.3 Regression Analysis Predicting Affective Commitment

Predictor variable	*B*	*Std. Error*	*Beta*	*t*	*Sig.*
• Affective commitment	.388	.054	.388	7.22	.0001
R^2=.447					

Hypothesis 3(b) predicted a positive relationship between transactional psychological contracts (TCs) and continuance commitment (CC). Transactional contracts explain 4.6% of the variance in continuance commitment. Contrary to expectations (see Table 6.4), transactional contracts significantly predict a negative relationship with continuance commitment (β=-.215, t=-3.185, p<.05). Therefore, hypothesis 3(b) was rejected.

TABLE 6.4 Regression Analysis Predicting Continuance Commitment

Predictor variable	*B*	*Std. Error*	*Beta*	*t*	*Sig.*
• Continuance commitment	–.206	.065	–.215	–3.185	.002
R^2=.215					

Hypothesis 3(c) suggested that the fulfilment of a balanced psychological contract (BC) positively predicts normative commitment (NC). Table 6.5's results show no significant effect of balanced psychological contracts on normative commitment (β= .017, t=.248, p>.05). In line with these findings, hypothesis 3(c) was rejected.

TABLE 6.5 Regression Analysis Predicting Normative Commitment					
Predictor variable	*B*	*Std. Error*	*Beta*	*t*	*Sig.*
• Normative commitment	.018	.072	.017	.248	.804
R^2=. 017					

DISCUSSION

This study aimed first, to analyse the effect of POS and psychological contract fulfilment on organisational commitment; and second, to analyse the effect of types of psychological contract on different dimensions of organisational commitment. Regarding the first aim, this study found that POS affects the organisational commitment of defence force members studying at SAMA: that is, that employees who perceive their organisation as more supportive reported higher levels of organisational commitment. Several studies concurred with these findings and demonstrated that when employees feel valued by an organisation, they develop feelings of attachment to that organisation (Tumwesigye, 2010). Scott (2014) and Satardien's (2014) studies made similar findings in a South African context.

Concerning the second aim, as expected, this study found that psychological contract fulfilment is positively related to organisational commitment. In other words, when an employee feels that the employer has kept its promises, they feel obligated to offer their loyalty in return and continue to work for the organisation. Considering that members studying at the SAMA are sent by the SANDF to empower themselves with knowledge, it is reasonable that employees will perceive the organisation's effort as a fulfilment of the psychological contract. In support of this, Pohl et al. (2016) recommended that since the military is a demanding working environment, military organisations should encourage commitment from soldiers by offering career support to them. These results are consistent with the findings of Van der Vaart et al. (2015) that employees generally desire to stay with an organisation that provides them with opportunities for development, which they believe cannot be replicated in another organisation. Thus, the findings of this study suggest that employers who fulfil their employees' psychological contracts give their employees the confidence to invest their time and effort in reaching organisational goals and objectives in return for job security and career development.

The study also investigated the effect of different types of psychological contracts on different dimensions of organisational commitment. Results showed a significant positive correlation between relational contracts and affective commitment, thus supporting the part of the third hypothesis (relational contracts affect employees' affective commitment). This implies that the greater the employees' relational contracts, the higher the level of affective commitment towards the organisation. The underlying reason is that employees with strong relational contracts generally identify with the organisation's values and culture (McDonald & Makin, 2000). To others, the military is more than just a job; some people joined because they have strong ties with the values and culture of the military. It is, therefore, reasonable to expect that they would have an emotional attachment to the organisation.

Contrary to expectations, the current study revealed a negative relationship between transactional psychological contract and continuance commitment. As mentioned previously, employees whose psychological contracts are predominantly transactional expect rewards for reaching performance standards at work, and, when no rewards are given, they may seek alternative employment (Harman & Doherty, 2014). The results suggest that members studying at the SAMA feel no obligation to remain with the organisation. Finally, no relationship was found between a balanced psychological contract and normative commitment. This implies that employees believe that they are responsible for their career development and long-term employability, and as a result, they do not feel a moral obligation to remain with the organisation. Although it appears as if balanced contracts have not been investigated extensively, these findings suggest that soldiers studying at the Academy have boundaryless career patterns and therefore are willing to change jobs whenever they feel like it (Hamilton & Von Treuer, 2012).

Limitations of the study

The limitations of this study are related to the generalisation of results, the use of self-reported data and the exclusion of demographic variables in the analysis. First, the sample of this study was limited to uniformed members studying only at SAMA. Although the sole aim of the study was to examine the relationships between variables, and not to generalise the results, the significance of this study necessitates ongoing research using a larger sample. Second, the use of self-report questionnaires posed the risk of distortions in responses, and caution should therefore be exercised when interpreting the results. Finally, the present study did not take into account the demographic factors (i.e. arms of service, rank group or tenure) that could have an impact on the organisational commitment of the members studying at the SAMA: future research should also examine the influence of demographic variables on organisational commitment.

CONCLUSION AND RECOMMENDATIONS

As highlighted, employment relationships based on mutual obligations or commitments by both the employer and the employee are crucial for the success of any organisation. Following the review of literature on employment relationships in the South African military context, the relationship between perceived organisational support, psychological contract fulfilment and organisational commitment has not been studied in the SANDF. This study aimed to begin to address this gap as evidenced in the literature. The primary objective of this study was to examine the effect of POS and psychological contract fulfilment on organisational commitment among students studying at SAMA. The results of the study indicate that both perceived organisational support and psychological contract fulfilment have a significant, positive effect on organisational commitment.

Relational psychological contracts were found to be a predictor of affective commitment. Contrary to what was expected, transactional contracts negatively predicted continuance commitment. Furthermore, no relationship was found between balanced psychological contracts and normative commitment. Based on these findings, it can be deduced that employees are actively seeking support in the form of empowerment and career mobility from the organisation, which is more than just emotional attachment.

This study confirmed that an organisation that values its employees, by fulfilling its obligations and supporting them, enhances employee commitment to the organisation, even in the context of the SANDF's Military Academy. It is therefore suggested that the military can enhance a soldier's commitment to the organisation by offering support in terms of career advancement, providing job security and reducing breaches of psychological contracts. Given that students at SAMA have expectations with regard to future utilisation in the SANDF (as implied by the career development plan between the individual and the career manager), a breach of this contract should be avoided. It is recommended that constant reconciliation of an individual's career plans and the organisation's goals must be initiated, and must be realistic.

APPENDIX TO CHAPTER 6: SUPPLEMENTARY TABLES

TABLE 6.6 Total Variance Explained for Perceived Organisational Support

Component	*Initial Eigenvalues*			*Extraction Sums of Squared Loadings*		
	Total	*% of Variance*	*Cumulative %*	*Total*	*% of Variance*	*Cumulative %*
1	2.729	61.077	61.077	2.729	61.007	61.077
2	.634	9.061	70.068			
3	.627	8.960	79.027			
4	.517	7.381	86.408			
5	.492	7.033	93.441			

Note:
Extraction method: principal component analysis.

TABLE 6.7 Total Variance Explained for Organisational Commitment Scale

Component	*Initial Eigenvalues*			*Extraction Sums of Squared Loadings*		
	Total	*% of Variance*	*Cumulative %*	*Total*	*% of Variance*	*Cumulative %*
1	3.561	29.679	29.679	3.561	29.679	29.679
2	2.105	17.544	47.223	2.105	17.544	47.223
3	1.264	10.534	57.757	1.264	10.534	57.757
4	.980	8.171	65.928			
5	.866	7.218	73.146			
6	.717	5.979	79.125			
7	.588	4.897	84.022			
8	.468	3.903	87.925			
9	.456	3.797	91.723			
10	.423	3.527	95.249			
11	.311	2.589	97.838			
12	.259	2.162	100.000			

Note:
Extraction method: principal component analysis.

TABLE 6.8 Total Variance Explained for Psychological Contract

Component	Initial Eigenvalues			Extraction Sums of Squared Lwoadings		
	Total	% of Variance	Cumulative %	Total	% of Variance	Cumulative %
1	7.574	27.050	27.050	7.574	27.050	27.050
2	5.222	18.649	45.698	5.222	18.649	45.698
3	2.344	8.373	54.072	2.344	8.373	54.072
4	1.724	6.156	60.228	1.724	6.156	60.228
5	1.600	5.714	65.942	1.600	5.714	65.942
6	1.163	4.154	70.096	1.163	4.154	70.096
7	.933	3.331	73.427			
8	.815	2.909	76.336			
9	.672	2.399	78.735			
10	.609	2.175	80.910			
11	.558	1.994	82.904			
12	.553	1.975	84.879			
13	.467	1.669	86.548			
14	.451	1.612	88.160			
15	.406	1.451	89.611			
16	.352	1.258	90.870			
17	.328	1.172	92.042			
18	.320	1.142	93.184			
19	.278	.994	94.177			
20	.266	.951	95.129			
21	.247	.882	96.010			
22	.229	.816	96.827			
23	.203	.724	97.550			
24	.193	.691	98.241			
25	.160	.570	98.811			
26	.137	.491	99.302			
27	.116	.413	99.716			
28	.080	.284	100.000			

Note:
Extraction method: principal component analysis.

REFERENCES

Agarwal, U.A. & Gupta, R.K. 2016. Examining the nature and effects of psychological contract: Case study of an Indian organization. *Thunderbird International Business Review*, 60(2). https://doi.org/10.1002/tie.21870

Arshadi, N. 2011. The relationships of perceived organizational support (POS) with organizational commitment, in-role performance, and turnover intention: Mediating role of felt obligation. *Procedia: Social and Behavioral Sciences*, 30:1103-1108.

Aselage, J. & Eisenberger, R. 2003. Perceived organizational support and psychological contracts: A theoretical integration. *Journal of Organizational Behavior*, 24(5):497-509. https://doi.org/10.1002/job.211

Balassiano, M. & Salles, D. 2012. Perceptions of equity and justice and their implications on affective organizational commitment: A confirmatory study in a teaching and research institute. *Brazilian Administration Review*, 9(3):268-286.

Bishop, J.W., Scott, K.D. & Burroughs, S.M. 2000. Support, commitment, and employee outcomes in a team environment. *Journal of Management*, 26(6):1113-1132.

Bless, C., Higson-Smith, C. & Sithole, S.L. 2013. *Fundamentals of social research methods: An African perspective* (5th Edition). Cape Town: Juta.

Cheung, M.F. & Chiu, W.C. 2005. Effects of psychological contract fulfilment, perceived organizational support, leader-member exchange, and work outcomes: A test of a mediating model. Conference paper, presented at Asia Academy Management Meeting 2004, Shanghai, 15–18 December. http://hdl.handle.net/10397/56557

Coetzee, M. & Schreuder, D. 2010. *Personnel psychology: An applied perspective*. Cape Town: Oxford University Press.

Conway N. & Briner R.B. 2005. *Understanding psychological contracts at work: A critical evaluation of theory and research*. Oxford: Oxford University Press.

Coyle-Shapiro, J.A. & Conway, N. 2005. Exchange relationships: Examining psychological contracts and perceived organizational support. *Journal of Applied Psychology*, 90(4):774-781.

Coyle-Shapiro, J. & Kessler, I. 2000. Consequences of the psychological contract for the employment relationship: A large scale survey. *Journal of Management Studies*, 37(7):903-930. https://doi.org/10.1111/1467-6486.00210

Cronbach, L. 1951. Coefficient alpha and the internal structure of tests. *Psychometrika*. 16(3):297-334.

Department of Defence. 2014. *South African Defence Review*. Available at http://www.dod.mil.za [Accessed 20 April 2017]

Department of Defence. 2015. *Annual Report 2014/2015*. Available at http://bit.ly/33nPBEH [Accessed 20 June 2015]

Du Plessis, L. 2010. The relationship between talent management practices, perceived organisational support, perceived supervisor support and intention to quit among generation Y employees in the recruitment sector. Unpublished Masters' thesis, University of Pretoria, Pretoria.

Du Plessis, L., Barkhuizen, N., Stanz, K. & Schutte, N. 2015. The management side of talent: Causal implications for the retention of generation Y employees. *Journal of Applied Business Research*, 31(5):1767-1780.

Eisenberger, R., Huntington, R., Hutchison, S. & Sowa, D. 1986. Perceived organizational support. *Journal of Applied Psychology*, 71(3):200-507. https://doi.org/10.1037/0021-9010.71.3.500

Eisenberger, R., Fasolo, P. & Davis-LaMastro, V. 1990. Perceived organizational support and employee diligence, commitment, and innovation. *Journal of Applied Psychology*, 75(1):51-59. https://doi.org/10.1037/0021-9010.75.1.51

Freese, C. & Schalk, R. 2008. How to measure the psychological contract? A critical criteria-based review of measures. *South African Journal of Psychology*, 38(2):269-286.

Gade, P.A. 2003. Organizational commitment in the military: An overview. *Military Psychology*, 15(3):163-166. https://doi.org/10.1207/S15327876MP1503_01

Guchait, P., Cho, S. & Meurs, J.A. 2015. Psychological contracts, perceived organizational and supervisor support: Investigating the impact on intent to leave among hospitality employees in India. *Journal of Human Resources in Hospitality & Tourism*, 14(3):290-315.

Guerrero, S. & Herrbach, O. 2008. The affective underpinnings of psychological contract fulfilment. *Journal of Managerial Psychology*, 23(1):4-17.

Hamilton, S.M. & Von Treuer, K. 2012. An examination of psychological contracts, careerism and ITL. *Career Development International*, 17(5):475-494.

Harman, A. & Doherty, A. 2014. The psychological contract of volunteer youth sport coaches. *Journal of Sport Management*, 28(6):687-699.

James, L.J. 2011. *The relationship between perceived organisational support and workplace trust: An exploratory study*. Unpublished Master's thesis, University of Western Cape, Cape Town South Africa. Available at http://hdl.handle.net/11394/3188

Judge, T.A. & Kammeyer-Mueller, J.D. 2012. Job attitudes. *Annual Review of Psychology*, 63:341-67. https://doi.org/10.1146/annurev-psych-120710-100511

LaMastro, V. 1999. Commitment and perceived organizational support. *National Forum of Applied Educational Research Journal*, 13(3):1-13.

Luddy, N. 2005. Job satisfaction among employees at a public health institution in the Western Cape. Unpublished Master's thesis, University of the Western Cape, Cape Town. Available at http://bit.ly/2xl0plj

Mapisa-Nqakula, N. 2019. *Minister Nosiviwe Mapisa-Nqakula: Media briefing on defence and military veterans department budget vote 2019/2020*. Media Advisory, 17 July. Available at http://bit.ly/2U8O9Sp [Accessed 29 October 2019].

Martin G. 2012. Inability to retain skills is SANDF's top challenge-CHR. DefenceWeb, 27 March. Available at http://bit.ly/38P7UUk

Martin, G. 2016. Department of Defence force forced to reduce personnel budget. DefenceWeb, 16 May. Available at http://bit.ly/2UblSdL

Masibigiri, V. & Nienaber, H. 2011. Factors affecting the retention of Generation X public servants: An exploratory study. *SA Journal of Human Resource Management*, 9(1): article 318 (11 pages). https://doi.org/10.4102/sajhrm.v9i1.318

Maslach, C., Schaufeli, W.B. & Leiter, M.P. 2001. Job burnout. Annual Review of Psychology, 52(1):397-422. https://doi.org/10.1146/annurev.psych.52.1.397

McDonald, D.J. & Makin, P.J. 2000. The psychological contract, organisational commitment and job satisfaction of temporary staff. *Leadership & Organization Development Journal*, 21(2):84-91. https://doi.org/10.1108/01437730010318174

Meyer, J.P. & Allen, N.J. 1991. A three-component conceptualization of organizational commitment. *Human Resource Management Review*, 1(1):61-89. https://doi.org/10.1016/1053-4822(91)90011-Z

Millward, L.J. & Hopkins, L.J. 1998. Psychological contracts, organizational and job commitment. *Journal of Applied Social Psychology*, 28(16):1530-1556. https://doi.org/10.1111/j.1559-1816.1998.tb01689.x

Moideenkutty, U., Blau, G., Kumar, R. & Nalakath, A. 2001. Perceived organisational support as a mediator of the relationship of perceived situational factors to affective organisational commitment. *Applied Psychology*, 50(4):615-634. https://doi.org/10.1111/1464-0597.00076

Moorman, R.H. 1991. Relationship between organizational justice and organizational citizenship behaviors: Do fairness perceptions influence employee citizenship? *Journal of Applied Psychology*, 76(6):845-855.

Mowday, R.T., Porter, L.W. & Steers, R.M. 1982. *Employee-organization linkages: The psychology of commitment, absenteeism, and turnover*. New York: Academic Press.

Muijs, D. 2010. *Doing quantitative research in education with SPSS* (2nd Edition). London: Sage.

Mullen, T.R., Kroustalis, C., Meade, A.W. & Surface, E.A. 2006. Assessing change in perceived organizational support due to training. Paper presented at the 21st Annual Conference of the Society for Industrial and Organizational Psychology, Dallas, Texas. Available at http://bit.ly/2WhWYMc

Neethling, T. 2011. The SANDF as an instrument for peacekeeping in Africa: A critical analysis of three main challenges. *Journal for Contemporary History*, 36(1):134-153. Available at https://hdl.handle.net/10520/EJC28535

O'Donohue, W., Donohue, R. & Grimmer, M. 2007. Research into the psychological contract: Two Australian perspectives. *Human Resource Development International*, 10(3):301-318.

Panaccio, A. & Vandenberghe, C. 2009. Perceived organizational support, organizational commitment and psychological wellbeing: A longitudinal study. *Journal of Vocational Behavior*, 75(2):224-236. https://doi.org/10.1016/j.jvb.2009.06.002

Pohl, S., Bertrand, F. & Ergen, C. 2016. Psychological contracts and their implications for job outcomes: A social exchange view. *Military Psychology*, 28(6):406-417.

Raina, M. 2013. Relating organizational commitment to eudaimonic Wellbeing. *European Journal of Business and Management*, 5(3):102-112.

Raja, U., Johns, G. & Ntalianis, F. 2004. The impact of personality on psychological contracts. *Academy of Management Journal*, 47(3):350-367. https://doi.org/10.2307/20159586

Rhoades, L. & Eisenberger, R. 2002. Perceived organizational support: A review of the literature. *Journal of Applied Psychology*, 87(4):689-714.

Robinson, S.L. 1996. Trust and breach of the psychological contract. *Administrative Science Quarterly*, 41(4):574-599.

Rousseau D.M. 1989. Psychological and implied contracts in organizations. *Employee Responsibilities and Rights Journal*, 2(2):121-139. https://doi.org/10.1007/BF01384942

Rousseau, D.M. 1995. *Psychological contracts in organizations: Understanding written and unwritten agreements*. Thousand Oaks CA: Sage.

Rousseau, D.M. 2000. *Psychological contract inventory: Technical report*. Pittsburgh PA: Carnegie Mellon University. Available at http://bit.ly/3cZkG69 [Accessed 3 March 2017]

Rousseau, D.M. 2004. Psychological contracts in the workplace: Understanding the ties that motivate. *The Academy of Management Executive*, 18(1):120-127.

Satardien, M. 2014. Perceived organisational support, organisational commitment and turnover intentions among employees in a selected company in the aviation industry. Master's thesis, University of the Western Cape. Available at http://bit.ly/33nw5lz

Scheepers, C.B. & Shuping, J.G. 2011. The effect of human resource practices on psychological contracts at an iron ore mining company in South Africa. *SA Journal of Human Resource Management*, 9(1):1-19.

Scott, C. 2014. Perceived organisational support and commitment among employees at a higher education institution in South Africa. Master's dissertation, North West University, Potchefstroom, South Africa. Available at http://bit.ly/38P8VM8

Serfontein, T. 2014. The role of perceived organisational support, diversity, engagement and burnout in the retention of employees. Doctoral dissertation. North-West University,Potchefstroom, South Africa. Available at https://repository.nwu.ac.za/handle/10394/11977

Shore, L.M. & Wayne, S.J. 1993. Commitment and employee behaviour: Comparison of affective commitment and continuance commitment with perceived organizational support. *Journal of Applied Psychology*, 78(5):774-780. https://doi.org/10.1037/0021-9010.78.5.774

Sonnenberg, M., Koene, B. & Paauwe, J. 2011. Balancing HRM: The psychological contract of employees: A multi-level study. *Personnel Review*, 40(6):664-683. https://doi.org/10.1108/00483481111169625

Theron, A.V.S. & Dodd, N.M. 2011. Organisational commitment in the era of the new psychological contract. *South African Journal of Economic and Management Sciences*, 14(3):333-345. https://doi.org/10.4102/sajems.v14i3.100

Tumwesigye, G. 2010. The relationship between perceived organisational support and turnover intentions in a developing country: The mediating role of organisational commitment. *African Journal of Business Management*, 4(6):942-952. Available at http://www.academicjournals.org/AJBM

Van der Nest, J.P. 2014. Positive employment relations and organisational outcomes: The role of the psychological contract and employability. Master's dissertation, North-West University, Potchefstroom, South Africa. Available at https://repository.nwu.ac.za/handle/10394/13092

Van der Vaart, L., Linde, B., De Beer, L. & Cockeran, M. 2015. Employee wellbeing, intention to leave and perceived employability: A psychological contract approach. *South African Journal of Economic and Management Sciences*, 18(1):32-44. https://doi.org/10.17159/2222-3436/2015/v18n1a3

Verma, J.P. 2013. *Data analysis in management with SPSS software*. New Delhi: Springer India. https://doi.org/10.1007/978-81-322-0786-3

Wöcke, A. & Sutherland, M. 2008. The impact of employment equity regulations on psychological contracts in South Africa. *The International Journal of Human Resource Management*, 19(4):528-542. https://doi.org/10.1080/09585190801953525

Yong, A.G. & Pearce, S. 2013. A beginner's guide to factor analysis: Focusing on exploratory factor analysis. *Tutorials in Quantitative Methods for Psychology*, 9(2):79-94. https://doi.org/10.20982/tqmp.09.2.p079

Zagenczyk, T.J., Gibney, R., Few, W.T. & Scott, K.L. 2011. Psychological contracts and organizational identification: The mediating effect of perceived organizational support. *Journal of Labor Research*, 32(3):254-281. https://doi.org/10.1007/s12122-011-9111-z

7

Measuring Conscientiousness Subscales in the Military Academy

Yolika Kleynhans

The Faculty of Military Science based at the Military Academy (SAMA) in Saldanha offers military-related education at undergraduate and postgraduate levels to employees of all four arms of service of the SANDF: the Military Health Service, the Air Force, the Navy, and the Army. Within this diverse environment, individuals are expected to perform in their professional military capacity and as students. Determining what personal factors lead to better performance and success is an important ongoing task for the armed forces. Considering their personnel requirements, and the effort and resources invested in military recruitment, selection and training processes (Sellman, Born, Strickland & Ross, 2010; Shamir, 2011), the identification of valid and reliable predictors within the military environment is important for optimising these processes.

PERSONALITY AND THE FIVE-FACTOR MODEL

Personality tests have regained popularity since the 1980s, as researchers found support for their use in predicting work-related outcomes (Barrick & Mount, 1991; Salgado, 1997). 'Personality' refers to the extent to which individuals display high levels of specific traits (Nye, Orel & Kochergina, 2013). Personality research has produced abundant literature and efforts to measure and quantify personality constructs have made it necessary to advance classification frameworks that consolidate the range of individual variances in personality. One such effort to effectively categorise the dimensions of personality led to the development of the five-factor structure. The five-factor structure, or five-factor model (FFM), proposes that there are five primary factors (also referred to as the Big Five) that are fundamental elements of human personality.

The FFM has functioned as a scale for defining personality structure for many years (Costa & McCrae, 1988; Hendriks, Hofstee & De Raad, 2002), and has come to be the model of choice for many companies aiming to recruit staff. It affords a simple and easily understandable model of personality (John & Srivastava, 1999). Salgado (2003) compared inventories that are framed by the FFM and those that are not. He established that the latter inventories had lower criterion validity in the conscientiousness and agreeableness dimensions, which indicates that the FFM upholds more validity in measurements of personality. Salgado's findings lend weight to the argument that the FFM is a more comprehensive model of personality than others, despite efforts by various researchers to produce alternative taxonomies for personality (Kumar, 2019).

Numerous personality measures have been developed drawing from the framework of the Big Five (Cattell & Mead, 2008). The most common labels given to the Big Five personality dimensions are: neuroticism (N, as juxtaposed with emotional stability), extraversion (E), openness (O), agreeableness (A), and conscientiousness (C). These labels can vary from one instrument to another, depending on the dimension's theoretical content, but the Big Five conscientiousness domain is arguably the most important in the workplace, given that it is the most consistent and robust personality-related predictor of factors relating to performance (Barrick, Mount & Judge, 2001; Caprara et al., 2011; Poropat, 2009).

Conscientiousness

When considering aspects of personality, conscientiousness is a popular variable in personnel recruitment and selection research, as it relates to work and academic performance criteria (Mount & Barrick, 1998; Sümer, Sümer, Demirutku & Çifci, 2001). In this regard, the most extensively used personality measuring instrument is the Neuroticism Extraversion Openness (NEO) Five-Factor Inventory (the NEO-PI) (Costa & McCrae, 1992), a wide-ranging and thorough assessment measure of typical adult personality attributes, which is aimed to test explicitly for the five-factor model (FFM). The initial version comprised only three factors (neuroticism, extraversion, and openness to experience), but was later expanded to include the current five factors of the FFM. The subsequent version, known as the NEO Personality Inventory-Revised (NEO-PI-R), comprises a 240-item questionnaire examining six trait facets within each of the FFM personality dimensions (Kumar, 2019; McCrae, Costa & Martin, 2005).

The current study examines the psychometric properties of NEO-PI-R for students at SAMA, to assess its utility as a psychometric tool for this population.

TABLE 7.1 Dimensions of the NEO Personality Traits

NEO Dimensions	*High*	*Low*
• Neuroticism (N)	Anxious, nervous, social fear, emotional, temperamental, worrying, vulnerable, self-conscious, self-pitying	Emotionally stable, confident, calm, even-tempered, self-satisfied, comfortable, unemotional, hardy
• Extraversion (E)	Outgoing, energetic, open, ambitious, assertive, sociable, affectionate, active, fun-loving, passionate	Introvert, reserved, work individually, shy, quiet
• Openness (O)	Broadminded, inventive, curious, creative, imaginative, prefer variety, liberal	Cautious, simple, narrow, concrete, conventional, conservative

Source:
Adapted from Kwon & Song (2011), and Block (1995).

TABLE 7.1 Dimensions of the NEO Personality Traits

NEO Dimensions	*High*	*Low*
• Agreeableness (A)	Friendly, tolerant, compassionate, flexible, cooperative, trusting, soft-hearted, generous	Competitive, outspoken, sceptical, obstinate, ruthless, suspicious, irritable, antagonistic
• Conscientiousness (C)	Careful, thorough, organised, diligent, hard-working, ambitious, methodical, competent, punctual, persevering	Easy-going, careless, inconsistent, impulsive, undisciplined, unreliable, lazy, disorganised, negligent, late, aimless

Source:
Adapted from Kwon & Song (2011), and Block (1995).

Personality traits can be described as consistent patterns of thoughts, feelings, motives and behaviour that a person typically exhibits in different situations (Fleeson & Gallagher, 2009). Someone with a high score on a specific trait will demonstrate a psychological state that manifests that trait more frequently and with greater magnitude than those with lower scores on that trait. As depicted in Table 7.1, an example would be that an individual who scores high on conscientiousness would tend to be more careful as opposed to a low-scorer, who would be more careless.

The NEO-PI-R as developed by Costa and McCrae (1988) and Costa Jr and McCrae (2010) incorporates a set of Big Five markers in an inventory that offers six-facet scales measuring each of the five domains, as set out in Table 7.2. Conscientiousness relates to an individual's ability to control their impulses, to exhibit task- and goal-directed behaviour, to plan, delay gratification, and to follow norms and rules (John & Srivastava, 1999).

TABLE 7.2 NEO-PI-R Domain and Associated Facet Scales

Domains	*Facets*			
• Neuroticism	N1 N2 N3	Anxiety Angry hostility Depression	N4 N5 N6	Self-consciousness Impulsiveness Vulnerability
• Extraversion	E1 E2 E3	Warmth Gregariousness Assertiveness	E4 E5 E6	Activity Excitement seeking Positive emotions
• Openness to experience	O1 O2 O3	Fantasy Aesthetics Feelings	O4 O5 O6	Actions Ideas Values
• Agreeableness	A1 A2 A3	Trust Straightforwardness Altruism	A4 A5 A6	Compliance Modesty Tender-mindedness
• Conscientiousness	C1 C2 C3	Competence Order Dutifulness	C4 C5 C6	Achievement–striving Self-discipline Deliberation

The following provides a breakdown of the six facets of conscientiousness as portrayed in Table 7.2 (Costa & McCrae, 1992; Costa Jr & McCrae, 2010; Roberts et al., 2005):

C1 *Competence.* The ability to complete tasks successfully, or an individual's confidence in their ability to accomplish things.

C2 *Order.* The extent to which one prefers structure and is well-organised, tidy and neat as opposed to leaving a mess.

C3 *Dutifulness.* Following the rules or fulfilling one's obligation as opposed to breaking rules.

C4 *Achievement–striving.* Dedicating time and effort to achieve excellence, as opposed to doing just enough to get by.

C5 *Self-discipline.* Persistence with difficult or unpleasant tasks until completion, as opposed to wasting one's time.

C6 *Deliberation.* Avoiding mistakes by thinking carefully before acting; avoiding precipitate actions.

Cross-cultural considerations

Various researchers have questioned the cross-cultural generalisability of the NEO-PI-R structure. In their research, McCrae and Costa (1997) drew samples from a range of countries, including China, Germany, Portugal, Israel, Korea, and Japan, and then compared them to the NEO-PI-R structure found in American samples. They established that there is acceptable congruence among the factors. The only disconcerting factors were extraversion and agreeableness within the Japanese sample. Rolland (2002) more recently revised the existing evidence and determined that there is cross-cultural structural equivalence for the neuroticism, openness, and conscientiousness scales. He upholds that the FFM can justifiably be used to measure personality constructs, even in non-westernised countries, where the agreeableness and extraversion scales remain problematic. The universality of the Big Five factors in trait psychology was, and is, accepted by the majority of researchers, among whom there tends to be ongoing consensus on the basic structure of personality (as cited in Boyle et al., 2008).

Some psychological professionals support the notion that the basic traits, as depicted in the FFM, would prove to be universal to all humans regardless of the countries they reside in or the cultural background and beliefs they may have. Supporting research indicates that there is a universal biological basis for human personality traits that transcends educational background, ethnicity and gender, giving rise to numerous studies that examine the impact on personality of neurological, biological, genetic and environmental factors. Such research has highlighted the significant impact that these factors have on how personality and intelligence are expressed (Boyle et al., 2008).

Ohlsson, Johansen and Larsson (2017) describe how organisations such as the military, operating within the public sector, concentrate on performance factors to improve service, production and effectiveness as a whole. In the military context, performance development revolved around 'hard factors' (hierarchy, routines, training exercises, and set procedures); but with the changing needs and complexity of organisations, 'soft factors' (leadership styles, interpersonal skills, team performance, and personality) have gained considerable importance (Bartone et al., 2009; Blass & Ferris, 2007; Laker & Powell, 2011; Ohlsson, Hedlund & Larsson, 2016). Scroggins, Thomas and Morris (2008) highlighted that with this rising complexity, researchers and psychologists are increasingly concerned with utilising statistically sound techniques and methods that will prove to be valid and reliable in testing individuals' or employees' personality factors.

PERSONALITY AND THE ORGANISATION

In many organisations, the personality test has become an integral part of the selection and hiring processes, mainly because it helps to determine whether potential candidates have the necessary traits to perform, and are an ideal fit, a particular job (Stabile, 2002). There is a tendency for greater retention and commitment in an organisation when candidates with the necessary traits for success are earmarked and employed (Anderson, Spataro & Flynn, 2008). Although some professionals are still opposed to the use of these tests in personnel selection processes, organisations that do use them gain financial and legal advantages because they avoid the cost and legal risks of poor hiring decisions (Stabile, 2002).

Barrick and Mount (1991) conducted a meta-analysis of 15 research findings from five occupational clusters in America consisting of professionals, managers, police, salespeople, and skilled and semi-skilled workers to examine the validity of the Big Five personality factors. The conscientiousness domain of personality emerged as the most accurate predictor of performance in all these occupational clusters. Studies in other countries yielded similar results (Kumar, 2019).

Tett, Jackson and Rothstein (1991) cautioned against generalising personality results in the military environment where validity in the previous studies was established on the basis of samples from the civilian population. However, it may be argued that their concerns point to the need to review military-related research in this field. Gade, Lakhani, and Kimmel (1991) established that military personnel who possess high levels of traits such as independence, self-discipline and confidence (which form part of the conscientiousness domain) are more inclined to positively rate and value their military experiences as opposed to members who scored lower. When United States Army officers were faced with realistic scenario testing and interviewing, it became apparent that conscientiousness influenced leadership performance positively and created a greater motivation towards leading others (Van Iddekinge, Ferris & Heffner, 2009).

THE MILITARY AND PERSONALITY TESTING

The popularity of personality testing surged during World War II (Vinchur & Koppes Bryan, 2012). At the time, the US military had to rapidly identify and exclude candidates who displayed traits that could hamper their abilities to perform their duty as aviators and soldiers (Gibby & Zickar, 2008). Later, Tupes and Christal (1961) took personality research forward in the military context, identifying five personality factors that emerged from evaluations in the United States Air Force. Their research led to the development of the Air Force Self Descriptive Inventory (AFSDI). Subsequently, the AFSDI has been adapted and utilised in selection and recruitment processes by various military establishments. In line with mainstream research, conscientiousness was the main predictor of job performance among military personnel (Ohlsson, Hedlund & Larsson, 2016).

Sümer et al. (2001), in a study among military officers on behalf of the Turkish Armed Forces, argued that, in the light of personality variables possessing generalisable validity across occupations, there would be a likelihood that military occupations would require individuals to possess certain personality attributes that would be specific to their military jobs. Their study also suggested that conscientiousness was an important personality factor to consider in officer-related jobs within the structure of the military, and had considerable predictive value.

Following identification by DeYoung, Quilty and Peterson (2007) of ten mid-level aspects (facets) under the Big Five domains, French researchers Congard, Antoine & Gilles (2012) proposed a new personality test, TAMI-P, for use as an admission test for military personnel in the French Navy. The five factors of their scale, essentially the same as FFM, were: emotional stability, ascendancy, openness, agreeableness, and conscientiousness. They assigned two facets to each domain, and each facet comprised seven items, so that their scales comprised 70 items, which they found to be "internally consistent and temporally stable" (Congard et al., 2012). Their research demonstrated that FFM domains do correspond to the skills needed for personnel to adapt to military structures, and have relevance not only to recruitment, but in terms of the conscientiousness factor also to life in the Navy, where personnel must follow orders, instructions and procedures to the letter.

Solomon (1954) conceptualised aspects of successful military life and concluded that it involved integrating and adopting new behaviours and attitudes while conforming to the expectations set out by superiors and instructors. Military professions tend to be physically and psychologically more demanding than the majority of civilian occupations (Krueger, 2001). Military professions also tend to value conscientiousness-related characteristics such as obedience and respect for the chain of command, together with secrecy, order and discipline, more highly than civilian professions.

In a factor analysis of performance ratings, Pulakos, White, Oppler, and Borman (1989), compared 19 military occupational specialities and found three dominant factors. Two of these factors, namely personal discipline (abiding by the rules, exerting self-control, and displaying integrity) and military bearing (upholding proper military form), were uniquely associated with what is expected and required from military members as opposed to the civilian workforce. These factors also reflect aspects of conscientiousness.

According to Bartone, Roland, Picano and Williams (2008), high levels of conscientiousness and agreeableness have been found to lead to better leadership performances. Halfhill, Nielsen, Sundstrom and Weilbaecher (2005) found that the military service teams that displayed higher levels of agreeableness and conscientiousness also had the highest effectiveness outcomes (DeRue, Nahrgang, Wellman & Humphrey, 2011; Judge, Bono, Ilies & Gerhardt, 2002). In a meta-analysis of 73 studies, conscientiousness and leader efficiency were significantly correlated (Judge et al., 2002). John and Srivastava (1999) highlighted that these dimensions are also suitable predictors of team-related behaviour and performance, which is imperative in the effective functioning of the armed forces. Kumar (2019) demonstrated that conscientiousness positively correlates with organisational cultures dominated by hierarchy (typically orientated towards detail and reliability), which is prominent in the military.

CONSCIENTIOUSNESS AND ACADEMIC PERFORMANCE

In terms of the academic context, O'Connor and Paunonen (2007) established that conscientiousness, neuroticism and extraversion (ambition) are essential contributing factors to performance in work and study settings. Conscientiousness has proved to be predictive of academic performance (Kappe & Van der Flier, 2010). Salgado (2002) pointed out that individuals who tend to steal, break the rules and have ill-discipline have lower conscientiousness, while Judge, Martocchio and Thoresen (1997) linked low conscientiousness to higher levels of absenteeism. These findings highlight how important the conscientiousness domain is for SAMA, as the Academy wishes to avoid delinquent behaviours that could tarnish the institution's reputation and performance outcomes.

Poropat (2009) conducted a meta-analysis of 80 studies that drew samples from over 70 000 students. In that analysis, conscientiousness was the Big Five trait that best correlated with academic performance. Conscientious people are more engaged and work harder toward attaining their goals. Bandura (1994) refers to conscientiousness as being a contributing factor towards individuals experiencing a greater sense of accomplishment and better regulation of their negative emotions, which then creates the potential to perform even better.

Armed forces including those in Norway, Australia, France and the United States of America are utilising and developing personality tests for the purpose of enhancing the effectiveness of military education (Chappelle, Novy, Sowin & Thompson, 2010; Congard, Antoine & Gilles, 2012; McCormack & Mellor, 2002).

In Norway's Army, Air and Sea War Colleges, much as at SAMA, military education entails mastering theory conveyed by lectures and in practical training exercises. When longitudinal data of the three military academies in Norway were explored both academic and military performance related to conscientiousness, and the findings suggested that academic and military performance may be predicted and enhanced through personality testing.

When considering the positive outcomes associated with being conscientious, it is unsurprising to discover that conscientious individuals tend to occupy themselves with many constructive behaviours. These competencies include self-management and self-directed studying in both educational and workplace settings. Conscientious individuals also tend to have a greater sense of right and wrong, which in effect means they will normally observe social rules and meet moral obligations (Fosse, Buch, Säfvenbom & Martinussen, 2015), as opposed to less conscientious individuals, who have been found to cheat in academic contexts (Williams, Nathanson & Paulhus, 2010).

Duckworth, Peterson, Matthews and Kelly (2007) found that conscientiousness predicts numerous academic outcomes. O'Connor & Paunonen (2007) also established, in their meta-analysis of post-secondary education, that the conscientiousness domain in its entirety proved to be valuable in predicting academic success. The two most influential conscientiousness facets were identified as achievement–striving and self-discipline. Additionally, Kelly (2001) concluded a study of undergraduate students indicating that more conscientious students were more able to acquire information and more focused on their academic tasks, in comparison to less conscientious students.

Fosse et al. (2015) commented on the compensatory role that certain features of conscientiousness play when an individual possesses lower intellectual abilities: beyond expectations, the self-discipline facet surpassed intellect in predicting academic performance among adolescents (Duckworth & Seligman, 2005). Credé and Kuncel (2008) indicated that conscientiousness traits influenced attitudes and habits that enable self-directed studying such as engaging in study sessions regularly, reviewing study materials, setting goals, and effective time management. The findings suggest that intellectual aptitude is only effectively exploited if there is a sufficient level of conscientiousness.

Zimmerman (2001) believes that even though personality traits are viewed as stable over time, study habits (specific behavioural patterns) are more malleable, and as a result, can be developed. Study skill interventions may be implemented to assist less conscientious students in developing useful study habits. These interventions could be of great value in SAMA to increase the throughput rate and increase graduation statistics.

Cheung (2016) reported unpublished research on conscientiousness in a sample of undergraduate nursing students. It indicated that the highly conscientious individuals (especially on the facets of self-discipline and organisation), generally had better academic performance outcomes. Additionally, more hours were dedicated to finding placements in hospitals by the students who scored higher on the achievement-focused (striving) facet. Achievement-focused individuals have greater aspirations and more drive to reach their goals (Baron & Dale, 2015). On the contrary, dropout rates correlated with lower conscientiousness scores (Cheung, 2016). Dudley, Orvis, Lebiecki and Cortina (2006) illustrated that focusing on specific facets of conscientiousness, such as achievement and order, generated better incremental validity predictions in areas of contextual performance that include interpersonal facilitation, job dedication and deviant workplace behaviours. Overall job performance among sales employees and managers were also better predicted by specific facets of conscientiousness (Dudley et al., 2006).

As extensive research has linked specific facets of the conscientiousness domain to specific academic and work outcomes, it becomes imperative for institutions such as SAMA to consider which facets are most relevant to achieve maximum success rates. Such research creates an opportunity to select stronger military and academic candidates and also to tailor interventions to individual needs.

RESEARCH OBJECTIVE

This main objective of this study was to examine the validity and reliability of the conscientiousness domain subscales as a predictor of success in work and study for military students at SAMA, and to ascertain whether they can be applied in selection processes in order to optimise the processes of recruitment, selection and training in the environment of the Military Academy.

RESEARCH METHOD

This study examines the psychometric properties of the six facets of conscientiousness derived from the NEO-PI-R conscientiousness scales. The scales were tested for internal consistency before using the test, to ensure that the items all measure the same construct. The scales were then factor analysed to determine the factorial stability of the scales.

Instrument

The study utilised a quantitative, cross-sectional, non-experimental research design, using self-administered assessments. Participants completed a battery of NEO-PI-R self-report questionnaires (self-report measures), on paper, by hand, in assessment settings.

The NEO–PI–R is a widely used and researched measure, and attested to by a wealth of research as being widely applicable across different cultures (McCrae & Costa, 1997; Rolland, 2002). It was operationalised by Costa and McCrae (1988) to measure the five factors (neuroticism, extraversion, openness, agreeableness and conscientiousness) of the five-factor model of personality, and was used for its appropriateness in eliciting detailed information about key concepts in the five domains (Laher, 2010).

DATA COLLECTION

Participants

Participants consisted of a sample of undergraduate students from SAMA. Stratified random sampling was used to select SAMA students from across three study areas (Human and Organisational Development, Security and Africa Studies, and Technology and Defence Management). The sample provided a confidence level of 95%. Undergraduate participants were selected from both genders (65% males, and 29% females) and varied ethnic backgrounds (Black 83%; Coloured 6%, Indian/Asian 2%, and White 3%) (Table 7.3). Most students at the Military Academy who participated in this study were males from the Army, the Military Health Services, the Air Force and the Navy between the ages of 18-25. The largest student complement stems from the SA Army and SAAF. The sample for this study comprised undergraduate students (males=108; females=47, missing=10). The sample's ages ranged from 18-47. Most students were Black males in their late twenties (M=27.47, SD=4.56).

TABLE 7.3 Demographic Variables of Faculty of Military Science Students (N=165)

Variables	*N*	*%*
Race		
• African	137	83.03%
• Coloured	9	5.45%
• Indian/Asian	4	2.42%
• White	5	3.03%
• Missing	10	6.06%
Gender		
• Female	47	28.48%
• Male	108	65.45%
• Missing	10	6.06%

Ethical compliance

Individuals were voluntary participants who were informed of the risks and benefits of the study. In accordance with professional psychological practice, the participants' rights to confidentiality and privacy were protected by practical security measures: confidential records were stored in a secure area; all identifying personal information was stripped from records; each participant was assigned a case identifier, and the list with full identifying information was stored in a password-protected file. The participants were told in advance what data would be shared and how research findings would be disseminated. All feedback was conducted in a secure, discreet venue where conversations could not be overheard.

Validity and reliability

The reliability and validity of the NEO-PI-R has been found to be acceptable both in South Africa and internationally among non-Western countries (Costa & McCrae, 1988; Laher, 2010; Rolland 2002), although some subscales such as 'openness to experience' have been found to be imperfectly applicable in the South African context (Laher, 2010). This study, however, analysed only the conscientiousness subscales, which have not been deemed problematic in previous research.

Procedure

Using a sampling frame that listed undergraduate residential students at SAMA, sorted by academic programme, a stratified random sample of N=165 was drawn. Each participant who agreed to contribute to the study completed a structured background questionnaire to collect biographical and historical data. Between 10 and 30 individuals were assessed at a time in group assessment conditions, in a well-lit, quiet and ventilated venue. The instructions for each assessment were read verbatim from the instruction manuals. All participants completed the NEO-PI-R inventory.

Once completed, the instruments were hand scored and the data captured in MS Excel, then imported into the computer-based Statistical Package for the Social Sciences (SPSS) version 24 (IBM Corp, 2016) to generate descriptive and inferential statistics. The validity and reliability of the instruments were assessed using factor analysis and Cronbach's coefficient alpha.

Scoring

The NEO-PI-R is a self-report instrument consisting of 240 items that take approximately 40 minutes to complete. Items are scored on a five-point Likert scale where zero is 'strongly disagree' and four is 'strongly agree'. For the purposes of this study, only the conscientiousness subscale was analysed.

RESULTS

The sample demonstrated a high score on conscientiousness (M=81.85, SD=8.227). Cronbach's coefficient alpha is the most commonly used objective measure of reliability. Developed by Lee Cronbach in 1951, the alpha offers a means of assessing the internal consistency of a test or scale, alpha being a number between zero and one.

There are differing opinions about what constitutes an acceptable Cronbach's coefficient alpha, with a range between α=.70 and α=.95. A low alpha could be due to a low number of questions, poor inter-relatedness between items, or heterogeneous constructs. If the alpha is too high, then some items may be redundant. A maximum alpha value of α=.90 has been recommended (Cohen & Swerdlik, 2009; Thompson, 2003).

TABLE 7.4 Correlation Coefficients						
Variable	*1*	*2*	*3*	*4*	*5*	*6*
1. Competence	–					
2. Order	.447	–				
3. Dutifulness	.739	.442	–			
4. Achievement–striving	.709	.429	.653	–		
5. Self-discipline	.783	.523	.654	.655	–	
6. Deliberation	.79	.445	.808	.623	.680	–
Note: Correlation for all data significant at the 0.01 level						

The correlations between the items according to the inter-item correlation matrix (Table 7.4) are all above .60, except for the correlation between 'achievement-striving' and 'order'; 'order' did not have significant correlation with any of the other items. If deleted from the scale, the Cronbach's alpha for conscientiousness will increase. The Cronbach's alpha for the SAMA sample is α=.90. The reliability test results in Table 7.5 show that the reliability coefficient has exceeded the minimum value of α=.70. The Kaiser-Meyer-Olkin test score was 0.87, indicating sampling adequacy and the data's suitability for factor analysis.

TABLE 7.5 Conscientiousness Components and Cronbach's Alpha (α)	
Conscientiousness	**α=.897**
Components	α
• Competence	.678
• Order	.678
• Dutifulness	.715
• Achievement–striving	.561
• Self-discipline	.638
• Deliberation	.821
Numbering is comparable to numbering in Table 7.6	

Factor analysis

According to Rummel (1970), factor analysis helps when one needs to identify the relationship between variables in complicated concepts such as psychological assessments. Factor analysis enables researchers to investigate concepts that are not easily measured directly, by collapsing many variables into their underlying factors, based on the assumption that the observed variables have similar response patterns because they all reflect a latent variable.

In every factor analysis, there are as many factors as there are underlying or latent variables. Every factor explains some of the variances in the observed variables. Eigenvalues communicate how much variance each factor explains.

Any factor with an eigenvalue that is greater than 1 explains more variance than a single observed variable on its own. What this means is that the combined items explain more variance than any single item in the questionnaire. When factors explain very little of the variance, then they tend to be discarded (Bartholomew, Knott & Moustaki, 2011). Other uses of factor analysis include data transformation, hypothesis-testing, mapping, and scaling (Rummel, 1970). Factor loadings are moderately high if they are above 0.30 and high if they are greater than 0.60.

The six components of conscientiousness are set out in order in Table 7.5; variance is demonstrated in Table 7.6.

Table 7.6 Total Variance Explained

Component	*Initial eigenvalues*			*Extraction sums of squared loadings*		
	Total	*% of Variance*	*Cumulative %*	*Total*	*% of Variance*	*Cumulative %*
1	4.088	68.129	68.129	4.088	68.129	68.129
2	.690	11.497	79.626			
3	.481	8.012	87.638			
4	.327	5.449	93.087			
5	.238	3.968	97.055			
6	.177	2.945	100.000			

Note:
Extraction method: principal component analysis.
Components are numbered as displayed in Table 7.5.

Component 1 (competence) has a loading of 68%, thus loading the most out of all the factors, as displayed in Table 7.6. Furthermore, when extraction of items was done, it indicated that if items 35, 95 and 155 are removed from the competence subscale, the Cronbach's alpha will increase from α=.68 to α=.80. The alpha of component 4 (achievement–striving) increases from α=.56 to α=.87 if items 20, 80, 230 and 140 are discarded. Component 5 (self-discipline) has α=.63 alpha with an increase to α=.79 if items 85, 55, 115, 175 and 205 are removed. The NEO-PI-R conscientiousness scale can, therefore, be shortened further to improve reliability and validity within the SAMA context.

Reliability and validity of NEO-PI-R

As per Table 7.5, the Cronbach alpha score for the NEO-PI-R scale is α=.90, which means that this scale has high internal consistency and is reliable and valid. It meets the minimum required level of α=.70.

Analysis of internal consistency of scales revealed that the scales with the highest internal consistency measured deliberation (eight items; α=.82) and dutifulness (eight items; α=.72). Competence and order each with eight items had Cronbach's alphas of α=.68, followed by self-discipline (eight items; α=.64) and achievement striving (eight items; α=.56). As noted by Nunnally (1978), scales with internal reliabilities of $\alpha=.70$ to $\alpha=.80$ are acceptable for research purposes because correlations with such scales are not diminished to any great degree by measurement error. As indicated by Cronbach's alphas, two of the six conscientiousness scales demonstrated acceptable internal consistency for reliable scale construction. The scree plot confirmed the above findings showing the distinct presence of one main factor influencing a large portion of variance for all scales together. Thus, factor analysis confirms that conscientiousness is the main factor that influences scores on all six scales. Reliability analysis revealed that conscientiousness demonstrated sufficient alpha levels for use ($\alpha>.90$) (Foxcroft & Roodt, 2015).

Given the disciplined and structured nature of the military profession, it was in line with expectations that the Academy's students demonstrated very high levels of this trait ($M=133.02$, $SD=23.96$) when compared with Laher's (2010) Witwatersrand sample ($M=115.40$, $SD=21.45$) with $t(480)=5.73$, $p=.001$; and Costa and McCrae's (2010) international norm ($M=121.1$, $SD=19.9$) with $t(690)=4.25$, $p=.001$).

There was a significant difference in conscientiousness between the international norm group (Costa Jr & McCrae, 2010), Laher's (2010) Witwatersrand sample of students, and the Military Academy students at the $p<.05$ level [$F(2, 1.114)=22.34$, $p=.001$].

DISCUSSION

Scales constructed to evaluate the six facets of conscientiousness from the NEO-PI-R inventory were examined for their factorial stability and psychometric properties. Reliability analysis of each scale separately indicated that the reliability coefficients ranged from $\alpha=.64$ to $\alpha=.82$. Four scales fell below the target reliability of $\alpha=.70$ which was aimed for when the six scales were constructed. Overall, the size of the reliability coefficients indicated that scales were internally consistent, thereby leading to the conclusion that the conscientiousness scales have an acceptable level of internal consistency to be useful for personality research at SAMA.

Factor analysis was conducted to test the overall factorial stability of the six conscientiousness scales. Factor analysis of all six scales overall led to the extraction of a one-factor solution to describe conscientiousness data. This finding is in keeping with expectations that all six scales of conscientiousness measure one core facet of conscientiousness. Factor loadings and percentage of variance accounted for by the conscientiousness factor indicated that all six scales loaded on the main factor and were representative of the facet of conscientiousness.

Conscientious individuals, whether they are military professionals, students or part of the private sector workforce, tend to be driven and motivated towards achieving their goals and working hard to successfully attain those goals (Roberts et al., 2005). This being said, the conscientiousness domain possibly predicts military performance in military professionals to a greater extent, due to the nature of the military environment.

The military culture is one that necessitates the ability to adhere to rules, regulations and procedures, while also being able to persevere during challenging circumstances. Furthermore, military professionals, especially officers, are required to display and exercise self-control and integrity in their actions and conduct (Pulakos et al., 1989). This emphasises the utility that personality inventories may have in the military educational environment of SAMA.

The present study suggests that the scales measuring the six facets of conscientiousness in the NEO–P–IR are valid and reliable in the SAMA environment and become even more so when certain items are removed.

RECOMMENDATIONS

Descriptive statistics showed that SAMA students in general had high levels of conscientiousness. The data suggested that conscientiousness levels among SAMA students are higher than in other contexts within and outside of SA. These constructs can, therefore, be considered in the selection criteria for students at SAMA. The relationship between particular personality domains (such as conscientiousness and its respective facets) and performance of military personnel, indicates that personality should be considered in recruitment and selection processes. Furthermore, it provides information and guidance as to what types of interventions or skills training need to be addressed for military professionals to perform optimally in the daily execution of their duties.

Barrick et al. (2001) suggested that it would be ideal for organisations to identify and develop an understanding of relevant criteria that would predict desired organisational outcomes. By linking the personality factors and the relevant facets to the identified criteria, the validity of personality inventories in the military setting would improve. Once there is an understanding of why and how certain personality factors influence desired outcomes, it will be possible to identify items in the inventories that would be more relevant in predicting those outcomes. This will allow organisations such as SAMA to customise these inventories to increase their predictive capabilities, including by removing items that appear to be irrelevant or that hamper the results of the Cronbach alphas.

As already indicated, organisational and personnel research should continue to examine the utility of personality measures within the unique environment of the military, given the distinctive expectations and demands of military life. In conclusion, it can be positively asserted that the conscientiousness scale of the NEO-PI-R is valid as a measure to predict desirable personality traits and likely success of soldier-students in the SAMA context.

LIMITATIONS AND FUTURE RESEARCH

The research was conducted in the military education context, which limits the applicability of the findings to other contexts; but the uniqueness of the military education context makes this research appropriate and essential for this environment. The NEO-PI-R was distributed to students in English, and as SAMA consists of students with diverse ethnic and cultural backgrounds, this may have impeded the understanding or interpretations of certain questions. More culturally appropriate terms could be researched. Future research can also aim to determine the differences in conscientiousness levels and the experience thereof in other military education contexts.

Further research should replicate the study using larger sample sizes and in other academic and work contexts. Longitudinal research should also be conducted to determine how the constructs in the study change over time, and how changes in these constructs within individuals may influence the applicability and levels of the conscientiousness scale.

REFERENCES

Anderson, C., Spataro, S.E. & Flynn, F.J. 2008. Personality and organizational culture as determinants of influence. *Journal of Applied Psychology*, 93(3):702-710. https://doi.org/10.1037/0021-9010.93.3.702

Bandura, A. 1994. Self-efficacy. In: V. S. Ramachaudran (ed.), Encyclopedia of human behavior, Vol. 4, 71-81. New York: Academic Press. (Reprinted in Friedman, H. [Ed.], *Encyclopedia of mental health*. San Diego: Academic Press, 1998).

Baron, H. & Dale, L.E. 2015. Validation of CPSQ for student recruitment in the City University School of Health. Cambridge Assessment, internal briefing document.

Barrick, M.R. & Mount, M.K. 1991. The Big Five personality dimensions and job performance: A meta-analysis. *Personnel Psychology*, 44(1):1-26.

Barrick, M.R., Mount, M.K. & Judge, T.A. 2001. Personality and performance at the beginning of the new millennium: What do we know and where do we go next? *International Journal of Selection and Assessment*, 9(1/2):9-30

Bartholomew, D., Knott, M. & Moustaki, I. 2011. *Latent variable models and factor analysis: a unified approach*. Hoboken NJ: Wiley.

Bartone, P.T., Eid, J., Johnsen, B.H., Laberg, J.C. & Snook, S.A. 2009. Big five personality factors, hardiness, and social judgment as predictors of leader performance. *Leadership & Organization Development Journal*, 30(6):498-521. https://doi.org/10.1108/01437730910981908

Bartone, P.T., Roland, R.R., Picano, J J. & Williams, T.J. 2008. Psychological hardiness predicts success in US Army Special Forces candidates. *International Journal of Selection and Assessment*, 16(1):78-81. https://doi.org/10.1111/j.1468-2389.2008.00412.x

Blass, F. & Ferris, G. 2007. Leader reputation: The role of mentoring, political skill, contextual learning, and adaptation. *Human Resource Management*, 46(1):5-21. https://doi.org/10.1002/hrm.20142

Block, J. 1995. A contrarian view of the Five-Factor Approach to personality description. *Psychological Bulletin*, 117(2):187-215.

Caprara, G.V., Vecchione, M., Alessandri, G., Gerbino, M., Barbaranelli, C. 2011. The contribution of personality traits and self-efficacy beliefs to academic achievement: A longitudinal study. *British Journal of Educational Psychology*, 81(1):78-96.

Cattell, H. & A.D., Mead. 2008. The Sixteen Personality Factor Questionnaire (16PF). In: Boyle, G.J., Matthews, G. & Saklofske, D.H. (eds), *The SAGE handbook of personality theory and assessment, Vol. 2*, pp.135-159. Los Angeles CA: Sage.

Chappelle, W., Novy, P.L., Sowin, T.W. & Thompson, W.T. 2010. NEO PI-R normative personality data that distinguish U.S. Air Force female pilots. *Military Psychology*, 22(2)158-175

Cheung, K.Y.F. 2016. Initial findings from a study of CPSQ predictive validity with undergraduate nursing. Cambridge Assessment, internal briefing document.

Cohen R. & Swerdlik. M. 2009. *Psychological testing and assessment: An introduction to tests and measurement* (7th Edition). New York: McGraw-Hill Higher Education.

Congard, A., Antoine, P. & Gilles, P.-Y. 2012. Assessing the structural and psychometric properties of a new personality measure for use with military personnel in the French Armed Forces. *Military Psychology*, 24(3):284- 307. https://doi.org/10.1080/08995605.2012.678242

Costa, P.T. & McCrae, R.R. 1988. From catalog to classification: Murray's needs and the five-factor model. *Journal of Personality and Social Psychology*, 55(2):258-265.

Costa, P.T. & McCrae, R.R. 1992a. *NEO PI-R: Professional Manual: Revised NEO PI-R and NEO-FFI*. Lutz FL: Psychological Assessment Resources.

Costa, P.T. & McCrae, R.R. 1992b. Normal personality assessment in clinical practice: the NEO Personality Inventory. *Psychological Assessment*, 4(1):5-13.

Costa, P.T. Jr & McCrae, R.R. . 2010. *NEO Inventories for the NEO Personality Inventory-3 (NEO-PI-3), NEO Five-Factor Inventory-3 (NEO-FFI-3), and NEO Personality Inventory-Revised (NEO-PI-R): Professional manual*. Lutz FL: Psychological Assessment Resources (PAR).

Credé, M. & Kuncel, N.R. 2008. Study habits, skills, and attitudes: The third pillar supporting collegiate academic performance. *Perspectives on Psychological Science*, 3(6):425-453.

Cronbach, L. 1951. Coefficient alpha and the internal structure of tests. *Psychometrika*. 16(3):297-334.

Darr, W.A. 2009. *The Trait Self Descriptive (TSD) Inventory: A facet-level examination. Technical Memorandum 2009-010*. Ottawa, Canada: Director General Military Personnel Research and Analysis.

DeRue, D. S., Nahrgang, J. D., Wellman, N. & Humphrey, S. E. 2011. Trait and behavioral theories of leadership: An integration and meta-analytic test of their relative validity. *Personnel Psychology*, 64(1):7-52.

DeYoung, C.G., Quilty, L.C. & Peterson, J.B. 2007. Between facets and domains: 10 Aspects of the Big Five, Journal of Personality and Social Psychology, 93(5):880-896.

Duckworth, A. L., Peterson, C., Matthews, M. D. & Kelly, D. R. 2007. Grit: Perseverance and passion for long-term goals. *Journal of Personality and Social Psychology*, 92(6):1087-1101.

Duckworth, A.L., Seligman, M.E.P. 2005. Self-discipline outdoes IQ in predicting academic performance of adolescents. *Psychological Science*, 16(12):939-944.

Dudley, N.M., Orvis, K.A., Lebiecki, J.E. & Cortina, J.M. 2006. A meta-analytic investigation of conscientiousness in the prediction of job performance: Examining the intercorrelations and the incremental validity of narrow traits. *Journal of Applied Psychology*, 91(1):40-57. https://doi:org/10.1037/0021-9010.91.1.40

Fleeson, W. & Gallagher, P. 2009. The implications of Big Five standing for the distribution of trait manifestation in behavior: Fifteen experience-sampling studies and a meta-analysis. *Journal of Personality and Social Psychology*, 97(6):1097-1114.

Fosse, T., Buch, R., Säfvenbom, R. & Martinussen, M. 2015. The impact of personality and self-efficacy on academic and military performance: The mediating role of self-efficacy. *Journal of Military Studies*. 6(1):47-65. https://doi.org/10.1515/jms-2016-0197

Foxcroft, C. & Roodt, G. 2015. *Introduction to psychological assessment in the South African context* (4th Edition). Cape Town: OUP

Gade, P.A., Lakhani, H. & Kimmel, M. 1991. Military Service: A good place to start? *Military Psychology*, 3(4):251-267.

Gibby, R.E. & Zickar, M.J. 2008. A history of the early days of personality testing in American industry: An obsession with adjustment. *History of Psychology*, 11(3):164-184. https://doi.org/10.1037/a0013041

Halfhill, T., Nielsen, T.M., Sundstrom, E. & Weilbaecher, A. 2005. Group personality composition and performance in military service teams. *Military Psychology*, 17(1):41-54.

Hendriks, A.A.J., Hofstee, W.K.B. & De Raad, B. 2002. The Five-Factor Personality Inventory: Assessing the Big Five by means of brief and concrete statements. In: de Raad, B. & Perugini, M. (eds), *Big five assessment*, pp.79-108. Seattle WA: Hogrefe & Huber.

Hogan, T.P., Benjamin, A. & Brezinski, K.L. 2000. Reliability methods: A note on the frequency of use of various types. *Educational and Psychological Measurement*, 60(4):523-531. https://doi.org/10.1177/00131640021970691

IBM Corp. Released 2016. IBM SPSS Statistics for Windows, Version 24.0. Armonk, NY: IBM Corp.

John, O.P. & Srivastava, S. 1999. The Big Five Trait taxonomy: History, measurement, and theoretical perspectives. In: L. A. Pervin & O.P. John (eds), *Handbook of personality: Theory and research* (2nd Edition) pp.102-139. New York: Guilford Press.

Judge, T.A., Bono, J.E., Ilies, R., Gerhardt, M.W. 2002. Personality and leadership: A qualitative and quantitative review. *Journal of Applied Psychology*, 87(4):765-780.

Judge, T.A., Martocchio, J.J. & Thoresen, C.J. 1997. Five-factor model of personality and employee absence. *Journal of Applied Psychology*, 82(5):745-755. https://doi.org/10.1037//0021-9010.82.5.745

Kappe, R. & Van der Flier, H. 2010. Using multiple and specific criteria to assess the predictive validity of the Big Five personality factors on academic performance. *Journal of Research in Personality*, 44(1):142-145. https://doi.org/10.1016/j.jrp.2009.11.002

Krueger, G.P. 2001. Military psychology: United States. *International Encyclopedia of the Social & Behavioral Sciences*, pp.9868-9873. Oxford: Elsevier.

Kumar, R. 2019. The use of personality testing in personnel selection. BA thesis, Claremont McKenna College, Claremont, California. https://scholarship.claremont.edu/cmc_theses/2038

Kwon, N. & Song., H. 2011. Personality traits, gender, and information competency among college students. *Malaysian Journal of Library & Information Science*, 16(1):87-107.

Laher, S. 2010. Using exploratory factor analysis in personality research: Best-practice recommendations. *SA Journal of Industrial Psychology/SA Tydskrif vir Bedryfsielkunde*, 36(1) article 873 (7 pages). https://doi.org/10.4102/sajip.v36i1.873

Laker, D.R. & Powell, J.L. 2011. The difference between hard and soft skills and their relative impact on training transfer. *Human Resource Development Quarterly*, 22(1):111-122. https://doi.org/10.1002/hrdq.20063

McCormack, L. & Mellor, D. 2002. The role of personality in leadership: An application of the five-factor model in the Australian military. *Military Psychology*, 14(3):179-197.

McCrae, R.R. and Costa, P.T. 1997 'Personality trait structure as a human universal', *American Psychologist*, 52(5): 509-16.

McCrae, R.R., Costa, J.P. & Martin, T.A. 2005. The NEO–PI–3: A more readable revised NEO Personality Inventory. *Journal of Personality Assessment*, 84(3):261-270. https://doi.org/10.1207/s15327752jpa8403_05

Mount, M.K. & Barrick, M.R. 1998. Five reasons why the "Big Five" article has been frequently cited. *Personnel Psychology*, 51(4):849-857.

Nunnally, J.C. 1978. *Psychometric Theory* (2nd Edition). New York: McGraw Hill.

Nye, J., Orel, E. & Kochergina, E. 2013. *Big Five personality traits and academic performance in Russian universities*. Higher School of Economics (HSE), Research Paper No. WP BRP 10/PSY/2013. Moscow: National Research University, https://doi.org/10.2139/ssrn.2265395

O'Connor, M.C. & Paunonen, S.V. 2007. Big Five personality predictors of post-secondary academic performance. *Personality and Individual Differences*, 43(5):971-990. https://doi.org/10.1016/j.paid.2007.03.017

Ohlsson, A., Hedlund, E. & Larsson, G. 2016. Examining the relationship between personality, organizational political skill and perceived team performance in a multinational military staff exercise context. *Journal of Military Studies*, 7(1):24-30.https://doi.org/10.1515/jms-2016-0003

Ohlsson, A., Johansen R.B., Larsson G. 2017. An exploratory study of the relationship between the Big-Five personality dimensions and political skills with military staff members' perceived performance. *Scandinavian Journal of Work and Organizational Psychology*, 2(1):1-7. https://doi.org/10.16993/sjwop.31

Poropat, A. 2009. A meta-analysis of the five-factor model of personality and academic performance. *Psychological Bulletin*, 135(2):322-338.

Pulakos, E.D., White, L.A., Oppler, S.H., Borman, W.C. 1989. Examination of race and sex effects on performance ratings. *Journal of Applied Psychology*, 74(5):770-780.

Rankin, G. & Stokes, M. 1998. Reliability of assessment tools in rehabilitation: An illustration of appropriate statistical analyses. *Clinical Rehabilitator*, 12(3):187-199.

Roberts, B.W., Chernyshenko, O.S., Stark, S.E. & Goldberg, L.R. 2005. The structure of conscientiousness: An empirical investigation based on seven major personality questionnaires. *Personnel Psychology*, 58(1):103-139.

Rolland, J.P. 2002 'The cross-cultural generalizability of the Five-Factor Model of personality.' In: McCrae, R.R. & Allik, J. (eds), *The Five-Factor Model of Personality Across Cultures*, pp.7-28. New York: Kluwer Academic/Plenum Publishers.

Rummel, R.J. 1970. *Applied factor analysis*. Evanston IL: Northwestern University Press.

Salgado, J.F. 1997. The Five Factor Model of personality and job performance in the European Community. *Journal of Applied Psychology*, 82(1):30-43.

Salgado, J.F. 2002. The Big Five personality dimensions and counterproductive behaviors. *International Journal of Selection and Assessment*, 10(1-2):117-125.

Salgado, J.F. 2003. Predicting job performance using FFM and non-FFM personality measures. *Journal of Occupational and Organizational Psychology*, 76(3):323-346. https://doi.org/10.1348/096317903769647201

Scroggins, W.A., Thomas, S.L. & Morris, J.A. 2008. Psychological Testing in Personnel Selection, Part I: A Century of Psychological Testing. *Public Personnel Management*, 37(1):99-109. https://doi.org/10.1177/009102600803700107

Sellman, W.S., Born, D.H., Strickland, W.J. & Ross, J.J. 2010. Selection and Classification in the US Military. In: Farr, J.L. & Tippins, N.T. (eds), *Handbook of Employee selection*, pp.679-699. London: Routledge.

Shamir, E. 2011. *Transforming Command. The Pursuit of Mission Command in the U.S., British and Israeli Armies*. Stanford CA: Stanford Security Studies (Stanford University Press).

Solomon, D.N. 1954. Civilian to soldier: Three sociological studies of infantry recruit training. *Canadian Journal of Psychology*, 8(2):87-94. https://doi.org/10.1037/h0083601

Stabile, S.J. 2002. The use of Personality Tests as a Hiring Tool: Is the Benefit worth the Cost? *University of Pennsylvania Journal of Business Law*, 4(2):279-313. https://scholarship.law.upenn.edu/jbl/vol4/iss2/1

Sümer, H., Sümer, N., Demirutku, K. & Çıtcı, O. 2001. Using a personality-oriented job analysis to identify attributes to be assessed in officer selection. *Military Psychology*, 13(3):129-146. https:/doi.org/10.1207/S15327876MP1303_1

Tett, R.P., Jackson D.N. & Rothstein, M. 1991. Personality measures as predictors of job performance: A meta-analytic review. *Personnel Psychology*, 44:703-742. https://doi.org/10.1111/j.1744-6570.1991.tb00696.x

Thompson, B. 2003. Understanding reliability and coefficient alpha, really. In: Thompson, B. (ed.), *Score reliability: Contemporary thinking on reliability issues*, pp.3-23. Thousand Oaks CA: Sage.

Tupes, E.C. & Christal, R.E. 1961. Recurrent personality factors based on trait ratings (Originally released as an ASD Technical Report in 1961: No. 61-97). Lackland Air Force Base, Texas: Aeronautical Systems Division, Personnel Laboratory. Available at https://doi.org/10.1111/j.1467-6494.1992.tb00973.x

Van Aarde, N., Meiring, D. & Wiernik, B.M. 2017. 'The validity of the Big Five personality traits for job performance: Meta-analyses of South African studies', *International Journal of Selection and Assessment*, 25(3):223-239. https://doi.org/10.1111/ijsa.12175

Van Iddekinge, C.H., Ferris, G.R. & Heffner, T.S. 2009. Test of a multistage model of distal and proximal antecedents of leader performance. *Personnel Psychology*, 62(3):463-495. https://doi.org/10.1111/j.1744-6570.2009.01145.x

Vinchur, A.J. & Koppes Bryan, L.L. 2012. A History of Personnel Selection and Assessment. In: Schmitt, N. (ed.), *The Oxford handbook of personnel assessment and selection*. Oxford Handbooks Online series. Available at https://doi.org/10.1093/oxfordhb/9780199732579.013.0002

Williams, K.M., Nathanson, C. & Paulhus, D.L. 2010. Identifying and profiling scholastic cheaters: their personality, cognitive ability, and motivation. *Journal of Experimental Psychology Applied*, 16(3):293-307.

Zimmerman, B.J. 2001. Theories of self-regulated learning and academic achievement: An overview and analysis. In: Zimmerman, B.J. & Schunk, D. H. (eds), *Self-regulated learning and academic achievement: Theoretical perspectives* (2nd Edition), pp.1-37. Mahwah NJ: Erlbaum.

8

Exploring Psychological Resilience in the South African Navy

Danille Arendse
Petrus Bester
Charles van Wijk

Since the establishment of the South African National Defence Force (SANDF) in 1994, its utilisation has not been restricted to a passive role of peacekeeping; it also escalated to peace enforcement where SANDF soldiers were actively engaged in combat. For example, Martin (2019) reported that an SANDF platoon (led by a female SANDF commander) engaged in a battle with Arab militia during a peace-support operation (PSO) in the Sudan in late 2018. The SANDF's exposure to armed conflict has also occurred where SANDF members were deployed as part of a bilateral agreement, such as in the case of the Central African Republic (CAR). In the battle of Bangui in March 2013, South African soldiers engaged in battle with rebel forces while they were in fact deployed on a mission for training and renovation of military infrastructure in the CAR (Mphofu & Van Dyk, 2016). The above emphasises the critical importance of soldiers being ready for deployments that can escalate, sometimes abruptly, from low-intensity operations to intense combat, as in the case of the battle of Bangui.

Readiness for deployment involves three interrelated factors: personnel, equipment, and training. Mphofu and Van Dyk (2016) emphasise that 'human factors' (ergonomics, or the technological and psychological support of a work unit) play a crucial role in ensuring the readiness of soldiers for deployment. Closely related to human factors is a concept referred to as psychological capital, which includes characteristics such as resilience, self-efficacy, optimism and hope (Grundlingh, 2016). Grundlingh (2016) points out that resilience, in particular, enables soldiers to face the intense stress of multiple deployments and repeated combat. In view of deployments such as those mentioned above, it is clearly of significance to explore the measurement of psychological resilience in the context of the SANDF.

THEORETICAL BACKGROUND

Resilience

Resilience is defined as the process of adapting well in the face of adversity, trauma, tragedy or threats (American Psychological Association, 2019). The concept of resilience is often located within the positive psychology movement, which in the past four decades has been characterised by a surge in developments across resilience-related constructs, such as salutogenesis (Antonovsky, 1979), hardiness (Kobasa, 1979), learned resourcefulness (Rosenbaum, 1990), mental toughness (MT) (Clough, Earle & Sewell, 2002) and locus of control (Rotter, 1966). These constructs are generally thought of as dispositional, in that they are approaches or orientations towards life that an individual develops over time.

Psychological hardiness

Psychological hardiness is one of the most researched constructs found in the resilience literature (Sandvik et al., 2019). It is defined as a personal worldview that is fairly stable over time and comprises the following components:

- commitment (vs. alienation), referring to the ability to feel deeply involved in activities of life;
- control (vs. powerlessness), the belief that one can control or influence the events of one's experience; and
- challenge (vs. threat), an attitude that regards change as normal, and as an opportunity for personal development rather than a threat to personal security.

Hardiness is a psychological orientation associated with people who remain healthy and continue to perform well in a range of stressful conditions (Bartone, Roland, Picano & Williams, 2008; Kobasa, Maddi & Kahn, 1982).

An extensive body of research has developed showing that hardiness protects against the ill effects of stress on health and performance among a wide variety of civilian occupations and contexts (Bartone, 1989; Maddi & Hess, 1992; Maddi & Kobasa, 1984; Topf, 1989). Hardiness has been shown to influence outcomes among soldiers in training, combat duty and peacekeeping, and across various national contexts (Bartone, 1996, 1999; Bartone, Johnsen, Eid, Laberg & Brun, 2002; Florian, Mikulincer & Taubman, 1995; Johnsen et al., 2013; Westman, 1990). There is evidence that hardier soldiers are less likely to develop posttraumatic stress disorder and other mental health conditions after exposure to combat (Bartone, 1999, 2000; Bartone, Hystad, Eid & Brevik, 2012; Escolas, Pitts, Safer & Bartone, 2013; Pietrzak, Johnson, Goldstein, Malley & Southwick, 2009; Sandvik et al., 2019), and may adapt better both during and after operational deployments (Britt, Adler & Bartone, 2001). There is some support for the cross-national validity of the hardiness construct (Hystad, Eid, Johnsen, Laberg & Bartone, 2010; Maddi & Harvey 2006; Sinclair & Tetrick, 2000), suggesting that the psychological description and measurement of hardiness may apply across cultures.

Mental toughness

A related construct, partially derived from the theoretical foundations of hardiness, is that of mental toughness (MT), originally developed within the field of sport psychology (Cherry, 2005; Clough et al., 2002). MT adds a fourth component to the three dimensions of hardiness theory (commitment, control and challenge), namely confidence. It has been suggested that confidence in one's abilities and interpersonal skills distinguishes MT from hardiness (Crust, 2008; Gerber et al., 2013). MT is moderately associated with other psychological constructs such as optimism and self-efficacy (Clough et al., 2002; Kaiseler, Polman & Nicholls, 2009). MT is also a predictor of relative tendency towards depressive symptoms, life satisfaction over time, and burnout (Gerber et al., 2013, 2015), and is strongly associated with behavioural perseverance (Giles et al., 2018; Gucciardi, Peeling, Ducker & Dawson, 2016) – or what is often referred to as 'grit'.

The presence of psychological hardiness appears to confer positive personal benefits. Within the military, the value of hardiness to influence outcomes – from general performance to mental health – has been extensively researched (as reviewed above). In the South African Navy (SA Navy), several occupational groups work in isolated, confined and/or extreme (ICE) environments. These range from ship-based sailors and submarine crews to navy divers. Given the stressful environmental demands under such circumstances, positive resilience may be particularly advantageous for navy specialists working in ICE environments.

Measuring resilience

If resilience can be meaningfully measured in terms of a specific research population (i.e. sectors of the SANDF), it may support two initiatives. The first is the identification of personnel who are at risk of sub-optimal outcomes (in terms of work performance or mental health), leading to provision of interventions to support their psychological adaptation. The second is the identification of factors associated with resilience, as a basis for programmes equipping individuals to optimise personal psychological adaptation. Based on available research (as reflected in the literature), this study assumes that both hardiness and MT contribute to an overarching construct of resilience.

Many of the constructs in the resilience literature have their own associated measuring tools, such as the ER89, the Connor Davidson Resilience Scale, the Resilience Scale for Adults, and the Brief Resilience Scale (Windle, Bennett & Noyes, 2011). This study makes use of two measuring tools that have specific relevance to hardiness and MT, The Dispositional Resilience Scale (DRS), and the Mental Toughness Questionnaire (MTQ).

Bartone developed 45-, 30-, and 15-item versions of the DRS (Bartone, 1989, 1995, 2014), which has been extensively used to measure hardiness in military as well as non-military samples (Britt et al., 2001). The literature views the DRS facets as supposedly independent of one another, although all load onto a latent secondary factor, called 'hardiness'. Bartone sometimes treats them as independent concepts, and at other times as one unitary concept (hardiness) across his publications. The DRS-15 (Bartone, 2014) is a 15-item self-report scale that taps into attitudes regarding commitment, control and challenge (each represented by five items). Good psychometric properties have been reported from samples in well-resourced contexts (Bartone, 1995, 1999). Kardum, Hudke-Knezevic and Krapic (2012), however, found high correlations between the facets and suggested that they may not be quite independent (as measured by the DRS-15).

The MTQ comes in 48- and 18-item versions (Clough et al., 2002). The 48 items are aggregated to the following dimensions: challenge, commitment, emotional control, life control, interpersonal confidence, and confidence in one's own ability. This six-component factor structure has been confirmed in large-scale studies conducted in well-resourced contexts (Perry et al., 2013). Although the factor structure for the 48-item version has been established (Perry et al., 2013), an extensive review of the dimensionality of MT (Lin et al., 2017) indicates that serious concerns remain (Gucciardi, 2018). Recent publications questioned the independence of the theorised constructs (Vaughan, Hanna & Breslin, 2018). Based on the literature for the DRS-15 and MTQ-18, there seems to be mixed consensus on the factor structure, yet most appear to indicate that the constructs are related to one another in the respective tests. In both instances, with the DRS and the MTQ, one can expect that exploratory factor analysis (EFA) may yield interesting results in relation to this debate on the factor structure, particularly in a South African context.

As mentioned, there is some support for the cross-national validity of the hardiness construct, and the DRS has been translated into a number of European languages (Hystad et al., 2010; Kardum et al., 2012). As mentioned, the DRS was successfully used across various well-resourced contexts in the global North (Bartone et al., 2012; Johnsen et al., 2013). However, resilience in under-resourced settings – typically found in lower-income countries – may require a different psychological orientation, and it is not clear whether the underlying components of the DRS and/or MTQ will remain valid in the cultural contexts of middle- and lower-income countries (for example, in sub-Saharan Africa).

Research purpose and objectives

From the above it is clear that resilience is important for military personnel in general and more specifically for SA Navy personnel; and that it can be measured in various ways. Two constructs applicable to the military context are identified, namely hardiness and MT. This study set out to explore the characteristics of two dispositional resilience scales in a South African population: the DRS-15 measures hardiness, and has been applied extensively to military populations; and the MTQ-18, which was developed in a sports context, measures the ability to perform under stress, and thus seems at face value applicable to the military context. Participants were selected from the SA Navy using convenience sampling (Bryman, 2012) based on the following rationale:

- resilience remains of enduring interest in military populations, because of the nature of the work context, psychological adaptation during and after operational deployments, and risks to long-term mental health;
- the sample would provide access to a low- to middle-income population (in contrast to samples from well-resourced populations in previous studies); and
- the scales have previously been used with navies of high-income countries, which would enable preliminary comparisons.

The aim of this study is to explore the psychometric properties of the DRS-15 and MTQ-18 in the South African context and to compare results across other studies done internationally, particularly in developing countries, with the following specific objectives:

- to inspect the items of the test using classical test theory;
- to explore the factor structure of the scales by conducting EFA;
- to explore the internal consistency of the scales using a reliability analysis; and
- to compare the results obtained with existing research on the scales.

RESEARCH METHOD AND DESIGN

The research design used is a cross-sectional quantitative approach. In keeping with psychometric test theory (Goldstein, 1989), the analyses conducted for the study are aimed at establishing the reliability of the instruments and preliminary validation of the instruments for a South African context since this is the first time that analyses have been conducted on these instruments in an SA Navy sample, thus requiring exploration. Since this is an exploratory study, no hypothesis is stated: rather, the analyses conducted forms a baseline for further investigations.

Participants

Table 8.1 represents the age, gender, and language distribution of the participants, who numbered 1 008 for the DRS-15 piloting (N=1 008). Although the average age of the sample was M=31 years, most participants were aged 25. In gender distribution, males (70%) outnumbered females (30%). The home languages were coded as English and non-English (this comprises the remaining 10 official languages). Only 6% of participants reported as English-speaking and 17% as non-English-speaking; the remainder of the sample did not report their home language.

The piloting of the MTQ-18 involved 893 participants (N=893). Most of the participants were 29 years old, but the average age of the sample was M=34 years. The gender distribution again included more males (68%) than females (32%). In terms of home language, 27% of participants reported as English-speaking and 73% as non-English-speaking. All participants (across both samples) had a minimum of 12 years of formal education. The samples further included all occupational classes in the SA Navy excluding divers, and as the scales were administered during routine health surveillance cycles, could be considered as representative of the SA Navy in terms of occupational class and language.

TABLE 8.1 Age, Gender and Language Distribution

Variables	*DRS-15 (N=1 008)*	*MTQ-18 (N=893)*
First Language		
• English	25.6%	26.7%
• Non-English	74.4%	73.3%
Gender		
• Women	29.9%	32.4%
• Men	70.1%	67.6%
Age		
• Mean ± SD	31.3 ± 8.4 years	34.1 ± 9.2 years
• Range	20–59 years	19–59 years

Instruments

DRS-15

The DRS-15 (Bartone, 2014) was used in its standard format. It is scored on a four-point Likert scale, anchored at zero (not true at all) and three (completely true), with six items reverse-scored. Higher scores reflect greater hardiness. Good psychometric properties and criterion-related validity across multiple samples have been reported, with a Cronbach's alpha reliability coefficient of .82 for the total scale (Bartone, 1995, 1999). The three-week test–retest reliability coefficient for the DRS-15 is .78 (Bartone, 2007). Other studies that found support for the three hardiness dimensions (Hystad et al., 2010) reported Cronbach's alpha coefficients of .70 for the total scale, .62 for commitment, .54 for control, and .57 for the challenge subscale (Kardum et al., 2012).

MTQ-18

The MTQ-18 (Clough et al., 2002) was used in its standard format. It is scored on a five-point Likert scale anchored at 1 (strongly disagree) and 5 (strongly agree), with nine items reverse-scored. Higher scores reflect greater MT. The MTQ-18 provides an overall score for MT, but not of the subscales of the MTQ-48 (Clough et al., 2002). High test–retest reliability, high internal consistency, and good content, construct, and criterion validity have been reported for the MTQ-48, which has a correlation of r=.87 with the MTQ-18 (Clough et al., 2002; Gerber et al., 2013). Scores do not appear to discriminate across gender (Clough et al., 2002). Despite the absence of robust psychometric examination, the shorter 18-item version was chosen to enhance ease of completion. A Cronbach's alpha reliability coefficient of .70 has been reported for the MTQ-18 (Gerber et al., 2013).

Data collection procedure

Participants were SA Navy personnel and were recruited during their annual occupational health assessment and then completed the scales. It is important to note that most participants completed only one of the two instruments. All completed the instruments anonymously.

Ethical considerations

The study was conducted according to the principles set out in the Declaration of Helsinki (World Medical Association, 2013). Participants were briefed on the purpose of the scales and invited to complete them. For the DRS-15, after the briefing, participants signed a consent form for their data to be used in the research. Their data were anonymised prior to analysis. For the MTQ-18, after the briefing, participants were invited to complete the scale anonymously. The forms were completed in group sessions, and then placed in a box, so that there would be no way to identify any individual. Because official Department of Defence information would be published, the research findings first had to be vetted by Defence Intelligence, who gave authorisation to publish this research.

Data analysis

The data analysis for this study consists of descriptive statistics, item analysis, item correlations, EFA, and reliability, for each of the instruments. These methods of analysis are part of dissecting the items and structures of the test and elucidating how the test is functioning.

The descriptive statistics serve to describe the data characteristics for the piloting of the two measures. These statistics were generated on the Statistical Package for the Social Sciences Software (SPSS) and include the range of values observed for the two measures and the normality statistics (George & Mallery, 2010).

The item analysis provides an indication of the performance of items in the test. The item analysis for this study was guided by classical test theory and generated using SPSS. The items of a Likert scale (the DRS-15 and MTQ-18 are structured as Likert scales) are dependent on the sample because the items are generated by calculating the mean value for the different items. The item difficulty was therefore interpreted in terms of the associated mean of the answer options for the respective tests (Schwarz, 2011). In the evaluation of item discrimination, a range between 0.30 and 0.79 is used to depict moderate discrimination (Field, 2017). The items that have values outside this discrimination range can be classified as problematic items (Field, 2017).

EFA is a method used to investigate the underlying structure of a test or questionnaire and involves reducing the items of the test into factors (Martin & Savage-McGlynn, 2013). EFA is usually used as a preliminary method to examine the structure of a test or questionnaire and is guided by theory (Martin & Savage-McGlynn, 2013).

Principal axis factoring (PAF), which was used for this study, is regarded as a method of EFA and can be used when the data are not normally distributed (Yong & Pearce, 2013). Since the literature suggests that the factors are related, Promax rotation was used, which is a common oblique rotation method (Tabachnick & Fidell, 2013). In the execution of the EFA, the Kaiser-Meyer-Olkin measure of sampling adequacy was assessed, as it should be above 0.50 for the sample to be considered adequate for factor analysis (Yong & Pearce, 2013). This is observed in Table 8.2 for the DRS-15 and MTQ-18 respectively. The Bartlett's test for sphericity was significant ($p<.001$) and indicates the data's appropriateness for factor analysis (Field, 2017).

Table 8.2 Sample Adequacy for DRS-15 and MTQ 18

Measure		*DRS-15 (N=1 008)*	*MTQ-18 (N=893)*
• Kaiser-Meyer-Olkin		0.805	0.932
• Bartlett's test of sphericity	Approx chi-square	5 923.695	2 746.587
	df	153	105
	Significance	0.001	0.001

In the selection of the number of factors to be extracted from the data, the Kaiser criterion, which states that factors that contain eigenvalues greater than 1 should be retained, and the scree plot of eigenvalues was consulted (Field, 2017). The naming of these factors was influenced by the item loadings and theory. Identical procedures were followed for the DRS-15 and MTQ-18. The factor correlation matrix was interpreted to evaluate the relationship between the factors of the DRS-15 and MTQ-18 separately. These factor correlations were interpreted as follows: 0–.29 (small correlation), .30–.49 (moderate correlation) and .50–1.00 (large correlation) (Cohen, 1988).

Reliability is referred to as the internal consistency of a measure in that it refers to lack of measurement errors in the measure (Suhr & Shay, 2009). The reliability of the DRS-15 and MTQ-18 was calculated using Cronbach's alpha (Suhr & Shay, 2009). The coefficient alpha was interpreted as follows: a value of .60 to .69 was acceptable for research purposes, a value ranging from .70 to .79 was acceptable for a newly developed measure, a value ranging from .80 to .89 was acceptable for an aptitude test and a value of .90 and above was acceptable for selection purposes (Nunnally & Bernstein, 1994; Suhr & Shay, 2009).

RESULTS

Descriptive data

The normality of the data was determined by skewness, kurtosis and the Kolmogorov-Smirnov and Shapiro-Wilk tests. In Table 8.3, the total values for skewness and kurtosis for the DRS-15 suggest that the data are negatively skewed with a peaked distribution (Field, 2017). The mean, median and mode suggest that the participants in the test were generally scoring 35, which suggests high hardiness, as a score between 34 and 38 indicated high hardiness for the American samples. Moreover, the participants scored a minimum of 15 and a maximum of 45, suggesting that they used the full range of expression, because these are the minimum and maximum scores for the DRS-15.

TABLE 8.3 Descriptive Statistics for the DRS-15 (N=1 008)

Statistic	*Value*
Mean	35.2
Median	35
Mode	36
Skewness	−0.432
Std. error of skewness	0.077
Kurtosis	0.592
Std. error of kurtosis	0.154
Minimum	15
Maximum	45

The Kolmogorov-Smirnov value (.056) and Shapiro-Wilk value (.982) (Table 8.4) indicate that the data are not normally distributed ($p<.001$) to a significant extent.

TABLE 8.4 Tests of Normality for the DRS-15 (N=1 008)

Normality tests	*Statistic*	*df*	*Sig*
• Kolmogorov-Smirnov	.056	1008	.001
• Shapiro-Wilk	.982	1008	.001

In Table 8.5, the total values for skewness and kurtosis for the MTQ-18 indicate that the data are negatively skewed with a pointy distribution (Field, 2017). The mean, median and mode suggest that participants' performance in the test varied, with an average performance of 68. Gerber et al. (2013) indicated that values above 60 were typical for 'well-adjusted' participants. Moreover, the participants scored a minimum of 29 and a maximum of 90, which indicates that the scores of the participants may be skewed towards the higher end, as 18 is the minimum score and none of the participants scored lower than 29. This was, however, suggested by the skewness and kurtosis values.

TABLE 8.5 Data statistics for the MTQ-18 (N=893)

Statistic	*Value*
Mean	68.16
Median	69
Mode	72
Skewness	−0.981
Std. error of skewness	0.082
Kurtosis	2.108

TABLE 8.5 Data statistics for the MTQ-18 (N=893)	
Statistic	*Value*
Std. error of kurtosis	0.163
Minimum	29
Maximum	90

In Table 8.6, the Kolmogorov-Smirnov value (.118) and Shapiro-Wilk value (.936) indicate that the data are not normally distributed ($p<.001$) to a significant extent.

TABLE 8.6 Tests of Normality for the MTQ-18 (N=893)			
Normality tests	*Statistic*	*df*	*Sig*
• Kolmogorov-Smirnov	.118	893	.001
• Shapiro-Wilk	.936	893	.001

Item analysis

Table 8.7, presents the item difficulty and item discrimination for the DRS-15. It demonstrates that 12 of the items had mean values above 2. This indicates that items 1, 2, 4, 6, 7, 8, 9, 10, 12, 13 and 15 were well above 2, showing that participants in the study were more in favour of answering "Quite true" and "Completely true" for these items. The remaining items, 3, 5, 11 and 14, elicited responses in favour of "A little true" and "Quite true". Overall, the "Quite true" option appears to have been the most commonly used response among the participants.

In terms of item discrimination, most of the items have acceptable discrimination values, as they are above .30 and below .79 (Field, 2017). The items below .30 require investigation, as they are not effectively discriminating between participant's responses. These items (marked in bold italics in Table 8.7) are items 1, 3, 4, 8, 11 and 14. These items are either worded in a manner that is problematic or the answer options are not discriminating enough.

TABLE 8.7 Item Analysis of the DRS-15 (N=1 008)			
Item	*Item difficulty*	*Standard deviation*	*Item discrimination*
1	2.22	.817	***.279***
2	2.67	.565	.337
3	1.91	.855	***.197***
4	2.83	.496	***.284***
5	2.01	.811	.404
6	2.46	.655	.371
7	2.30	.718	.478
8	2.69	.685	***.228***
9	2.16	.746	.366
10	2.32	.694	.528
11	1.90	.898	***.157***

TABLE 8.7 Item Analysis of the DRS-15 (N=1 008)

Item	*Item difficulty*	*Standard deviation*	*Item discrimination*
12	2.58	.641	.370
13	2.87	.429	.336
14	1.84	.862	***.191***
15	2.42	.672	.426

The item difficulty and discrimination for the MTQ-18 are indicated in Table 8.8. The majority of the items are over .3, which is normal for a five-point Likert scale. Thus, most of the responses to items were "Neither agree nor disagree" or "Agree". There are no responses below .3, indicating that most participants did not choose the "Strongly disagree" or "Disagree" options to any of the items. There were only three items that had .4 means, which indicates that most participants only chose to respond "Agree" and "Strongly Agree" to these specific items.

In terms of the item discrimination for the MTQ-18, only the last item was found to score below .30, which suggests that the item is not discriminating effectively. The other 17 items have acceptable discrimination values and can be regarded as having plausible answer options.

TABLE 8.8 Item nalysis of the MTQ-18 (N=893)

Item	*Item difficulty*	*Standard deviation*	*Item discrimination*
1	3.92	.878	.621
2	3.21	1.118	.355
3	3.78	.915	.611
4	3.94	.824	.620
5	4.26	.947	.585
6	3.70	.953	.532
7	3.87	.986	.431
8	3.61	1.021	.448
9	3.63	1.050	.401
10	3.95	.897	.655
11	3.40	1.010	.347
12	3.53	.990	.453
13	3.87	.876	.485
14	4.13	.896	.666
15	4.22	.925	.692
16	3.89	.915	.637
17	3.72	.923	.595
18	3.52	1.008	.254

Exploratory factor analysis

The analyses of the DRS-15 identified four components that explained 36% of the variance on the test, while three components explained 33% of the variance on the test. The scree plot was also consulted, which indicated that three or four factors should be retained. When using the four-factor solution for the DRS-15, 14 items loaded on the four factors, with only two items loading on one factor and one item not loading on any of the four factors. For this reason, a three-factor solution was chosen for the DRS-15 (seen in Table 8.9), which had 14 items loaded on the three factors and a cross-loading of two items.

TABLE 8.9 Pattern Matrix for the DRS-15

Items	*Control*	*Commitment*	*Challenge*
@6	.653		
@12	.613		
@15	.553		
@9	.508		
@5	.475		
@2	.462		
@10	.440	.352	
@7	.407	.391	
@4		.713	
@13		.643	
@1		.319	
@14			.702
@3			.546
@11			.524

Factor 1 is labelled 'control' because of the items loading on this factor, as most of the items pertain to the control factor of the DRS-15 (Bartone, 2014). Factors 2 and 3 are labelled 'commitment' and 'challenge' respectively, because of the items loading on them that resemble the DRS-15 factor structure (Bartone, 2014). The cross-loading of items 10 and 7 on both factor 1 and factor 2 suggests that these items are tapping into both factors (control and commitment), yet the strongest loading for these items is observed for control. It should also be noted that although the item loadings on the commitment and challenge factors are the same as those of Bartone's (2014) factor structure, the control factor is significantly different, as it contains items that were theorised to belong to both the challenge and commitment factors.

TABLE 8.10 Factor Correlation Matrix the DRS-15 (N=1 008)

Factor	*Control*	*Challenge*
• Challenge	.010	

Note:
a Correlation is significant at $p<.001$

TABLE 8.10 Factor Correlation Matrix the DRS-15 (N=1 008)

Factor	*Control*	*Challenge*
• Commitment	.507[a]	.057

Note:
a Correlation is significant at p<.001

The control factor has a moderate relationship with the commitment factor and a negligible relationship with the challenge factor (seen in Table 8.10). The commitment factor has a similarly negligible relationship with the challenge factor. This would suggest that the control and commitment factors are similar in nature but not identical, and these two factors measure opposite constructs to the challenge factor.

The MTQ-18 analyses identified three components that explained 43% of the variance and two components that explained 41% of the variance of the test. The scree plot was also consulted, which indicated that two or three factors should be retained. When using the three-factor solution for the MTQ-18, all 18 items loaded on the three factors, with three items (specifically from the third factor) cross-loading across factors. The two-factor solution for the MTQ-18 (seen in Table 8.11) was chosen and indicated that all 18 items loaded on the two factors, with a cross-loading of one item.

TABLE 8.11 Pattern Matrix for the MTQ-18 (N=893)

Items	*Self-control*	*Self-confidence*
@15	.845	
@14	.808	
@5	.748	
@7	.675	
@10	.640	
@1	.575	
@13	.543	
@18	.538	
@4	.537	
@2		.707
@6		.681
@8		.635
@17		.606
@12		.599
@11		.550
@3		.459
@16	.354	.395
@9		.335

Note:
Rotation converged in three iterations

Factor 1 is labelled self-control because the items loaded under this factor are related to the challenge factor and a combination of the control and confidence factors of the MTQ-18 factor structure. Since the items related to the control factors of the MTQ-18 have more loadings compared to the confidence factors, it was suitable to name this factor self-control. Factor 2 is labelled self-confidence because these items consist of the commitment factor and the combination of the control and confidence factors; however, there were more item loadings related to the confidence factor. Item 16 cross-loads on both the self-control and self-confidence factors, with similar loadings across both factors, suggesting that the item taps into both factors.

The results of the Pearson correlation indicated that there was a significant positive association between self-control and self-confidence, $r(893)=.618$, $p<.001$. Thus, the self-control and self-confidence factors have a moderate relationship. This suggests that these two factors are closely related and are measuring constructs that are similar in nature.

Reliability

The DRS-15 full scale produced a Cronbach alpha of =.714 (which can be observed in Table 8.12), which could be marginally improved to =.723 if item 11 should be excluded. This alpha value indicates that the scale is sufficient for research purposes (as it is not a newly developed measure) (Foxcroft & Roodt, 2009; Nunnally & Bernstein, 1994). The MTQ-18 full scale produced a Cronbach alpha of =.884 (which is indicated in Table 8.7), and no improvement was observed through any exclusions. This alpha value therefore indicates that this scale is sufficiently reliable for measuring MT (Foxcroft & Roodt, 2009; Nunnally & Bernstein, 1994).

The Cronbach's alphas for the subscales across the DRS-15 and MTQ-18 are presented in Table 8.12.

TABLE 8.12 Cronbach's Alpha for DRS-15 and MTQ-18

Scale	*Component*	α
DRS-15 (N=1008)	Total scale	.714
	Control	.764
	Commitment	.686
	Challenge	.608
MTQ-18 (N=893)	Total scale	.884
	Self-control	.875
	Self-confidence	.813

In Table 8.12, the Cronbach's alpha subscales of the DRS-15 range between .6 and .7, indicating that the subscales are also not sufficiently reliable, yet may be reliable enough for research purposes. Thus, the internal consistency of these scales is low, which suggests they are only suitable for research purposes (Foxcroft & Roodt, 2009; Nunnally & Bernstein, 1994).

In Table 8.12, the ranges of Cronbach's alpha for the different subscales of the MTQ-18 are both over .8. The subscale self-control produced the highest Cronbach's alphas compared to the self-confidence subscale, yet both subscales are sufficiently reliable for measuring MT (Foxcroft & Roodt, 2009; Nunnally & Bernstein, 1994).

DISCUSSION

This study set out to explore the characteristics of two dispositional resilience scales (DRS-15 and MTQ-18) in the SA Navy. The exploration of both the DRS-15 and MTQ-18 yielded several important findings. These findings are further discussed in terms of psychometric properties of the questionnaires; comparison of questionnaire results; and the value of resilience scales (hardiness and MT) for researchers and military mental health practitioners.

Psychometric properties of the questionnaires

The description of data indicated that the data were negatively skewed, yet the full range of expression was used by the participants for both the DRS-15 and the MTQ-18. The mode across the two measures suggested that 'high hardiness' and 'well-adjusted' behaviour were indicated by the responses to these measures.

DRS-15

The analysis of items suggested that most participants were in favour of answering "Quite true" and "Completely true" to questions in the test. However, six items were marked as not discriminating sufficiently. These six items form part of the commitment and change factors. This would suggest that the language use is either not clear or allows different interpretations across language groups. In South Africa, where there are 11 official languages, language can produce bias in instruments from different contexts (Van de Vijver & Rothmann, 2004).

The three factors of hardiness are represented by five items each in the DRS-15 (Bartone, 2014), which differs from the factor structure of this study in South Africa. The control factor generally represents the positively formulated items of control, but also includes the positively formulated items of challenge and commitment factors from the original DRS-15 validated by Bartone (2014). The commitment factor represents the five items of commitment (with the three positively formulated items also cross-loading on the control factor). The challenge factor represents the negatively formulated items of the challenge factor described by Bartone (2014). So, although there is a structure that vaguely reflects the original three facets of hardiness, the direction of item formulation may have played a strong role in how the scale was completed. Moreover, the relationship between factors closely follows a finding from a meta-analysis (Eschleman, Bowling & Alarcon, 2010) that described a close relationship between control (factor 1) and commitment (factor 2), but only a moderate relationship between those two and challenge (factor 3).

The DRS-15 as well as the control factors are sufficiently reliable for research purposes, yet the other two factors are ultimately not sufficiently reliable. The DRS-15 factors therefore have questionable internal consistency among the items of the test for this sample. It should, however, be noted that the full-scale reliability of the DRS 15 for this study is lower than .82 of the measure of Bartone (1995, 1999), and similar to .70 of that of Kardum et al. (2012). This finding is therefore in agreement with previous research conducted on the DRS 15.

MTQ18

The item analysis indicated that most of the participants in the study answered, "Neither agree nor disagree" or "Agree" to the questions in the test. Moreover, only one item, which belongs to the self-control factor, was identified as not discriminating well.

The self-control factor clustered the positively formulated items, while the self-confidence factor clustered the negatively formulated items. The original positive-negative formulation of these factors was done randomly, and the current factor structure of this study appears to be following the direction of item formulation; for example the self-control factor contains items associated with the challenge, control and confidence factors of the validated MTQ-18. The self-confidence factor contains items associated with the commitment, control and confidence factors of the validated MTQ-18. This factor structure could possibly be viewed as supporting previous findings suggesting that the 18-item version only provides an overall score for MT (Clough et al., 2002; Gerber et al., 2013).

The full MTQ-18, as well as the factors identified, shows good reliability, which suggests that there is sufficient internal consistency for measuring a construct such as MT. Moreover, the full-scale reliability of the MTQ-18 for this study is higher than .70 and .81, as reported by Gerber et al. (2013, 2015).

There is a factor differentiation in the MTQ-18, a scale that purportedly provides an overall score of MT, along the positive and negatively worded items. Similarly, although the DRS-15 'factors' vaguely resemble the theoretical model, these are also strongly associated with the direction of positively and negatively phrased items.

Comparison of questionnaire results

When the DRS-15 scores of the SA Navy sample were compared to the means of published groups, the SA Navy sample in general scored significantly higher than all other samples (civilian and military), except for a sample of active duty Royal Norwegian Navy sailors (see Table 8.13).

TABLE 8.13 DRS-15 Comparison of Means of SA Navy Sample and Other Published Groups

Group	Scale	M	SD	t	p
• US Army Special Forces[a]	Total	34.07	4.3	7.469	<.001
• US Military Academy students[b]	Total	30.8	4.6	29.113	<.001
• Working adults[c]	Total	28.85	5.14	42.021	<.001
	CM	10.39	2.47	31.761	<.001
	CO	10.45	2.07	36.577	<.001
	CH	8.01	2.59	22.942	<.001
• Post-deployed service members[d]	Total	28.69	6.16	43.080	<.001
• Norwegian adults[e]	Total	30.37	5.21	31.960	<.001
	CM	10.20	2.48	34.560	<.001
	CO	10.27	2.08	39.347	<.001
	CH	9.90	2.31	-.930	.353
• US Military Academy students[f]	Total	29.15	4.63	40.035	<.001
	CM	10.42	2.04	31.319	<.001
	CO	10.10	1.99	41.964	<.001
	CH	8.62	2.67	15.238	<.001
• Sailors of the Royal Norwegian Navy[g]	Total	48.19	2.68	-85.992	<.001
• US Reserve Officer Training Corps[h]	Total	31.40	5.31	25.142	<.001

Sources:
a - Bartone et al. (2008)
b - Bartone et al. (2009)
c - Kardum et al. (2012)
d - Escolas et al. (2013)
e - Bartone (2014)
f - Bartone (2014)
g - Nordmo, Hystad, Sanden & Johnsen (2017)
h - Johnston (n.d.)

Similarly, when the MTQ-18 scores of the SA Navy sample were compared to the means of published groups, the SA Navy sample scored significantly higher than the available (civilian) samples (see Table 8.14).

TABLE 8.14 MTQ-18 Comparison of Means of SAN Sample and Other Published Groups

Group	M	SD
• SAN sample[a]	68.16	9.978
• Swiss adolescent students[b]	58.23	6.66
• Swiss adolescent students[c]	62.09	7.48

Sources:
a - Current study
b - Gerber et al. 2013
c - Gerber et al. 2015

Value of these resilience scales for military mental health

In general, the issue of language is an important point of discussion, as most of the individuals in this study are English second- or third-language speakers and their interpretation of words may differ from the intended meaning. This may in some instances explain the differences across the items in the factor structure. When inspecting the DRS-15, which has been marked as problematic in both the reliability and item analysis, the wording and phrasing of sentences in the questionnaire may present problems for English second/third-language speakers. The addition of negatively worded items is also problematic for individuals who are not English first-language speakers. In the field of research (Hinz, Michalski, Schwarz & Herzberg, 2007; Salazar, 2015), the inclusion of negatively worded items is generally designed to reduce incidence of two kinds of responses: extreme response bias; and acquiescence bias. However, such inclusions tend to create more difficulties than they prevent (this happens through various mechanisms), and result in, for example, lowering of the internal reliability of scales, and distortion of the factor structure, which may be particularly problematic in cross-cultural settings (Salazar, 2015; Sauro & Lewis, 2011; Van Sonderen, Sanderman & Coyne, 2013). Interestingly, in cases where items use Likert scale responses, there is some evidence of a significant effect of item direction on the factorial construction, but not on the criterion validity, of scales (Qasem & Gul, 2014). Furthermore, scales with positively worded items show higher values for Cronbach alpha coefficients, and better fit of theoretical factor structures (Salazar, 2015).

The South African naval context therefore requires questionnaires to be adapted for the South African population, especially in terms of language. The use of negatively phrased items can be problematic when used interchangeably to evaluate a sample of predominantly English second/third-language speakers. Thus, the measurement of constructs such as hardiness and MT needs to be presented in a manner that will enable understanding and ensure fair assessment. It is interesting to note that although the MTQ-18 presents relatively well in terms of item analysis and reliability, the words used could be problematic for English second/third-language speakers. However, the phrasing of the sentences may have countered the effect of the possibly problematic words in the questionnaire.

LIMITATIONS AND RECOMMENDATIONS

Although the sample presents relatively representative features, the use of convenience sampling limits the generalisability of the study. The fact that the DRS-15 and MTQ-18 were not administered to the same sample denotes that it is impossible to determine the possibility of concurrent validity between the two instruments. The results of the factor analysis and reliability are limited to the SA Navy. The issue of language, particularly the use of negatively phrased questions, appears to have interfered with how participants responded to some of the items in the questionnaires, yet only the DRS-15 yielded concerning results, suggesting that the DRS-15 requires more investigation into the items of the test and may require adaptation for use in the South African military. The MTQ-18, however, shows promising results, but still requires more research to validate it for the South African military population. It can also be argued that the MTQ-18, which has shown promising results, may serve as a better measure of a resilience-related subscale than the DRS-15.

Considerably more research is required before more definitive statements can be made about the psychometric properties and usability of these two instruments. Further studies on these instruments can include analysis to assess differential performances across genders and language groups (although this is restricted to English and non-English). The reason for this is that the same construct should emerge across language and gender groups to establish fairness in testing and reduce bias as far as possible. Research conducted in other arms of service in the SANDF will allow for comparison, as this study can serve as a baseline for follow-up studies. Rasch analysis (Linacre, 2012) should also be conducted in a follow-up study, because this analysis of item performance will yield rich information in terms of separating individual and item performance on the two measures. Thus, one will be able to see clearly how the items are performing and how the individuals completing the test were answering, providing a better indication of the test item quality as opposed to the person response patterns. Research among military members actively engaging in tasks that could compromise their MT and/or hardiness may prove interesting and may serve to confirm the findings of the exploratory study.

If both questionnaires can be applied to the same sample and both demonstrate good validity and reliability, one can test for concurrent validity to determine whether the two instruments measure the same construct or not. Lastly, future research on both instruments could include a qualitative study where the theoretical components of the questionnaires are validated against the participants' perceptions of the characteristics of mentally tough and/or hardy military personnel.

CONCLUSION

The exploratory nature of this study makes it the first step towards validating these instruments for the South African military population and as such, these questionnaires cannot yet be used to make decisions, although they serve as a good baseline. Practitioners should be cautious when applying these instruments until more research can be conducted using these scales with larger and more varied samples.

REFERENCES

American Psychological Association. 2019. The road to resilience. *Psychology Help Center*. Available at http://www.apa.org/helpcenter/road-resilience

Antonovsky, A. 1979. *Health, stress and coping*. San Francisco CA: Jossey-Bass.

Bartone, P.T. 1989. Predictors of stress-related illness in city bus drivers. *Journal of Occupational Medicine*, 31(8):657-663.

Bartone, P.T. 1995. *A short hardiness scale*. Paper presented at the July 1995 Annual Convention of the American Psychological Society, New York, NY.

Bartone, P.T. 1996. Stress and hardiness in US peacekeeping soldiers. Paper presented at the (August) 1996 Annual Convention of the American Psychological Association, Toronto, Canada.

Bartone, P.T. 1999. Hardiness protects against war-related stress in Army Reserve forces. *Consulting Psychology Journal: Practice and Research*, 51(2):72-82. https://doi.org/10.1037/1061-4087.51.2.72

Bartone, P.T. 2000. Hardiness as a resiliency factor for United States forces in the Gulf War. In: Violanti, J.M., Paton, D. & Dunning, C. (eds), *Posttraumatic stress intervention: Challenges, issues, and perspectives*, pp.115-133. Springfield, IL: C. Thomas.

Bartone, P.T. 2007. Test-retest reliability of the Dispositional Resilience Scale-15, a brief hardiness scale. *Psychological Reports*, 101(3):943-944. https://doi.org/10.2466/pr0.101.3.943-944

Bartone, P.T. 2014. *Dispositional Resilience Scale-15: Normative data, adults and college students*. www.kbmetrics.com

Bartone, P.T., Eid, J., Johnsen, B.H., Laberg, J.C. & Snook, S. 2009. Big five personality factors, hardiness, and social judgment as predictors of leader performance. *Leadership & Organization Development Journal*, 30(6):498-521. https://doi.org/10.1108/01437730910981908

Bartone, P.T., Hystad, S.W., Eid, J. & Brevik, J.I. 2012. Psychological hardiness and coping style as risk/resilience factors for alcohol abuse. Military Medicine, 177(5):517-524.

Bartone, P.T., Johnsen, B.H., Eid, J., Brun, W. & Laberg, L.C. 2002. Factors influencing small-unit cohesion in Norwegian Navy officer cadets. *Military Psychology*, 14(1):1-22.

Bartone, P.T., Roland, R.R., Picano, J.J. & Williams, T.J. 2008. Psychological hardiness predicts success in US Army special forces candidates. *International Journal of Selection and Assessment*, 16(1):78-81. https://doi.org/10.1111/j.1468-2389.2008.00412.x

Britt, T.W., Adler, A.B. & Bartone, P.T. 2001. Deriving benefits from stressful events: The role of engagement in meaningful work and hardiness. *Journal of Occupational Health Psychology*, 6(1):53-63.

Bryman, A. 2012. *Social research methods* (4th Edition). Oxford: Oxford University Press.

Cherry, H.L. 2005. Psychometric analysis of an inventory assessing mental toughness. Master's thesis, University of Tennessee-Knoxville. Available at http://bit.ly/2xQ494j

Clough, P., Earle, K. & Sewell, D. 2002. Mental toughness: The concept and its measurement. In: Cockerill, I. (ed.), *Solutions in Sport Psychology*, pp.32-46. London: Thomson Learning.

Cohen, J. 1988. *Statistical power analysis for the behavioural sciences* (2nd Edition). Mahwah NJ: Erlbaum.

Cronbach, L. 1951. Coefficient alpha and the internal structure of tests. *Psychometrika*, 16(3):297-334.

Crust, L. 2008. A review and conceptual re-examination of mental toughness: Implications for future researchers. *Personality and Individual Differences*, 45(7):576-583.

Eschleman, K.J., Bowling, N. & Alarcon, G.M. 2010. A meta-analytic examination of hardiness. *International Journal of Stress Management*, 17(4):277-307.

Escolas, S.M., Pitts, B.L., Safer, M.A. & Bartone, P.T. 2013. The protective value of hardiness on military posttraumatic stress symptoms. *Military Psychology*, 25(2):116-123. https://doi.org/10.1037/h0094953

Field, A.P. 2017. *Discovering statistics using IBM SPSS statistic* (5th Edition). London: Sage.

Florian, V., Mikulincer, M. & Taubman, O. 1995. Does hardiness contribute to mental health during a stressful real life situation? The role of appraisal and coping. *Journal of Personality and Social Psychology*, 68(40):687-695.

Foxcroft, C.D. & Roodt, G. 2009. *An introduction to psychological assessment in the South African context* (3rd Edition). Cape Town: Oxford University Press.

George, D. & Mallery, M. 2010. *SPSS for Windows step-by-step: A simple guide and reference* (10th Edition). Boston MA: Pearson.

Gerber, M., Brand, S., Feldmeth, A.K., Lang, C., Elliot, C., Holsboer-Trachsler, E. & Pühse, U. 2013. Adolescents with high mental toughness adapt better to perceived stress: A longitudinal study with Swiss vocational students. *Personality and Individual Differences*, 54(7):808-814.

Gerber, M., Feldmeth, A.K., Lang, C., Brand, S., Elliott, C., Holsboer-Trachsler, E. & Pühse, U. 2015. The relationship between mental toughness, stress and burnout among adolescents: A longitudinal study with Swiss vocational students. *Psychological Reports: Employment Psychology & Marketing*, 117(3):703-723. https://doi.org/10.2466/14.02.PR0.117c29z6

Giles, B., Goods, P.S.R., Warner, D.R., Quain, D., Peeling, P., Ducker, K.J., Dawson, B. & Gucciardi, D.F. 2018. Mental toughness and behavioural perseverance: A conceptual replication and extension. *Journal of Science and Medicine in Sport*, 21(6):640-645. https://doi.org/10.1016/j.jsams.2017.10.036

Goldstein, H. 1989. Psychometric test theory and educational assessment. In: Elliott, J. & Simons, H. (eds), *Rethinking appraisal and assessment*, pp.140-148. Milton Keynes: Open University Press.

Grundlingh, A. 2016. New military leaders for new wars in Africa. In: Van Dyk, G.A.J. (ed.), *Military psychology for Africa*, pp.323-347. Stellenbosch: African Sun Media.

Gucciardi, D.F. 2018. Commentary: Mental toughness and individual differences in learning, educational and work performance, psychological wellbeing, and personality: A systematic review. *Frontiers in Psychology*, 8: article 2329. https://doi.org/10.3389/fpsyg.2017.02329

Gucciardi, D.F., Peeling, P., Ducker, K.J. & Dawson, B. 2016. When the going gets tough: Mental toughness and its relationship with behavioural perseverance. *Journal of Science and Medicine in Sport*, 19(1):81-86. https://doi.org/10.1016/j.jsams.2014.12.005

Hinz, A., Michalski, D., Schwarz, R. & Herzberg, P.Y. 2007. The acquiescence effect in responding to a questionnaire. *GMS Psycho-Social Medicine*, 4: Doc 07. Available at http://bit.ly/2vB3wul

Hystad, S.W., Eid, J., Johnsen, B.H., Laberg, J.C. & Bartone, P. 2010. Psychometric properties of the revised Norwegian dispositional resilience (hardiness) scale. *Scandinavian Journal of Psychology*, 51(3):237-245. https://doi.org/10.1111/j.1467-9450.2009.00759.x

Johnsen, B.H., Bartone, P., Sandvik, A.M., Gjeldnes, R., Morken, A.M., Hystad, S.W. & Stornæs, A.V. 2013. Psychological hardiness predicts success in a Norwegian armed forces border patrol selection course. *International Journal of Selection and Assessment*, 21(4):368-375. https://doi.org/10.1111/ijsa.12046

Johnston, S.M. n.d.. An examination of the influence of psychological hardiness on retention in US Army Reserve Officer Training Corps (ROTC) programs. Paper (c.2009), Workforce Development and Education, Department of Educational Studies, Ohio State University, Dayton, Ohio.

Kaiseler, M., Polman, R.C.J. & Nicholls, A.R. 2009. Mental toughness, stress, stress appraisal, coping and coping effectiveness in sport. *Personality and Individual Differences*, 47(7):728-733.

Kardum, I., Hudke-Knezevic, J. & Krapic, N. 2012. The structure of hardiness, its measurement invariance across gender and relationship with personality traits and mental health outcomes. *Psychological Topics*, 21(3):487-507.

Kobasa, S.C. 1979. Stressful life events, personality, and health: An inquiry into hardiness. *Journal of Personality and Social Psychology*, 37(1):1-11. https://doi.org/10.1037/0022-3514.37.1.1

Kobasa, S.C, Maddi, S.R. & Kahn, S. 1982. Hardiness and health: A prospective study. *Journal of Personality and Social Psychology*, 42(1):168-177. https://doi.org/10.1037/0022-3514.42.1.168

Lin, Y., Mutz, J., Clough, P.J. & Papageorgiou, K.A. 2017. Mental toughness and individual differences in learning, educational and work performance, psychological wellbeing, and personality: A systematic review. *Frontiers in Psychology*, 8: article 1345 (15 pages). https://doi.org/10.3389/fpsyg.2017.01345

Linacre, M. 2012. *Winsteps tutorials 2: Fit analysis and measurement models*. Available at http://bit.ly/3d9KXyB

Maddi, S.R. & Kobasa, S.C. 1984. *The hardy executive: Health under stress*. Burr Ridge IL. Irwin Professional Publishing.

Maddi, S.R. & Hess, M. 1992. Personality hardiness and success in basketball. *International Journal of Sports Psychology*, 23(4):360-368.

Maddi, S.R. & Harvey, R.H. 2006. Hardiness considered across cultures. In: Wong, P.T.P. & Wong L.C.J. (eds), *Handbook of multicultural perspectives on stress and coping*, pp.409-426. New York: Springer.

Martin, C.R. & Savage-McGlynn, E. 2013. A 'good practice' guide for the reporting of design and analysis for psychometric evaluation. *Journal of Reproductive and Infant Psychology*, 31(5):449-455. https://doi.org/10.1080/02646838.2013.835036

Martin, G. 2019. Female SANDF commander leads combat engagement in Sudan. DefenceWeb, 16 January. Available at http://bit.ly/2UjSphN

Mphofu, R. & Van Dyk, G.A.J. 2016. A model to apply military psychology in Africa: The case of Bangui. In: Van Dyk, G.A.J. (ed.), *Military psychology for Africa*, pp.401-423. Stellenbosch: African Sun Media.

Nordmo, M., Hystad, S.W., Sanden, S., Johnsen, B.J. 2017. The effect of hardiness on symptoms of insomnia during a naval mission. *International Maritime Health*, 68(3):147-152. https://doi.org/10.5603/IMH.2017.0026

Nunnally, J.C. & Bernstein, I. H. 1994. *Psychometric theory* (3rd Edition). New York: McGraw Hill.

Perry, J.L., Clough, P.J., Crust, L., Earle, K. & Nicholls, A.R. 2013. Factorial validity of the Mental Toughness Questionnaire-48. *Personality and Individual Differences*, 54(5):587-592. http://dx.doi.org/10.1016/j.paid.2012.11.020

Pietrzak, R.H., Johnson, D.C., Goldstein, M.B., Malley, J.C. & Southwick, S.M. 2009. Psychological resilience and post-deployment social support protect against traumatic stress and depressive symptoms in soldiers returning from Operations Enduring Freedom and Iraqi Freedom. *Depression and Anxiety*, 26(8):745-751. https://doi.org/10.1002/da.20558

Qasem, M.A. & Gul, S.B.A. 2014. Effects of item direction (positive or negative) on the factorial construction and criterion related validity in Likert scale. *Asian Journal of Research in Social Sciences and Humanities*, 4(4):114-121.

Rosenbaum, M. 1990. *Learned resourcefulness: On coping skills, self-control, and adaptive behavior*. New York: Springer.

Rotter, J.B. 1966. Generalised expectancies for internal versus external control of reinforcement. *Psychological Monographs*, 80(1):1-28. https://doi.org/10.1037/h0092976

Salazar, M.S. 2015. The dilemma of combining positive and negative items in scales. *Psichothema*, 27(2). 192-200. https://doi.org/10.7334/psicothema2014.266

Sandvik, A.M., Gjevestad, E., Aabrekk, E., Øhman, P., Kjendlie, P., Hystad, S.W., Bartone, P., Hansen, A.L. & Johnsen, B.J. 2019. Physical fitness and psychological hardiness as predictors of parasympathetic control in response to stress: A Norwegian police simulator training study. *Journal of Police and Criminal Psychology*. https://doi.org/10.1007/s11896-019-09323-8.

Sauro, J. & Lewis, J.R. 2011. When designing usability questionnaires, does it hurt to be positive? Proceedings of the Conference in Human Factors in Computing Systems (CHI 2011), 7-12 May, Vancouver BC, Canada.

Schwarz, J. 2011. Research methodology: Tools. Lecture 02: Measurement scales and item analysis. Lecture in the personal collection of Professor J. Schwarz, Lucerne University of Applied Sciences and Arts (Hochschule Luzern), Switzerland.

Sinclair, R.R. & Tetrick, L.E. 2000. Implications of item wording for hardiness structure, relation with neuroticism, and stress buffering. *Journal of Research in Personality*, 34(1):1-25. https://doi.org/10.1006/jrpe.1999.2265

Suhr, D.D. & Shay, M. 2009. Guidelines for reliability, confirmatory and exploratory analysis. Paper presented at the SAS Global Forum, 22-25 March, Washington DC, USA.

Tabachnick, B. G. & Fidell, L. S. 2013. *Using multivariate statistics* (6th Edition). Upper Saddle River NJ: Pearson Education.

Topf, M. 1989. Personality hardiness, occupational stress, and burnout in critical care nurses. *Research in Nursing Health*, 12(3):179-186. https://doi/org/10.1002/nur.4770120308

Van de Vijver, A.J.R. & Rothmann, S. 2004. Assessment in multicultural groups. The South African case. *South African Journal of Industrial Psychology*, 30(4):1-7. https://doi.org/10.4102/sajip.v30i4.169

Van Sonderen, E., Sanderman, R. & Coyne, J.C. 2013. Ineffectiveness of reverse wording of questionnaire items: Let's learn from cows in the rain. *Plos One*, 8(9).e https://doi.org/10.1371/annotation/af78b324-7b44-4f89-b932-e851fe04a8e5.

Vaughan, R., Hanna, D. & Breslin, G. 2018. Psychometric properties of the Mental Toughness Questionnaire 48 (MTQ48) in elite, amateur and nonathletes. *Sport, Exercise, and Performance Psychology*, 7(2):128-140. https://doi.org/10.1037/spy0000114

Westman, M. 1990. The relationship between stress and performance: The moderating effects of hardiness. *Human Performance*, 3(3):141-55. https://doi.org/10.1207/s15327043hup0303_1

Windle, G., Bennett, K.M. & Noyes, J. 2011. A methodological review of resilience measurement scales. *Health and Quality of Life Outcomes*, 9: article 8. http://www.hqlo.com/content/9/1/8

World Medical Association. 2013. *WMA declaration of Helsinki: Ethical principles for medical research involving human subjects*. Available at http://bit.ly/2vzmyBC

Yong, A.G. & Pearce, S. 2013. A beginner's guide to factor analysis: Focusing on exploratory factor analysis. *Tutorials in Quantitative Methods for Psychology*, 9(2):79-94. https://doi.org/10.20982/tqmp.09.2.p079

9

Human Resources Keys to Military Effectiveness for South Africa

Tumelo Mahlelehlele
Nicole Dodd
Lindiwe Masole

The success of modern organisations centres on the efficient management of its most critical resource – its personnel. In the South African National Defence Force (SANDF), military personnel are key to the accomplishment of the organisation's mandate is to secure and protect the sovereignty of the republic. In this endeavour, the changing battle landscape poses unique challenges for the military. This change is summarised in Kaldor's concept of 'new wars', which points to the unconventional nature of conflicts in which the military is required to intervene (Kaldor, 2013). In 'new wars' military members are likely to have to perform activities beyond the scope of what they were trained for (Masole & Van Dyk, 2016), resulting in numerous challenges at both individual and organisational level. The efficient management of human resources could make a significant contribution to alleviating the impact of these challenges.

Human resource management (HRM) is recognised as a pillar of any successful modern organisation and has undergone radical changes in the decades since the last world war. There has been a significant shift from the traditional focus on maintenance of personnel records to more advanced and complex functions that have a vital impact on organisational management (Mohan & Sudarsan, 2014). According to Balducci, Fraccaroli and Schaufeli (2010), many earlier studies in occupational psychology focused on negative aspects of psychology such as stress, burnout and turnover intentions. Consistent with the greater sophistication of HRM functions, researchers are now focusing more on aspects of positive psychology, such as employee wellbeing, using the positive aspects of work (Naudé & Rothmann, 2004).

COMPONENTS OF POSITIVE ORGANISATIONAL BEHAVIOURS

Bakker, Schaufeli, Leiter and Taris (2008) noted the need for research into positive organisational behaviour (POB). Luthans and Church (2002, p.59) defined POB as "the study and application of positively oriented human resource strengths and psychological capacities that can be measured, developed, and effectively managed for performance improvement in today's workplace". Based on this theory of POB, the capacities of emotional intelligence (EI), job satisfaction (JS) and work engagement

(WE) were selected as the variables of interest in this study. Job satisfaction needs no introduction. In an organisational context and engagement terms, a satisfied employee is more committed and is expected to serve the organisation for a longer period, thus enhancing the performance and productivity of the company (Markos-Kompaso & Sridevi, 2010). JS thus serves as an important factor in enhancing the standard and quality of services, no less in the military profession than in commercial organisations. The other two variables, EI and WE, also play an important role in boosting organisational effectiveness. According to Deshwal (2015), organisations with high employee engagement (WE) levels are more productive and more profitable than those with low levels of employee engagement. Employee engagement is positively linked to an increase in profitability through higher productivity, customer satisfaction and employee retention (Bakker & Leiter, 2010). EI is also touted as making a positive contribution to effective organisations, with Goleman (1998) making strong claims about the contribution of EI to individual success, and specifically to success in the workplace.

Although POB constructs have been explored in other organisational settings, very little research has been carried out within the South African military environment. The Joint Operational Headquarters (J Ops HQ) of the South African National Defence Force (SANDF), as the strategic headquarters responsible for all deployment of administrative and executive duties of military forces within and beyond the borders of South Africa, provided the specific organisational context for this study. We explored the relationship between the capacities of emotional intelligence, job satisfaction and work engagement, and also focused on personal factors (age, gender and level of education) as the moderators of the relationship between these capacities. It is proposed that an understanding of the variables of EI, JS, personal factors and their relationship with WE would be valuable in assisting HR personnel and line managers to improve both unit and organisational effectiveness.

Components of work engagement

Work engagement can be understood as a passion for work, the enthusiasm someone feels towards their job, or a willingness to extend one's efforts beyond requirements (Ashforth & Humphrey, 1995). WE has also been defined as "a positive, fulfilling, work-related state of mind", which is characterised by three critical sub-constructs: "vigour, dedication, and absorption" (Schaufeli, Salanova, González-Romá & Bakker 2002, p.74).

Vigour

Vigour is characterised by high levels of energy and mental resilience while an individual is doing the work. Vigorous individuals are willing to invest effort in their work and persist in the face of difficulties (Schaufeli & Bakker, 2004a). This depicts those soldiers with an invisible drive towards their work even when the situation is said to be dysfunctional, or the work atmosphere is presumed to be unfavourable.

Dedication

Dedication, on the other hand, refers to being strongly involved in one's work and experiencing a sense of significance, enthusiasm, and challenge from one's work. Such dedicated employees attach strong personal importance to and display a passion for their work. There exists a consistent experience of pride, stimulation, and encouragement which is conceptually comparable to job involvement (WE) (Schaufeli et al., 2002). Dedicated soldiers will then be characterised by unit and professional pride, self-motivation and immense pleasure in the service they provide.

Absorption

Lastly, absorption is characterised by being fully focused and happily occupied in one's work, in such a way that time passes quickly, and one has difficulties with detaching oneself from one's work. This state could be likened to Csikszentmihalyi's concept of 'flow', which is defined as a "subjective state that a person reports when they are completely involved in something to the point of forgetting time, fatigue and everything else but the activity itself' (Csikszentmihalyi, 2014, p.15). An employee who is fully absorbed or experiences flow, is someone with focused attention, "a clear mind, mind and body unison, effortless concentration, complete control, loss of self-consciousness", who experiences a "distortion of time and also intrinsic enjoyment" (Csikszentmihalyi, 1990).

Bakker and Demerouti (2008) highlighted that engaged employees have a high level of energy and are enthusiastic about their work. Such employees, due to their positive attitude and activity level, often create their positive feedback using appreciation, recognition, and success. Bakker and Hakanen (2013) mention that engaged employees are more passionate about their work. They are enthusiastic and often have the willingness to extend their efforts to invest in their work, not only using their hands and heads but investing their hearts in their work as well (Ashforth & Humphrey, 1995).

The potential benefits of such an engaged military workforce could be numerous. Bakker and Demerouti (2008) highlighted that engaged employees create value to the organisation through greater job performance, more creative and proactive thinking, more innovative work behaviour, reduced absenteeism and turnover, more committed/loyal employees and significant growth of organisational citizenship

Components of emotional intelligence

Emotional intelligence plays an important role in influencing other psychological capacities in the workplace (Ashforth & Humphrey, 1995). Rauf et al. (2013, p.1), define EI as "the ability to monitor one's own and other's feelings and emotions, to discriminate among them and to use this information to guide one's thinking and actions." For this study, EI is described as an individual's ability to perceive, control, and to evaluate their emotions, so enabling them to manage relationships more effectively (Zijlmans et al., 2011).

According to Goleman, Boyatzis, and McKee (2002), emotional intelligence competencies are classified into four major components and are subdivided into 20 competencies. The four major components include self-awareness, social awareness, self-management and relational management.

Self-awareness

Self-awareness is the ability to recognise and understand personal moods, emotions, drives and their ultimate effect on other people. This component includes the skill to focus on one's emotional state and knowledge of which emotions are experienced at any given moment. People who have high emotional self-awareness recognise the relationship between their thoughts and feelings and they are mindful of their beliefs, values and goals (Boyatzis, Goleman & Rhee, 2000). Furthermore, the self-awareness cluster measures a couple of competencies, such as self-assessment and self-confidence. Individuals who score highly in these competencies are said to know their strengths, limits and have a strong sense of self-worth (Yaya & Ebunuwele, 2016). Military practitioners at the J Ops HQ are expected to meet job demands within their respective capacities, for instance in taking criticism constructively, presenting themselves assertively, and improving their abilities through appropriate action.

Social awareness

The second cluster within EI, social awareness entails reading other people's emotions accurately. The social awareness cluster measures several competencies such as empathy, service orientation, organisational awareness, organisational commitment and leadership (Boyatzis et al., 2000). Individuals who have high social awareness understand others' emotional states, nurture relationships, understand group dynamics, align their goals to those of the organisation and are good at inspiring and guiding others to achieve. Military administrators or managers who are dealing daily with people are expected to be sensitive to the feelings of others, provide customer centred service, abide by rules and regulations, be committed to organisational goals, and exhibit leadership skills that will promote the achievement of a unit's daily responsibilities.

Self-management

This third cluster of EI refers to the management of internal states, impulses, and resources, in order to achieve the desired goals of the organisation (Goleman, 1998). This cluster comprises eight competencies namely: self-control; trustworthiness; conscientiousness; adaptability; achievement drive; optimism; initiative; and growth orientation. Individuals with high scores in this cluster do well by regulating and managing their reactions, displaying standards of honesty and integrity, taking responsibility for personal performance, and being flexible in handling change.

Furthermore, such individuals always strive to meet standards of excellence, are persistent, take advantage of opportunities and have a continuous drive for knowledge development (Ziv, 2014). Administrators working in stressful areas are expected to know their feelings, be reliable, have self-discipline, be flexible, be goal-driven and be proactive to meet contemporary organisational challenges without difficulties.

Relationship management

Relationship management is the last cluster in Goleman's (1998) EI framework, and it involves inducing desirable responses in others. This cluster contains a set of seven essential competencies useful for the development of social skills of workers in the organisation. Such competencies comprise developing others, communication, conflict management, positive impact on others, building bonds, teamwork, and collaboration. Within this cluster, people possess the skills of supporting others in their personal growth, and of assertive communication, conflict resolution competency, being an exemplary figure and being a team player (Yaya & Ebunuwele, 2016). Military personnel should take pleasure in enhancing organisational effectiveness by: mentoring others to develop their talents, in developing effective communication skills and conflict resolution skills, offering constant counselling to career-troubled employees, nurturing positive relationships, and cooperating with fellow employees.

The relationship between emotional intelligence and work engagement

Kahn (1990) stated that the engagement challenge has a lot to do with emotions: how the employees feel about the work experience and about the way they are treated. In a study with information technology employees, Lindebaum and Cartwright (2010) a found a positive but weak correlation between EI and WE. Such results indicate that EI may influence WE of employees to a certain extent, but that other factors such as personality characteristics and cultural differences play a significant role in that regard. Bezuidenhout & Cilliers (2011) found that WE relates positively to the demographic variables of age and gender. Similarly, the research of Schaufeli and Bakker (2004b) found that men seem more engaged with their work than women. In another study, Foos and Boone (2008) found that older employees show good adaptation skills, while younger employees display more creative personality.

Job satisfaction and work engagement in the organisation

According to Xanthopoulou, Bakker, Demerouti, and Schaufeli (2009), job satisfaction (JS) has a significant role to play in WE. For the purposes of this study, job satisfaction is defined as "a pleasurable or positive emotional state resulting from the appraisal of one's job or job experience" (Locke, 1976, p.1300). Furthermore, job satisfaction, according to Bruck, Allen and Spector (2002) is the extent to which people like or dislike their jobs: JS depends on the extent to which a person's work environment fulfils their expectations, needs, values or personal characteristics. Bakker, Schaufeli, Leiter and Taris (2008), suggested that WE may have a positive effect on employee

JS, which in turn influences their overall life satisfaction. Halbesleben and Wheeler (2008) argued that much of the academic literature on engagement has concentrated on the identification of engagement measures that reflect a distinct psychological state rather than being contextually connected to constructs such as EI and JS.

In the work of Mohr et al. (2011), employee JS was declared essential to employee WE. The identification of this outcome was based on survey results that revealed that engagement levels varied across the sample group based on organisational size, gender, workplace structure, and functions. Furthermore, younger employees were less engaged than older and married employees. However, a study of personal, family and academic factors revealed contrary outcomes that certain personal factors (ethnicity, level of education and geographical location) have little or no influence on EI compared to aspects such as gender and age (Rauf et al., 2013). Saks (2006) argued that JS is one of the key attitudes related to WE. Yalabik, Popaitoon, Chowne and Rayton (2013) also found a positive relationship between JS and WE.

Military job satisfaction

Locke and Lathan (1990) described job satisfaction as an emotional state which gives pleasure and positive energy to employees when they believe that their needs are fulfilled. In terms of retaining talented personnel, one of the most important and critical factors of employee engagement is JS (Kaye & Jordan-Evans, 2005).

In a study conducted on the British military by Limbert (2004), it was discovered that when individuals are engaged in positive thinking and acceptance of a situation, and they perceive social support from those helping them cope with stressful situations, they present higher levels of job satisfaction and psychological wellbeing. Furthermore, the results of this study also showed that JS and psychological wellbeing were significantly related. Regarding the advantages of JS as an attitude, Sanchez, Bray, Vincus and Bann (2004) demonstrated that military personnel who reported greater job satisfaction were more likely to stay, or indicated an intention to stay, in the army.

The relationship between job satisfaction, emotional intelligence and work engagement

Carmeli (2003) found that EI is positively associated with JS. Emotionally intelligent employees are more likely to be satisfied with their jobs as they can easily manage their work-family conflict, behaviour and outcome. Previous studies on JS and WE revealed a positive and strong relationship between these two constructs (Wefald & Downey, 2009). Some authors argue that this causal relationship is not straightforward. In Biswas and Bhatnagar (2013), it was argued that higher levels of JS are a result of WE. Consistent with this, JS is perceived as a passive and affective state, while engagement represents an active and content state. WE could potentially be enhanced through satisfying employees, and it can, therefore, be assumed that JS is an antecedent of WE (Schaufeli & Bakker, 2004a).

In the JS and WE correlation study of Judge, Higgins, Thoresen and Barrick (1999), a significant positive correlation was found between the two variables ($r(1893)=.628$, $p<.05$). In a study by Lundquist (2008), regarding the relationship between gender and JS, the findings indicated that men were more satisfied than women. Gender difference in values could explain this. According to Jones (1997), men attribute greater importance to career-related rewards such as pay, benefits or security, whereas women attach greater importance to social rewards such as the quality of established relationships with their co-workers and supervisors.

A more consistent result was, however, found concerning age, which is commonly found to be a stronger predictor of the JS of military personnel. According to the results obtained by Sanchez et al. (2004), JS is lower among younger military personnel, and similar results were obtained by Abedi and Mazruee (2010) with a sample of soldiers. Levels of education produced inconsistent results about JS levels of military personnel. In a study conducted by Rashid and Sultan (2013), well-educated officers were found to have higher JS levels than those who were less educated. Another study by Abedi and Mazruee (2010), found precisely the opposite, whereas in a study by Sanchez et al. (2004) the relationship between education and job satisfaction was not significant. These different findings leave the door open for more research to be conducted to resolve the inconsistencies.

RESEARCH OBJECTIVES

The primary objective of this research was to investigate the nature of the relationship between EI, JS and WE of employees at J Ops HQ. The secondary objectives were: first, to determine the existence of a relationship between emotional intelligence and work engagement in a sample of military personnel; second, to determine the existence of a relationship between job satisfaction and work engagement; third, to analyse the moderating role of personal factors (age, gender and level of education) between emotional intelligence and work engagement; and finally, to analyse the moderating role of personal factors (age, gender, and level of education) in the relationship between job satisfaction and work engagement.

RESEARCH HYPOTHESES

- H1 There is a significant correlation between emotional intelligence and work engagement of military personnel
- H2 There is a significant correlation between job satisfaction and work engagement of military personnel.
- H3 Emotional intelligence and job satisfaction have a significant effect on work engagement.

H4 Personal factors (age, gender and level of education) moderate the relationship between emotional intelligence and work engagement.

H5 Personal factors (age, gender and level of education) moderate the relationship between job satisfaction and work engagement.

RESEARCH DESIGN AND METHODOLOGY

The study adopted a quantitative cross-sectional approach to investigate the relationship between the constructs of EI, WE, JS, and the factors moderating their relationship. The independent variables measured were EI and JS, and the dependent variable was WE. The moderating factors were age, gender, and level of education

Population and sampling approach

The population for this study consisted of 260 military personnel from J Ops HQ. A sample of 156 participants was drawn using simple random sampling. The technique catered for a confidence level of 95%, and a five percent margin of error. The study participants comprised military personnel of various ranks, gender, race and age. The questionnaires were distributed randomly among the military personnel of various corps from different sections, and their responses were collected upon completion. Each participant was expected to complete all three questionnaires.

Measuring instruments

The data for this study were collected using three different instruments.

Emotional Competence Inventory (ECI)

The first section of the questionnaire was designed to gather biographical information such as gender, age and level of education respectively. The first instrument was the Emotional Competence Inventory (ECI), which is a questionnaire developed by Boyatzis and Goleman in partnership with the Hay Group, measuring 22 competencies of EI (Goleman, 1995). The instrument was developed as a measure of emotional intelligence based on the emotional intelligence competencies discovered by Goleman in conjunction with the Self-Assessment Questionnaire (SAQ), an earlier measure of competencies for line managers, executives, and leaders designed by Boyatzis (1994). The ECI is a multi-rater instrument that provides ratings for self, manager, direct report, and peer, on a series of behavioural indicators of emotional intelligence. The 22 competencies are organised into the four constructs outlined by Goleman's model. The respondents are required to rate themselves on level of agreement based on a scale from one to five; one being "low" (indicating that the behaviour is only slightly characteristic of the individual) to five being "high" (that is, the behaviour is very characteristic of the individual). The ECI was used in numerous studies, and it was normed in the United Kingdom and North American ECI databases with a Cronbach's coefficient alpha value ranging from $\alpha=0.73$ to $\alpha=0.92$ (De Kok, 2013).

Utrecht Work Engagement Scale (UWES)

The second instrument is the Utrecht Work Engagement Scale (UWES), which was developed by Wilmar Schaufeli in 2002 and which was designed to measure WE according to the three dimensions of vigour, dedication and absorption (Schaufeli et al., 2002). The UWES comprises 17 items (UWES-17) which are designed to measure core competencies of WE and consequences of WE. This instrument was validated and extensively utilised in various countries, including South Africa. The questionnaire employs a seven-point frequency scale. For each item, the participants need to rate themselves on how often they experience feelings at the workplace based on a scale of zero to six; zero being "never" and six being "always". The UWES-17 instrument has proven reliable in previous research with a Cronbach's coefficient alpha ranging from α=0.72 to α=0.89 (Bakker et al., 2008).

Job Satisfaction Survey (JSS)

The third instrument is the Job Satisfaction Survey (JSS) developed by Spector in 1985 and revised in 1994. This instrument is used to evaluate nine dimensions of JS. The JSS consists of 36 items, or four items for each of the nine subscales (Spector, 1985). The instrument is based on a six-point Likert scale. For each item, the participants rate themselves on how often they experience the expressed feelings in the workplace based on choices ranging from "strongly disagree" to "strongly agree". The instrument has proven to be reliable in previous research with a Cronbach's coefficient alpha value ranging from α=0.77 to α=0.87 (Spector, 1997).

Data analysis

The collected data were analysed using the Statistical Package for Social Sciences (SPSS) (IBM Corp, 2015). SPSS was used because it is ready to use, sound and well-known statistical software (Pallant, 2007; Field, 2009). The analysis started with the computation of descriptive statistics (e.g. minimum, maximum, mean, and standard deviation) of the sample group. Reliability, validity and unidimensionality analysis on instruments was assessed, and then the hypotheses were tested. For this study, the Pearson correlation coefficient was used to test the correlational hypotheses. Multiple regression analysis was used to determine the variances of multiple factors.

RESULTS

Descriptive statistics

The sample is described in Table 9.1, which presents the Pearson correlation matrices representing the relationship between all independent variables and WE. To observe the variance in explaining WE in a military context, multiple regression analyses of all moderator variables are also provided.

TABLE 9.1 Personal Factors of Respondents in the Study (*N*=156)

Personal factors	*N*	*%*	*M*	*Std*	*Min*	*Max*
Gender						
• Male	108	69.2				
• Female	48	30.8				
Age			**38.32**	**9.23**	**23**	**60**
• 18 – 25	8	5.1				
• 26 – 33	49	31.4				
• 34 – 41	39	25.0				
• 42 – 49	40	25.6				
• 50 – 70	20	12.8				
Level of education			–	–		
• Below matric	6	3.8				
• Matric	72	46.2				
• Higher certificate	29	18.6				
• Diploma/Degree	49	31.4				
• Other	–	–				

Regarding the data provided in Table 9.1, participants comprised 108 males (69.2%) and 48 females (30.8%). The entire sample ranged between the ages of 23 and 60 years. The majority of participants (31.4%) were between 26 and 33 years of age, with 25.6% between 42 and 49, 25% between 34 and 41, and 12.8% between 50 and 70. Only 5.1% of the participants were aged between 18 and 25. In terms of the level of education, the majority comprised participants who had only acquired matric (46.2%), followed by participants with a diploma/degree (31.4%), those with higher education certificates (18.6%), and the minority (3.8%) whose qualification was below matric.

Reliability and validity analysis

Reliability analysis is the most common measure of internal consistency (Gravetter & Wallnau, 2011). Reliability of various instruments and components was estimated by using Cronbach's alpha (α). Internal consistency results generated by the analysis are presented in Table 9.2, followed by a discussion on the reliability coefficients.

TABLE 9.2 Components and Cronbach's Alpha (α)

Components	*Mean*	*SD*	⊠
Emotional Competence Inventory	**84.09**	**8.74**	**.87**
• Self-awareness	25.90	2.85	.72
• Self-management	29.01	3.93	.74
• Situational-awareness	33.11	3.36	.56
• Relationship management	29.17	3.46	.76
Job Satisfaction Survey	**112.56**	**17.69**	**.79**
Utrecht Work Engagement Scale	**63.53**	**18.80**	**.93**
• Vigour	23.38	6.64	.82

TABLE 9.2 Components and Cronbach's Alpha (α)

Components	*Mean*	*SD*	⊠
• Dedication	22.82	7.74	.90
• Absorption	17.33	5.83	.74

According to Ray and Ray (2011), in the instance where α is≥0.9 the internal consistency is regarded to be excellent, 0.9>α≥0.8 is good, 0.8>α≥0.7 is acceptable, 0.7>α≥0.6 is questionable, and 0.6>α≥0.5 is a poor internal consistency. With data illustrated on Table 9.2, the different clusters or components of ECI (e.g. self-awareness, self-management and relationship management) were used to measure EI and yielded acceptable reliability coefficients of α=0.72; α=0.74; and α=0.76 respectively. Only one cluster (situational awareness) yielded poor internal consistency results, and that cluster was removed. The second instrument, the JSS, yielded an acceptable reliability coefficient (α=0.79). The third and final instrument, the UWES 17, subdivided into three components (e.g. vigour, dedication and absorption) was used to measure WE and yielded both good α=0.82; excellent α=0.90; and acceptable α=0.74 reliability coefficients respectively.

In terms of validity analysis, Anastasi and Urbina (1997) stipulated that high validity and reliability of a measurement scale are established through item analysis. In this regard, the measuring instrument is improved through the selection, removal, or revision of problematic items. Various factors were assessed through dimensionality analysis to confirm the unidimensionality of each subscale and to remove the items that showed insufficient factor loadings. Based on the acquired sample size of 156, the factor loading cut-off point of .45 was utilised. The following items of ECI were excluded due to poor factor loadings below the cut-off point: ECI 2, 15, 16, 17, 19, 21, 22, 26, 28 and 30 respectively. In terms of JSS, several items were also excluded due to poor factor loading, namely JSS 6, 7, 9, 14, 23, 33 and 34 respectively, and finally, in the UWES 1, 14 and 16 items were also eliminated for poor factor loading.

Inferential statistics

Gravetter and Wallnau (2005) expressed the importance of inferential statistics in terms of enabling the researchers to draw generalised conclusions from the generated sample group to the general population of the study, based on probabilities. Moreover, inferential statistics enable the researcher to confirm or reject hypotheses (or predictions). Utilising the Pearson correlation to measure and describe the relationship between two observed variables, several analyses were conducted. Correlation coefficients reflect the direction (negative or positive) and the magnitude of the relationship between two or more variables (Field, 2009). In an attempt to understand the interpretation of a correlation coefficient, the correlation of ±0.80 to ±1.00 is regarded as a high correlation (most preferred); correlation of ±0.60 to ±0.79 is moderately high (acceptable), and correlation of ±0.40 to ±0.59 (also acceptable) is regarded as moderate. Furthermore, a correlation of ±0.20 to ±0.39 is regarded as low; and any correlation below 0.20 is regarded as negligible/insignificant (Field, 2009). The correlation between the independent variables (EI and JSS) and dependent variable WE are provided in Table 9.3.

TABLE 9.3 The Correlations Matrix of EI, JS and WE

Variables	*M*	*SD*	*1*	*2*
1. Emotional intelligence (EI)	84.09	8.74		
2. Job satisfaction (JS)	112.56	17.69	214[a]	
3. Work engagement (WE)	63.53	18.80	.087	.416[a]

Note:
a - Correlation is significant at the 0.01 level.

Table 9.3 reports the relationship between EI and WE; and relating to the data illustrated above, a non-significant positive correlation is evident between EI and WE ($r(154)=0.087$, $p=$n.s). Therefore, regarding hypothesis 1 (there is a significant correlation between emotional intelligence and work engagement of military personnel), the null is not rejected as there is not enough statistical evidence to reject it. Thus, as emotional intelligence of military employees increases, their level of engagement may or may not increase concurrently with changes in other factors. This leaves room for a thorough analysis of the correlation between the variables mentioned above, as there is the probability of a third variable playing a role between these two factors.

Next, the relationship between JS and WE was explored and relating to the data illustrated above, a significant (sig) positive correlation is evident between JS and WE ($r(154)=.416$, $p<.01$). Therefore, concerning hypothesis 2 (there is a significant correlation between job satisfaction and work engagement of military personnel), the null is rejected, and the alternative hypothesis is accepted due to significant positive correlation depicted between JS and WE. Thus, a significant increase or decrease in employees' level of job satisfaction will also result in an increase or decrease in their level of work engagement. Although it was not the objective of this study, a significant positive correlation is also depicted between JS and EI ($r(154)=.214$, $p<.01$). Thus, a significant increase or decrease in employees' level of emotional intelligence will also result in an increase or decrease in their level of job satisfaction.

Multiple linear regressions

The regression analyses were computed to test the following: whether EI positively predicts WE, JSS positively predicts WE and whether personal factors affect this relationship. Stepwise multiple regression was conducted using EI, JS and personal factors as the independent variables and WE as the dependent variable. According to Field (2009), these analyses are conducted to measure different aspects of behaviour to see which behavioural aspects are related. Tables 9.4, 9.5 and 9.6 outline the regression analyses of these psychological constructs.

TABLE 9.4 Multiple Regression Analysis of EI and JS on Work Engagement

Model	*B*	*SE b*	β
Step 1[a]			
• Constant	47.84	14.60	
• Emotional intelligence (EI)	0.19	0.17	.09
Step 2[b]			
• Constant	14.12	14.69	
• Emotional intelligence (EI)	−0.01	0.16	−.00
• Job satisfaction (JS)	0.44	0.08	.42[c]

Notes:
a - R^2=0.01 for step 1
b - R^2=0.17 for step 2
c - $p<.001$

Regarding the information illustrated above, to test the predictor or moderator effect of each aspect, the first part of the table outlines estimates of coefficient (b) values which indicate the individual contribution of each predictor in the model. The standard error (SE b) values depict the relationship between WE and each predictor and depict the degree to which each predictor affects the outcome if predictors are held constant. Another important value provided by SPSS is the standardised beta values (β) which give clearer insight regarding the importance and variance of each predictor in the model (Field, 2009). In this regard, the higher the level of (β) and the lower the significance level, the better the impact of a variable in the model. The R^2 values provided below the table depict variability in the outcome that is accounted for by predictors.

When measured together, the EI (β) is -.00. For JS, it is .42. EI accounts for 0.01=1% of the variation in work engagement while JS accounts for 0.17=17% of the variance in WE. This implies that job satisfaction has a more significant effect in the model than EI as it accumulates to (17-1) 16% of the variance in WE scores. This tells us that concerning hypothesis 3 (emotional intelligence and job satisfaction have a significant effect on work engagement), job satisfaction is a better predictor of work engagement of military personnel than emotional intelligence. Therefore, the null hypothesis is partially rejected, and the alternative hypothesis is partially accepted.

TABLE 9.5 Multiple Regression Analysis of Personal Factors (Age, Gender & Level of Education) and EI on WE

Model	*B*	*SE b*	β
Step 1[a]			
• Constant	47.84	14.60	
• Total Emotional Competence Inventory	0.87	0.17	.09
Step 2[b]			
• Constant	43.73	14.73	
• Total Emotional Competence Inventory	0.19	0.17	.09
• Gender	5.34	3.24	.13
Step3[c]			
• Constant	43.20	15.19	
• Total Emotional Competence Inventory	0.17	0.17	.08
• Gender	5.12	3.25	.13
• 18–25	14.22	7.02	.17[e]
• 34–41	−1.68	3.98	−.04
• 42–49	7.57	4.00	.18
• 50–70	0.06	4.97	.00
Step 4[d]			
• Constant	41.28	14.98	
• Total Emotional Competence Inventory	0.22	0.17	.10
• Gender	5.07	3.23	.13
• 18–25	13.76	6.95	.16[e]
• 34–41	−1.78	3.98	−.04
• 42–49	8.34	4.01	. 19[e]
• 50–70	3.81	5.21	.07
• Below matric	−22.62	8.10	−.23[f]
• Higher certificate	−3.48	4.15	−.07
• Degree	−3.21	3.43	−.08

Notes:
a - R^2=0.01 for step 1
b - R^2=0.17 for step 2
c - R^2=0.08 for step 3
d - R^2=0.13 for step 4
e - $p< 0.05$
f - $p< 0.01$

The moderator effect of personal factors between emotional intelligence and work engagement is measured (see Table 9.5). The EI (β) value increases gradually as each personal factor is being loaded, and when measured together, the EI (β) is .10 and for personal factors varies accordingly per loadings. Ultimately EI accounts for 1% of the variation in work engagement while overall personal factors account for 13% of the variance in WE. This implies that personal factors moderate the relationship between emotional intelligence and work engagement to some extent (hypothesis 4), as it accumulates to (13-1) 12% of the variance in WE scores. On that note, the null hypothesis is rejected.

TABLE 9.6 Multiple Regression Analysis of Personal Factors (Age, Gender & Level of Education) and JS on WE			
Model	*B*	*SE b*	β
Step 1[a]			
• Constant	13.75	8.87	
• Total Job Satisfaction Survey	0.44	0.08	.42[g]
Step 2[b]			
• Constant	12.42	8.93	
• Total Job Satisfaction Survey	0.43	0.08	.41[g]
• Gender	3.52	2.99	.09
Step3[c]			
• Constant	12.59	9.24	
• Total Job Satisfaction Survey	0.41	0.08	.39[g]
• Gender	3.11	3.03	.08
• 18–25	10.77	6.51	.13
• 34–41	0.28	3.69	.01
• 42–49	7.55	3.67	.18[e]
• 50–70	0.55	4.52	.01
Step 4[d]			
• Constant	11.39	9.14	
• Total Job Satisfaction Survey	0.42	0.08	.40[g]
• Gender	3.30	2.98	.08
• 18–25	10.27	6.40	.12
• 34–41	−0.01	3.65	.00
• 42–49	8.27	3.65	.19[e]
• 50–70	4.67	4.73	.08
• Below matric	−23.17	7.63	−.24[f]
• Matric	0.53	3.10	−.01
• Higher certificate	−1.73	3.98	−.04

Notes:
a - R^2=0.17 for step 1
b - R^2=0.18 for step 2
c - R^2=0.22 for step 3
d - R^2=0.27 for step 4
e - $p< 0.05$
f - $p< 0.01$
g - $p<0.001$

The moderator effect of personal factors between job satisfaction and work engagement is measured (see Table 9.6). The JS (β) value fluctuates per each personal factor being loaded and when measured together, the JS (β) is .40 and for personal factors increases gradually per loadings. Ultimately, JS accounts for 17% of the variation in work engagement while overall personal factors account for 27% of the variance in WE. This implies that personal factors moderate the relationship between job satisfaction and work engagement to some extent as it accumulates to (27-17) 10%

of the variance in WE scores (hypothesis 5). Therefore, the null hypothesis is rejected, and the alternative hypothesis is accepted.

DISCUSSION OF RESULTS

In this section, the research results are discussed in comparison with previous research and findings. The aim is, therefore, to determine the extent to which the current results support the findings of research conducted in a similar or related context. Correlational analyses were utilised to determine the relationship between emotional intelligence, job satisfaction and work engagement. Furthermore, multiple regression analyses were utilised to determine the effect of EI and JS on WE, and to evaluate the moderator effect of personal factors between the relationship of EI and WE, and between JS and WE respectively.

The primary objective of this research, as outlined earlier, was to investigate the nature of the relationship between EI, JS and WE for employees at J Ops HQ. Hypothesis 1 aimed at determining the existence of a significant relationship between EI and WE. The null hypothesis was not rejected in this case. The existence of a weak and non-significant correlation between these two variables did not come as a surprise as it was consistent with the findings of Lindebaum and Cartwright (2010). Kgosana (2010) highlighted that military organisations rely heavily on the physical and mental contributions of their personnel to succeed. In such demanding circumstances, soldiers depend on available support structures (e.g. colleagues, social workers etc.) although, in some instances where the perceived support is insufficient, they have to draw from their natural survival kit (e.g. personality factors) to cope (Ditsela, 2012).

Therefore, soldiers may not need to be emotionally inclined to perform the mission tasks, as most tasks are governed using command structures as envisaged by the military. EI accounts for one percent of changes observed in the WE regression model. These findings leave room for more extensive research to determine the association between these two variables.

Hypothesis 2 was aimed at determining the existence of a significant relationship between JS and WE. Consistent with previous studies (Wefald & Downey, 2009) a significant positive correlation ($r(154)=0.416$; $p=.0001$) was found to exist between JS and WE (see Table 9.3). These findings imply that as job satisfaction levels of personnel increase, the work engagement levels will increase significantly with changes on the other variable. Schaufeli and Bakker (2004) commented that work engagement could be potentially enhanced through satisfying employees. Yet, JS accounts for only 16% of the changes observed in the WE regression model. Findings for Hypothesis 3 served as support for Hypotheses 1 and 2. EI and JS combined accounted for 17% of the variance observed in the WE regression model which illustrates that JS has more of an effect on WE than EI has. This supports the notion that job satisfaction is an antecedent of work engagement (Schaufeli & Bakker, 2004a).

Hypothesis 4 was aimed at evaluating the moderating effect of personal factors in the relationship between EI and WE. Consistent with the research findings of Bezuidenhout and Cilliers (2011), age and gender-related positively to work engagement. However, in their study, there was no research evidence to support the effect of education level on the EI and WE relationship. In this research, these personal factors showed a somewhat significant effect (see Table 9.6). EI on its own accounted for only one percent of the variance in the regression model; however, its variance increased gradually with each loading of personal factors. Ultimately, EI and personal factors accumulated up to 13% of the variance in the model.

Results in this study were found to be in line with the research findings of Schaufeli and Bakker (2004) that men seemed to be more engaged with their work than women. However, contrary to the research findings of Foos and Boone (2008), younger employees (aged 18-25) and older employees (aged 42-49) showed a positive significant level of engagement. Military employees with a low level of education (below Grade 12) showed a negative yet significant level of engagement, which implies that lack of education contributes negatively to members' level of engagement. Apart from the abovementioned contradictory findings, personal factors as a whole influenced the relationship between EI and WE. This implies that males, aged between 18-25 or 42-49, with grade 12 or higher education, at J OPs HQ are more likely to be engaged than other employees.

Hypothesis 5 was aimed at evaluating the moderating effect of personal factors in the relationship between JS and WE. Various theories explored the effect of personal factors on JS and WE. Consistent with the initial findings of Lundquist (2008), men seemed more satisfied with their work than women. Older employees were found to be more satisfied than younger employees (see Table 9.6). Similar results were obtained by Abedi and Mazruee (2010), and Sanchez et al. (2004) from a sample of military personnel. Regarding the level of education, Rashid and Sultan (2013) found that well-educated soldiers showed high levels of job satisfaction when compared to their less-educated counterparts. However, the opposite results were found by Abedi and Mazruee (2010). In this study less educated individuals were less engaged than their educated counterparts.

JS accounted for 17% of the variance in the model, and personal factors accounted for 10%, and when loaded in the WE regression model, total variance gradually accumulated to 27%. This implies that personal factors have a significant effect on the JS and WE regression model for South African soldiers.

LIMITATIONS AND RECOMMENDATIONS

The first limitation of this study is the sample size; although the acquired sample was adequate concerning the population size of the unit, in terms of generalisability of findings it is limited because the population of J OPs HQ is only a fraction of the entire SANDF.

Second, the research method applied in this study is a limitation in itself as it is simply exploratory and does not provide causality of the variables examined. Thus, the findings gathered from this study are not entirely conclusive. There is a possibility that other extraneous factors not observed in this study might have swayed the results.

Lastly, the environment in which the study was conducted is operational; more often when such surveys are undertaken, it is for deployment purposes. As a result, there is a likelihood that most answers were provided in a socially desirable manner rather than subjectively and with honesty.

Recommendations for future research

Due to inconclusive results discovered from the correlation studies of EI and WE, there is a need for more thorough efforts to determine the significance of their relationship. On the same note, it was evident that personal factors had a significant effect in moderating the relationship of EI and WE. Nevertheless, other factors, such as organisational commitment, subjective career success and work experience, might have an impact.

This study further suggests that military leaders need to focus the organisational resources on promoting the psychological and social wellbeing of their subordinates to enhance the effectiveness of the organisation. This can be done by establishing psycho-education and social awareness programmes in the workplace.

Managerial sensitivity towards soldiers' external circumstances that may directly or indirectly affect their work is recommended. Such circumstances may revolve around work-family balance and enrichment initiatives. Continuous job rotation and job enrichment intervention is also suggested to eradicate dissatisfaction and disengagements that derive from monotonous work roles or poor job design.

CONCLUSION

This study attempted to determine the relationship between EI and WE of military personnel. The results indicated a non-significant and weak positive correlation between these two variables. Furthermore, when evaluating factors involved in their relationship, it was discovered that gender, age and level of education have a significant effect in moderating this association for a South African military population. A significant correlation was found between JS and WE, concluding that soldiers who are satisfied with their jobs will most likely be engaged with their work. Lastly, multiple regression analysis proved the significant moderating effect of gender, age and level of education on the association of JS and WE within the members of J OPs HQ.

REFERENCES

Abedi, L. & Mazruee, H. 2010. Individual factors affecting military forces' job satisfaction. Iranian *Journal of Military Medicine*, 12:45-49.

Anastasi, A. & Urbina, S. 1997. *Psychological Testing* (7th Edition). Upper Saddle River NJ: Prentice Hall.

Ashforth, B.E. & Humphrey, R.H. 1995. Emotion in the workplace: A reappraisal. *Human relations*, 48(2):97-125.

Bakker, A.B. & Demerouti, E. 2008. Towards a model of work engagement, *Career Development International*, 13(3):209-223. https://doi.org/10.1108/13620430810870476

Bakker, A.B. & Hakanen, J.J. 2013. Work engagement among public and private sector dentists. In: Burke, R.J., Noblet, A.J. & Cooper, C.L. (eds), *Human Resource Management in the Public Sector*, pp.109-131. Cheltenham: Edward Elgar.

Bakker, A.B. & Leiter, M.P. (eds). 2010. *Work engagement: A handbook of essential theory and research*. Hove: Psychology press.

Bakker, A.B., Schaufeli, W.B., Leiter, M.P. & Taris, T.W. 2008. Work engagement: An emerging concept in occupational health psychology. *Work &Stress*, 22(3):187-200.

Balducci, C., Fraccaroli, F. & Schaufeli, W.B. 2010. Psychometric properties of the Italian version of the Utrecht Work Engagement Scale (UWES-9): A cross-cultural analysis. *European Journal of Psychological Assessment*, 26(2):143-149.

Bezuidenhout, A. & Cilliers, F. 2011. Age, burnout, work engagement and sense of coherence in female academics at two South African universities. *South African Journal of Labour Relations*, 35(1):61-80.

Biswas, S. & Bhatnagar, J. 2013. Mediator analysis of employee engagement: role of perceived organizational support, PO fit, organizational commitment and job satisfaction. *Vikalpa*, 38(1):27-40.

Boyatzis, R.E. 1994. Stimulating self-directed learning through the managerial assessment and development course. *Journal of Management Education*, 18(3):304-323.

Boyatzis, R.E., Goleman, D. & Rhee, K. 2000. Clustering competence in emotional intelligence: Insights from the Emotional Competence Inventory (ECI). In: Bar-On, R. & Parker, J.D.A. (eds), *Handbook of emotional intelligence*, pp.343-362. San Francisco CA: Jossey-Bass.

Bruck, C.S., Allen, T.D. & Spector, P.E. 2002. The relation between work–family conflict and job satisfaction: A finer-grained analysis. *Journal of Vocational Behaviour*, 60(3):336-353.

Carmeli, A. 2003. The relationship between emotional intelligence and work attitudes, behavior and outcomes: An examination among senior managers. *Journal of Managerial Psychology*, 18(8):788-813.

Cronbach, L. 1951. Coefficient alpha and the internal structure of tests. *Psychometrika*, 16(3):297-334.

Csikszentmihalyi, M. 1990. Flow: The psychology of optimal experience. *Journal of Leisure Research*, 24(1):93-94.

Csikszentmihalyi, M. 2014. Play and intrinsic rewards. In: M. Csikszentmihalyi, *Flow and the foundations of positive psychology: The collected works of Mihaly Csikszentmihalyi*, pp.135-153. Dordrecht: Springer.

De Bruin, G.P., Hill, C., Henn, C.M. & Muller, K.-P. 2013. Dimensionality of the UWES-17: An item response modelling analysis. *SA Journal of Industrial Psychology*, 39(2):1-8. https://dx.doi.org/10.4102/sajip.v39i2.1148

De Kok, C.A. 2013. Happiness at work: are job satisfaction, job self-efficacy and trait emotional intelligence related? Unpublished doctoral dissertation, University of South Africa, Pretoria.

Deshwal, S. 2015. Impact of emotional intelligence on employee engagement. *International Journal of Multidisciplinary Research and Development*, 2(3):255-256.

Ditsela, N.J. 2012. Factors involved in subjective career success of soldiers in the South African National Defence Force: An exploratory study. Unpublished Master's thesis, Stellenbosch University, South Africa.

Field, A.P. 2009. *Discovering statistics using SPSS* (3rd Edition). San Francisco CA: Sage.

Foos, P.W. & Boone, D. 2008. Adult age differences in divergent thinking: It's just a matter of time. *Educational Gerontology*, 34(7):587-594.

Goleman, D. 1995. *Emotional intelligence: Why it can matter more than IQ*. New York: Bantam Books.

Goleman, D. 1998. *Working with emotional intelligence*. New York: Bantam Books.

Goleman, D., Boyatzis, R.E. & McKee, A. 2002. The new leaders: Transforming the art of leadership into the science of results. London: Little, Brown/Time Warner.

Gravetter, F.J. & Wallnau, L.B. 2005. *Essentials of statistics for the behavioural sciences* (5th Edition). Belmont CA: Thomson Wadsworth.

Gravetter, F.J. & Wallnau, L.B. 2011. *Essentials of statistics for the behavioural sciences* (7th Edition). Belmont CA: Thomson Wadsworth.

Halbesleben, J.R.B. & Wheeler, A.R. 2008. The relative roles of engagement and embeddedness in predicting job performance and intention to leave. *Work & Stress: An International Journal of Work, Health & Organizations*, 22(3):242-256.

IBM Corp. Released 2015. IBM SPSS Statistics for Windows, Version 23.0. Armonk, NY: IBM Corp.

Jones, J.T. 1997. *Gender differences in job satisfaction in the U.S. Army (Study Report 97-04)*. Alexandria VA: U. S. Army Research Institute for the Behavioural and Social Sciences.

Judge, T.A., Higgins, C.A., Thoresen, C.J. & Barrick, M.R. 1999. The Big Five personality traits, general mental ability, and career success across the life span. *Personnel Psychology*, 52(3):621-652.

Kahn, W.A. 1990. Psychological conditions of personal engagement and disengagement at work. *Academy of Management Journal*, 33(4):692-724.

Kaldor, M. 2013. In defence of new wars. *Stability*, 2(1): article 4 (16 pages).

Kaye, B. & Jordan-Evans, S. 2005. Retaining talent. *Leadership Excellence*, 22(8):12.

Kgosana, M.C. 2010. An explanatory study of family stability under conditions of deployment. Master's thesis, University of Stellenbosch, Stellenbosch. Available at http://bit.ly/2wkdmRY

Limbert, C. 2004. Psychological wellbeing and job satisfaction among military personnel on unaccompanied tours: The impact of perceived social support and coping strategies. *Military Psychology*, 16(1):37-51. https://doi.org/10.1207/s15327876mp1601_3

Lindebaum, D. & Cartwright, S. 2010. A critical examination of the relationship between emotional intelligence and transformational leadership. *Journal of Management Studies*, 47(7):1317-1342. https://doi.org/10.1111/j.1467-6486.2010.00933.x

Locke, E.A. 1976. The nature and causes of job satisfaction. In: Dunnette, M.D. (ed.), *Handbook of industrial and organizational psychology* Vol 1, pp.1297-1343. Chicago: Rand McNally.

Locke, E.A. & Latham, G.P. 1990. Work motivation and satisfaction: Light at the end of the tunnel. *Psychological Science*, 1(4):240-246.

Lundquist, J.H. 2008. Ethnic and gender satisfaction in the military: The effect of a meritocratic institution. *American Sociological Review*, 73(3):477-496.

Luthans, F. & Church, A.H. 2002, Positive organizational behavior: Developing and managing psychological strengths, *Academy of Management Executive*, 16(1):57-75.

Markos-Kompaso, S. & Sridevi, M.S. 2010. Employee engagement: The key to improving performance. *International Journal of Business and Management*, 5(12):89-96. https://doi.org/10.5539/ijbm.v5n12p89

Masole, L. & Van Dyk, G.A.J. 2016. Military Work Readiness: A theoretical framework. In: Van Dyk, G.A.J. (ed.), *Military psychology for Africa*, pp.425-445. Stellenbosch: African sun Media.

Mohan, D. & Sudarsan, S. 2014. Studies on assessment of parameters influencing employee performance: A review, *International Journal of Advances in Management and Economics*, 3(1):69-86.

Mohr, D.C., Young, G.J., Meterko, M., Stolzmann, K.L. & White, B. 2011. Job satisfaction of primary care team members and quality of care. *American Journal of Medical Quality*, 26(1):18-25.

Naudé, J.L. & Rothmann, S. 2004. The validation of the Utrecht Work Engagement Scale for emergency medical technicians in Gauteng. *South African Journal of Economic and Management Sciences*, 7(3):459-468.

Pallant, J. 2007. *SPSS survival manual: A step-by-step guide to data analysis using SPSS* (Version 15) (3rd dition). New York: McGraw Hill.

Rashid, S. & Sultan, S. 2013. Military officers rank: Determining their job satisfaction, perceived stress and perceived social support. *Journal of Asian Development Studies*, 2(3):146-150.

Rauf, F.H.A., Tarmidi, M., Omar, M., Yaaziz, N.N. R. & Zubir, N.I.D.M. 2013. Personal, family and academic factors towards emotional intelligence: A case study. *International Journal of Applied Psychology*, 3(1):1-6.

Ray, S. & Ray, I.A. 2011. Human resource management practices and its effect on employees' job satisfaction: A study on selected small and medium sized iron and steel firms in India. *Public Policy and Administration Research*, 1(1):22-34.

Saks, A.M. 2006. Antecedents and consequences of employee engagement. *Journal of Managerial Psychology*, 21(7):600-619.

Sanchez, R.P., Bray, R.M., Vincus, A.A. & Bann, C.M. 2004. Predictors of job satisfaction among active duty and Reserve/Guard personnel in the U.S. military. *Military Psychology*, 16(1):19-35. https://doi.org/10.1207/s15327876mp1601_2

Schaufeli, W.B. & Bakker, A.B. 2004a. Job demands, job resources, and their relationship with burnout and engagement: A multi-sample study. *Journal of Organisational Behavior*, 25(3):293-315.

Schaufeli, W.B. & Bakker, A.B. 2004b. Utrecht work engagement scale: Preliminary manual. (Version 1.1) Occupational Health Psychology Unit, Utrecht University, Utrecht.

Schaufeli, W.B., Salanova, M., González-Romá, V. & Bakker, A.B. 2002. The measurement of engagement and burnout: A two sample confirmatory factor analytic approach. *Journal of Happiness Studies*, 3(1):71-92.

Spector, P.E. 1985. Measurement of human service staff satisfaction: Development of the Job Satisfaction Survey. *American Journal of Community Psychology*, 13(6):693-713. https://doi.org/10.1007/BF00929796

Spector, P.E. 1997. Job satisfaction: Application, assessment, causes, and consequences. London: Sage. https://doi.org/10.4135/9781452231549

Wefald, A.J. & Downey, R.G. 2009. Construct dimensionality of engagement and its relation with satisfaction. *The Journal of Psychology*, 143(1):91-112. https://doi.org/10.3200/JRLP.143.1.91-112

Xanthopoulou, D., Bakker, A.B., Demerouti, E. & Schaufeli, W.B. 2009. Work engagement and financial returns: A diary study on the role of job and personal resources. *Journal of Occupational and Organizational Psychology*, 82(1):183-200. https://doi.org/10.1348/096317908X285633

Yalabik, Z.Y., Popaitoon, P., Chowne, J.A. & Rayton, B.A. 2013. Work engagement as a mediator between employee attitudes and outcomes. *The International Journal of Human Resource Management*, 24(14):2799-2823. https://doi.org/10.1080/09585192.2013.763844

Yaya, J.A. & Ebunuwele, G.E. 2016. Exploring the correlation between emotional intelligence and job satisfaction of librarians in public universities in Nigeria. *IJRD-Journal of Social Science and Humanities Research*, 1(8):95-116. Available at http://bit.ly/2IXrTG3

Zijlmans, L.J.M., Embregts, P.J.C.M., Gerits, L., Bosman, A.M.T. & Derksen, J.J.L. 2011. Training emotional intelligence related to treatment skills of staff working with clients with intellectual disabilities and challenging behaviour. *Journal of Intellectual Disability Research*, 55(2):219-230. https://doi.org/10.1111/j.1365-2788.2010.01367.x

Ziv, T. 2014. What is emotional competence (EQ)? Website of Dr Talia Ziv. Available at http://bit.ly/33tIVVy [Accessed 5 October 2017]

10

Work Engagement and Turnover Intentions: 21st South African Infantry Battalion

Edward Mogaladi
Kyle Bester

Military organisations in the contemporary complex and turbulent environment are under pressure to acclimatise to changes, and contend with challenges and opportunities, in order to survive in a dynamic world (Louw & Martins, 2004; Martins & Coetzee, 2011). In this respect, members of the South African National Defence Force (SANDF) are not isolated from the pressures and demands that generally affect our society, and the military environment is similarly subject to a variety of challenges such as tightened budget constraints and the struggle to retain skilled human resources. Members of the military are not merely 'soldiers' but employees who are functioning within an organisation. For this study, we will mainly refer to them in these terms. As in any organisation, the human resources of the military – its employees – are considered to be the driving force of the organisation. Thus, not only securing but retaining human resources is crucial to the success of the mission and goals of the organisation (Wu & Polsaram, 2012).

As a military unit, infantry battalions – the 'foot soldiers' – are considered to be as old as warfare itself (Global Security, 2012). South African infantry battalions are regarded as elite units of the army: for more than a century, various infantry regiments of the South African Army Infantry Formation have participated in many wars and campaigns (Engelbrecht, 2010; Grundy, 1981). Within the greater infantry formation, the 21st South African Infantry Battalion (21st SAI Bn) is a notable unit and has a rich history dating back to 1947. The 21st SAI Bn unit is not trained traditionally in aspects of conventional warfare. Instead, skills development is geared toward combat skills related to counter-insurgency (Grundy, 1981). In addition to being trained as combatants, members of the 21st SAI Bn generally occupy the following specialisations, for which the SANDF has trained them: clerks and storemen, plumbers, electricians, carpenters, motor mechanics, chefs, and drivers (Global Security, 2012). As such – for human resources research – they can be regarded as comprising a representative cross-section of skilled army staff. The 21 South African Infantry Battalion (SAI bn) locates itself within the infantry battalion of the South African Army. More noticeably, 21 SAI bn is considered to be rich in diversity and has a wealth of history dating back to 1977 (Grundy, 1981). What makes the 21 SAI bn a unique population of interest is that not only is it a traditional training school for military personnel, but it also serves as a unit that is trained in operational combat.

This study focused on 21 SAI bn as a population group that has a vibrant South African past. However, the tale of work engagement is somewhat under researched, and information on this battalion can be considered limited in the public domain. Retaining staff is considered to be crucial and the level of engagement of personnel in the work place is paramount to maintain commitment (Schaufeli, 2012). This may be considered relevant in practical terms when viewing that battalion units are crucial in sustaining the nation's defence capabilities.

Like any organisation, the SANDF must limit the turnover of skilled staff. However, in recent years, it has experienced a surge in the retirement of military personnel, a phenomenon that is of greater concern because members are resigning before the customary retirement age (Defence web, 2011). Although there may be various incentives for early retirement, an increase in the rate must be addressed as an indicator of a trend or condition that is prejudicial to the organisation. Among reasons given for termination of contracts, the following have been cited: less-desirable working conditions; the monotony of life in the SANDF; and strict adherence to policies and guidelines (Heitman, 2019).

From this evidence, it seems likely that the increase in the rate of turnover is related to job satisfaction, which is widely recognised as a crucial factor in sustaining employment.

Closely related to job satisfaction is the construct of employee engagement, which, like job satisfaction, refers to the employees' affective orientation to their work: the extent to which they are emotionally committed to the organisation. Engaged employees are dedicated and loyal towards the organisation, and exhibit citizenship behaviour and heightened performance (Rhoades & Eisenberger, 2002), as well as reduced absenteeism and turnover. Typically, engaged employees operate in a climate in which they feel that the organisation is concerned about their wellbeing (Arnold & Feldman, 1986; Halbesleben & Wheeler, 2008), which includes functions such as facilitating employees' work performance, and providing a context that promotes work experiences that are pleasant and satisfying (Rhoades & Eisenberger, 2002).

Clearly, for the employer, the desired organisational environment is one where employees are engaged – willing to work hard for the organisation and themselves (Halbesleben & Wheeler, 2008). Thus employees, who are not passionate about their jobs, or the context of their jobs, are of great concern (Halbesleben & Wheeler, 2008).

Social exchange theorists see employment as an exchange of effort and loyalty for tangible benefits and perceived rewards, based on the notion that when individuals treat each other well, the norm of reciprocity obliges the return of that favourable treatment (Rhoades & Eisenberger, 2002). Thus the dynamic of social exchange requires that for mutually beneficial outcomes, both the employee and employer will apply the norm of reciprocity in the relationship.

Studies conducted in the domains of organisational behaviour and human resource management have identified multiple antecedents of turnover (see, for example, Halbesleben & Wheeler, 2008; Kuean, Kaur & Wong, 2010). Among the antecedents observed, turnover intention represents the strongest predictor of actual turnover behaviour (Hakanen, Perhoniem & Toppinen-Tanner, 2008; Kuean et al., 2010).

RATIONALE FOR THIS STUDY

The current study conducts a cross-sectional survey to investigate the extent to which poor work engagement can influence the intention to quit among the soldiers of the 21st South African Infantry Battalion in Johannesburg. Its purpose is to explore not only the impact that work engagement has on employees' intentions to terminate their contract of employment, but also to highlight contributing factors that may be regarded as driving turnover intentions; and thus may incline an employee to be attracted by other organisations, which are perceived to offer whatever the previous employer failed to deliver.

Work engagement has never been tested as a reason why soldiers terminate their contract of employment in the SANDF. Thus, it is intended that the findings of this study will assist in demonstrating the significance of the type of employment of an employee as a key aspect of dissatisfaction.

The most immediate employer–employee relationship is that of supervisor–supervisee, in which the norm of reciprocity may be encouraged since supervisors play a significant role, specifically in directing and evaluating employees. Given this, the present study focused on how employees perceive supervisory support and how it may impact their work effort and morale.

WORK ENGAGEMENT: THEORETICAL VIEWS

The term 'employee engagement' was initially developed by Kahn (1990), who observed that employees feel engaged when they find personal meaningfulness in their work and can do it wholeheartedly. He stressed that, for employees to be engaged, they need to receive positive social support at work, and to function in an organised and efficient environment (Kahn, 1990; Schreuder & Coetzee, 2009): one in which, moreover, human resource managers provide recognition, harness relationships, provide career opportunities and sustain a friendly work environment. Several researchers also found that employee engagement is an essential factor in employee wellbeing (Schaufeli et al., 2002). Kahn (1990) highlighted that a decrease in engagement could be directly associated with burnout and stress. That is the reason why employees who are less engaged experience poor physical and psychological wellbeing as opposed to those who are well engaged. Lehong and Hongguang (2012) found that engaged individuals are also satisfied with organisational objectives, suggesting that work engagement is a strong predictor of positive organisational performance, and showing the two-way relationship between the employer and the employee.

There is still a lack of consensus for the establishment of a unitary concept, but definitions of work engagement generally incorporate mental, emotional and behavioural factors or components (Ababneh & Macky, 2015; Halbesleben & Wheeler, 2008; Meyer & Gagné, 2008), and numerous theories on this construct are emerging. Macey and Schneider (2008) draw attention to the fact that the construct is often used ambiguously, as different researchers and human resources practitioners refer variously to employee engagement as "psychological states, traits, and behaviors as well as their antecedents and outcomes" (Macey & Schneider, 2008).

Schaufeli, Salanova, González-Romá and Bakker (2002) proposed a now classic definition of work engagement as "a positive, fulfilling, work-related state of mind that is characterised by vigour, dedication and absorption". The three 'dimensions' (Bakker, Van Emmerik & Van Riet, 2008) of vigour, dedication and absorption have further been identified as respectively encompassing the "physical, emotional and cognitive aspects of work engagement" (Bakker & Leiter, 2010). The construct represents both the ability to contribute to the organisation's success and the extent to which employees exert discretionary effort in their work (Kahn, 1990; Schreuder & Coetzee, 2009).

Goel, Gupta and Rastogi (2013) identify vigour as a facet that provides insight to time-investment by employees. It is an employee's willingness to devote time and put effort to work (Bakker et al., 2008; Schaufeli et al., 2002). It is characterised by high levels of energy and mental resilience, despite failure or challenging tasks (Bakker et al., 2008; Lunenburg, 2011). Rothmann (2008) defined work engagement as an energetic state whereby the employee is dedicated to exceptional performance. Lehong and Hongguang (2012) substantiated that an engaged employee may be expressing behaviour that is seen as confident due to their effectiveness within the organisation. Moreover, it can be stressed that work engagement is characterised by energy, efficacy and involvement (Bezuidenhout & Cilliers, 2010; Lehong & Hongguang, 2012). Dedication represents the task-commitment of employees. It signifies a strong sense of identification and involvement with tasks. Dedicated employees perceive their work as a significant and meaningful pursuit, and they typically exhibit feelings of enthusiasm, inspiration, pride and challenge (Bakker et al., 2008; Schaufeli et al., 2002).

Absorption emphasises employee task-investment. This concept refers to being fully concentrated on work, to the extent that employees find it challenging to disengage from their work after completing tasks (Schaufeli et al., 2002).

Organisations that understand their employees pay attention to work engagement (Bezuidenhout & Cilliers, 2010). Further, emphasis on the psychological component of work engagement promotes the success of an organisation, through greater understanding of the employees' psychological state of involvement, commitment and attachment to a specific work role (Bezuidenhout & Cilliers, 2010; Lehong & Hongguang, 2012). Bakker et al. (2008) found that even though the main focus is often on the organisation's wellbeing, work engagement focuses on the work itself and the enhancement of productivity.

Kahn's need satisfying approach

Kahn's "need satisfying approach" theory is built on the premise that certain cognitive aspects of employees' engagement at work include their beliefs about the organisation, its management, and its working conditions. Kahn (1990) suggests that when an individual is more invested in a role at work, it may channel both personal strengths and energies into role behaviours. Further, such constant role-investment may demonstrate the self within that role (self-expression). The theory explains that when the preferred self is expressed, the individual engages in task behaviours that have the potential to construct a personal connection to specific work-roles and colleagues (Kahn, 1990). Once the need to express oneself at work is satisfied, it generates energy in an employee which results in fully engaged employees.

Self-determination theory

The theory of self-determination, developed in the 1970s by Ryan and Deci, supports the concept that work engagement is related to an individual's need for autonomy. Meyer and Gagné (2008) highlighted that psychological maladjustment and behavioural difficulties may result from the absence of work engagement. Self-determination theory proposes that work engagement can function on two platforms of motivation: intrinsic and extrinsic. Intrinsic motivation is task performance for its own sake out of individual enjoyment and interest. Extrinsic motivation is task performance for instrumental reasons (Kahn, 1990; Meyer & Gagné, 2008). Since extrinsic, rather than intrinsic motivation dominates the work context, the engagement of an individual will depend on the relationship between the kinds of rewards valued by them and the rewards the organisation offers.

Antecedents of work engagement

There is wide divergence about the antecedents of work engagement, in part related to the question of whether engagement is a 'state' or a 'trait' (Ababneh & Macky, 2015), and how it should be measured. Saks (2006) and Kahn (1990) derived the following likely antecedents from various models that are focused on work engagement: job characteristics; rewards and recognition; and perceived organisational support.

Job characteristics

According to Kahn (1990), 'psychological importance' (meaningfulness) is related to a sense of return on investment when individuals invest themselves in their work. Therefore, the psychological importance of work – its meaningfulness to the individual – can be experienced through such components as challenging tasks; diversity of tasks; different skills; personal discretion; and the chance to make important contributions.

Rewards and recognition

Kahn (1990) revealed that employees differ in their engagement as a function of their understanding of the benefits they receive from a specific role. Moreover, a sense of return on investment can come from external rewards and recognition in addition to meaningful work. Therefore, one might expect that employees might be more likely to engage at work to the extent that they attach weight to the rewards and recognition received for their performances (Kahn, 1990). Rewards can also be linked to job satisfaction in employees. Employees who constantly receive positive affirmation about their work might experience intrinsic satisfaction. Martin and Roodt (2008) suggested that such responses to their work might bring about intrinsic satisfaction and may lead to experiencing feelings of triumph and self-actualisation.

Organisational and supervisor support

Kahn (1990) established that supportive and trusting relationships between managers and employees encourage a sense of psychological safety. Employees who experience a sense of safety in their work environments may, in turn, also exhibit aspects of honesty, openness and supportiveness. Supportive environments allow employees to experiment and try new things without the fear of facing judgment. Openness and supportiveness thus promote work engagement, and can reasonably be regarded as antecedents to it. Saks (2006) substantiated this by noting that receiving support from colleagues may predict engagement.

TURNOVER AND TURNOVER INTENTION

Many terms may be used to describe turnover, depending on context: quitting, attrition, exit, migration and succession. Looking at the phenomenon from the market perspective, Abbasi and Hollman (2000) describe employee turnover as “the rotation of workers around the labour market; between firms, jobs and occupations; and between states of employment and unemployment”. Voluntary turnover refers to employees’ “voluntary movement across the membership boundary of organisations” (Chimote & Srivastava, 2013; Saks, 2006; Schaufeli & Salanova, 2008). It denotes employees’ decisions to leave the organisation despite having the opportunity to stay (Mossholder, Settoon & Henagan, 2005). Nevertheless, various factors occurring in an organisation may force employees to leave the organisation.

A huge concern to most companies is that employee turnover is a costly part of doing business (Beam, 2009), especially for lower-paying job roles where the employee turnover rate is highest. Many factors play a role in the turnover rate of any company, and these can stem from both the employer and the employees. Significant factors include wages, company benefits, employee attitudes, and job performance.

Jacobs and Roodt (2008), however, explain that turnover is a multistage process, one of the stages in the process being intention to quit: that is, turnover intention.

Turnover intention

Unlike actual turnover, or quitting, intention to quit is not explicit in that it represents only statements about a specific behaviour of interest and not the actual behaviour (Beam, 2009). In terms of research into turnover, however, data collected is often based on intentions, rather than the actual statistics of outward mobility of employees. In this way, turnover intention becomes a proxy for turnover since the insights gained are typically used to address the issue of turnover (Perez, 2008).

Numerous studies report on the negative relationship between employee engagement and turnover intention (Saks, 2006; Schaufeli & Salanova, 2008). Tett and Meyer (1993) describe turnover intention as a "conscious and deliberate wilfulness to leave the organisation." Bothma and Roodt (2012) identify turnover intention as a type of withdrawal behaviour that is associated with under-identification with work, and as the last stage in a sequence of withdrawal cognitions. This multistage process includes attitudinal, decisional and behavioural components (Fox and Fallon, 2003; Jacobs & Roodt, 2008).

Schreuder and Coetzee's (2009) description of turnover intention as the last sequence of withdrawal in the turnover process finds resonance in Perez (2008), who states that it denotes the probability of imminent quitting. Fox and Fallon (2003) regard turnover intention to be a precursor to actual turnover. All turnover intentions may not lead to actual turnover behaviour. It can be stressed that employees' intention to leave an organisation may represent an important outcome, or dependent, variable (Jacobs & Roodt, 2008). A study conducted by Fox and Fallon (2003) found that a behavioural intention to leave is consistently correlated with turnover and that there is substantial support for the idea that intention to quit is the most crucial antecedent of turnover decisions.

WHAT WE KNOW ABOUT RELATIONSHIPS BETWEEN THE VARIABLES

Work stress and turnover intentions

Turnover may be the consequence of numerous factors, but stress is the most important one (Regts & Molleman, 2013). Stress can be considered the result of tensions and may aggravate employee turnover (Rahman & Iqbal, 2013). Job related tensions may badly influence job satisfaction, which may lead to a higher occurrence of turnover intentions (Rahman & Iqbal, 2013). According to Schreuder and Coetzee (2009), continuous stress may increase turnover intentions. Turnover intentions indicate high stress levels (Pitts, Marvel & Fernandez, 2011; Schreuder & Coetzee, 2009; Regts & Molleman, 2013; Rahman & Iqbal, 2013; Pitts et al., 2011).

Work overload and turnover intentions

Work overload – an excessive number of tasks allocated to an employee – is reported to have a significant impact on work exhaustion (Rahman & Iqbal, 2013; Martin & Roodt, 2008). In an increasingly competitive environment, an excessively high workload may not be an uncommon challenge for employees, but stress may occur in the workplace as a result of a highly demanding workload characterised by tight deadlines and great complexity (Martin & Roodt, 2008). Also, burnout may be considered the consequence of decreased job satisfaction (Martin & Roodt, 2008). Martin and Roodt (2008) and Kalliath and Beck, (2001) suggest that there is a direct relationship between workload, stress and turnover intentions. Burnout is a persistent, negative, work-related state of mind experienced by normal individuals, primarily characterised by exhaustion (Kalliath & Beck, 2001). This exhaustion can be accompanied by the following: distress; a sense of reduced effectiveness; decreased motivation; and development of dysfunctional attitudes and behaviours at work (Kalliath & Beck, 2001; Schreuder & Coetzee, 2010).

Working environment and turnover intentions

Poor working conditions are reported to be a crucial determinant of high turnover intentions (Miller, Cabrita & Vargas, 2011). This can be remedied, however. For example, flexible work arrangements result in higher job satisfaction which in turn paves the way for reduced turnover intentions (Martin & Roodt, 2008; Miller et al., 2011). Increased supervisory support and autonomy may have a positive impact on turnover intentions (Martin & Roodt, 2008; Miller et al., 2011). Inadequate supervision and lack of support towards the accomplishment of assigned tasks can be considered instrumental in causing high levels of stress, which may, in turn, increase the intention to quit (Janssen, 2001). Du Plooy and Roodt (2010) conducted a study on employee stress and satisfaction that revealed that satisfaction and turnover intentions are antecedents in the withdrawal process, which predict voluntary employee turnover.

Tett and Meyer (1993) found that the intention to quit an organisation might be the final step in a series of thoughts about quitting, which may include feelings of disengagement that eventually lead to actual turnover.

RESEARCH OBJECTIVE

This study aimed to examine the effects of work engagement on turnover intentions among a sample group selected from 21st SAI Bn. The objective of this study was to present findings that may lead to a deeper understanding of the nature and extent of the relationship between employee work engagement and turnover intentions

HYPOTHESIS

H1 Work engagement significantly affects turnover intentions.

RESEARCH METHODOLOGY

Design

This study utilised a correlational, cross-sectional research design, which is typically used when the purpose of the research is to predict certain outcomes in one variable from another variable that serves as the predictor. A self-report questionnaire was utilised as the survey instrument, consisting of three sections. The first section collected the biographical information of the participant. The second section held the Utrecht Work engagement scale. The final section comprised the Turnover Intentions Scale.

Population and sampling

The population for this study comprised approximately 500 military personnel of the 21st SAI Bn Johannesburg. A sample of 100 participants was drawn using simple random sampling, which provided for a confidence interval of 95%, with *p*-value smaller or equal to 0.05. Simple random sampling refers to the notion that each person in the population as an equal amount to chance to be select. In addition, each element in the population must be mutually exclusive so that there are no overlapping characteristics (Moshin, 2016). The study participants comprised male and female military personnel from junior to senior ranking. Age was not considered a pre-determined factor in the study; therefore, the study included the age range of 18-55 years. The questionnaires were completed in one sitting where participants were able to complete it individually. Each participant completed all three parts of the questionnaire.

Ethical considerations

The questionnaire consisted of a covering letter which provided a brief background of the study and its purpose, to give the participants insight into the study. It also included an informed consent section that assured the participants of their anonymity and the confidentiality of the study.

Measuring instruments

A self-report questionnaire was utilised as the survey instrument. All the constructs included in the study were assessed using a self-report measure. Responses to Work Engagement items were made on a four-point scale ranging from 1 (strongly agree), to 4 (strongly disagree), while responses to Turnover Intentions items were made on a six-point Likert scale ranging from 1 (strongly disagree), to 6 (strongly agree). The self-report questionnaire was a six-point scale and measured the items as indicated in the Likert scale range.

Biographical information

The first section of the questionnaire collected the biographical details of the participants. Age and gender were considered as variables of interest and were used to provide a profile of the participants in the study. Job types were considered variables of interest as biographical information also collected information on the job-types of military personnel.

Utrecht Work Engagement Scale (UWES)

The UWES scale measures three dimensions of work engagement: vigour, dedication, and absorption. The vigour dimension measures employees' energy and level of mental resilience while working, their willingness to invest effort in their work, and their persistence when facing difficulties. The dedication dimension determined whether employees experience a sense of significance at work and whether they are enthusiastic, inspired and proud of their work connection. The absorption dimension was utilised to establish whether employees are fully concentrated on their work, so that time passes quickly and they have difficulty detaching themselves from their work.

Turnover Intentions Scale (TIS-6)

The Turnover intention scale is a six-item scale that was adapted from the 15-item scale developed by Roodt (2004). Du Plooy and Roodt (2010) suggest that the items can be scored on a five-item scale varying between poles of frequency ranging from 1 (never) to 5 (always) (Du Plooy & Roodt, 2010). The Turnover intention survey was proved valid and reliable in two studies that focused on the validation of the scale (Jacobs, 2005; Martin & Roodt, 2007). Du Plooy and Roodt (2010) extended the validation of the Turnover Intention scale, which solidifies the utilisation of the initial instrument developed by Roodt (2004). Hence, this study included this scale in the study as it both valid and reliable

Data analysis technique employed for this study

The study was descriptive, as it sought to describe the relationship between work-engagement, turnover intention and intention to quit. The research investigated the empirical relationships between the variables through correlational statistical analysis. The data were statistically analysed using the Statistical Package for the Social Sciences version 23 (Statistical Package for Social Sciences Version 23, 2015).

Descriptive statistics showed the means and standard deviations. A 95% confidence interval with p-value smaller or equal to 0.05 was used for statistical significance. Correlational statistics were employed in the study to establish the direction and strength of associations between the constructs. Pearson product-moment correlation coefficients were calculated to indicate the relationships between the variables.

FINDINGS

The study aimed to examine the relationship between work engagement and turnover intentions. This study utilised one sample, which consisted of military personnel at 21st SAI Bn Johannesburg. The sample comprised of *N*=100 21 SAI Bn military personnel. A simple random sample was drawn from the population.

TABLE 10.1 Participants Per Gender Group (*N*=100)

Gender	*Frequency*	*%*
• Females	54	54
• Males	46	46
Total	**100**	**100**

Table 10.1 presents the gender profile of the participants. Regarding the gender groups of participants, of the *N*=100 participates, 54% of participants were females, and 46% were males.

TABLE 10.2 Participants Per Age Group (*N*=100)

Age	*Frequency*	*%*
• <24	12	12
• 25–34	56	56
• 35–44	14	14
• >45	18	18
Total	**100**	**100**

Table 10.2 illustrates the percentage of participants per age group. As for age, 12 respondents (12%) were 24 years and younger, 56 respondents (56%) were between 25 and 34 years of age, 14 respondents (14%) were between 35 and 44 years of age, 18 respondents (18%) were >45 years of age.

TABLE 10.3 Mean and Standard Deviation of Job-Engagement Variables (*N*=100)

Variable	*Min*	*Max*	*Mean*	*SD*
• Vigour	1.67	4.17	2.6167	.62023
• Dedication	1.00	4.00	2.1560	.77984
• Absorption	1.00	4.00	2.3783	.62892
• Turnover intentions	1.00	7.00	4.3900	1.59301

Table 10.3 demonstrates the breakdown of variables included in the study. The descriptive results in Table 10.3 record a vigour mean value of *M*=2.61, showing that the majority of the participants had relatively low levels of vigour; the dedication mean of *M*=2.15 shows that most employees are not dedicated to their work and are likely to quit, and the absorption score of *M*=2.37 also shows moderate to low levels of engagement.

TABLE 10.4 Correlations of Job-Engagement Variables (N=100)

Variable	*Vigour*	*Dedication*	*Absorption*
• Dedication	.693[a]		
• Absorption	.482[a]	.485[a]	
• Turnover intentions	–.368[a]	–.185	–.198[b]

Notes:
a - p<0.01
b - p <.05

Table 10.4 presents the correlations of the job-engagement variables. To test the hypothesis, a correlation analysis had to be employed as can be seen in Table 10.4, which shows the three dimensions of job-engagement: vigour, dedication, and absorption. Based on the information in the table, 'vigour' appears to have a significant relationship with 'dedication' ($r(98)=.693$, $p<.01$). Also, the subscale 'vigour' has a moderate association with 'absorption' ($r(98)=.482$, $p<.01$). 'Vigour' has a negative association with the variable 'turnover intention' ($r(98)=-.368, p<.01$). The relationship between the subscale 'vigour' and 'turnover intention' can be considered significant ($p<.01$. 'Dedication' has a moderate association with the two variables, 'vigour' and 'absorption' ($r(98)=.639$, $p<.01$; $r(98)=489$, $p<.01$). It can, therefore, be stated that these variables show positive associations with each other and are presented as being significant. These job-engagement subscales, as shown above, are negatively associated with 'turnover intentions'. This can be an indication that when 'dedication' and 'absorption' decrease or are non-existent, then employees are also planning to leave the organisation. Employees who express their desire to terminate their employment contract are more likely also to be disengaged.

The findings in Table 10.4 resulted in the rejection of the null hypothesis, as job-engagement is shown to have a significant relationship with turnover intentions within an organisation. The job-engagement variables present positive associations with each other. It is relevant to note that these variables or subscales can largely be considered positive for an organisation. The findings point toward a negative association between turnover intention and vigour and absorption.

DISCUSSION

The primary purpose of the study was to establish whether work engagement can be associated with the intention of military personnel to leave the 21st SAI Bn. Correlations exist among all three of the job-engagement subscales. Two of the job-engagement subscales (vigour and absorption) are significantly negatively associated with turnover intentions. Job-engagement (vigour and absorption) leads to a reduction in employee turnover intentions within the organisation. Accordingly, the findings have led to the conclusion that an employee's intention to leave the organisation is likely to depend on their vigour and absorption.

The effective resourcing, management and retention of human capital is a strategic issue for any organisation's survival, adaptation and competitive advantage (Martins & Coetzee, 2011). Organisations have increasingly stated that their employees are their most valuable assets (Glen, 2006). According to Kennedy (2006), there is no single identifiable variable that can be highlighted as the primary cause of turnover intention. Quan and Cha (2002) revealed in their study that turnover intention can be positively associated with age, years of employment, education, caseload complexity, self-esteem, organisational culture and job satisfaction. The SANDF is a diverse organisation with a multitude of rank systems and defence-related jobs.

Engaged employees demonstrate vigour, dedication and absorption (Glen, 2006). Employees' positive emotions and work experiences can cultivate organisational commitment. In turn, engaged employees' sense of commitment to their organisation makes them less inclined to want to leave (Schaufeli & Bakker, 2004). Allen, Shore and Griffeth (2003) revealed in their study that a negative relationship exists between employee engagement and turnover intention.

SIGNIFICANCE

The SANDF is a unique and multifaceted organisation that employs thousands of South African military personnel. Furthermore, as stressed, the SANDF is experiencing a surge in the retirement of military personnel. This study only assessed a small sample within the SANDF and therefore, results cannot be generalised to the entire SANDF population. However, the study provided insight into the current engagement and turnover levels of 21st SAI Bn. The SANDF is an organisation that relies on command and control structures, and with such structures, the ordinary employee might be susceptible to being overlooked or overburdened with work. The findings contribute to the existing body of literature on work-engagement within the SANDF. The findings of this study can be utilised to proactively develop strategies or interventions aimed at improving retaining strategies within the military context, thereby reducing employee turnover.

LIMITATIONS AND RECOMMENDATIONS

The study used cross-sectional data, which entails data collected at one specific time. The study, therefore, took a 'snapshot' of the studied phenomenon, which prevents the researcher from drawing causal conclusions (Taris & Kompier, 2006). To enhance the accuracy of the reported research, it might be viable to conduct a longitudinal study. This will enable the researcher to draw more definitive causal conclusions, but also to identify recurring behavioural patterns among employees of the SANDF. The 21st South African Infantry Battalion, does not constitute a representative sample of the SANDF.

Talent retention strategies should consider the relationships between job satisfaction and turnover intention within the SANDF. The findings of the study demonstrate the influence of various work engagement dimensions on constructs such as turnover intentions.

CONCLUSION

This study explored the relationship between turnover intention and employee engagement among participants employed in the SANDF. The study also contributed to the theoretical framework of turnover intention and work engagement, providing the reader with an understanding of the challenges facing the SANDF. The research has shown the relationship that exists between work engagement and intention to quit in the population under study.

REFERENCES

Ababneh, O.M.A. & Macky, K. 2015. The meaning and measurement of employee engagement: A review of the literature. *New Zealand Journal of Human Resources Management*, 15(1):1-35.

Allen, D.G., Shore, L.M. & Griffeth, R.W. 2003. The role of perceived organizational support and supportive human resource practices in the turnover process. *Journal of Management*, 29(1):99-118.

Arnold, H.J. & Feldman, D.C. 1986. *Organizational behavior*. New York: McGraw Hill

Bakker, A.B. & Leiter, M.P. 2010. Where to go from here: Integration and future research on work engagement. In: Bakker, A.B. & Leiter, M.P. (eds), *Work engagement: A handbook of essential theory and research*, pp.181-196. Hove: Psychology Press.

Bakker, A.B. 2011. An evidence-based model of work engagement. *Current Directions in Psychological Science*, 20(4):265-269.

Bakker, A.B., Van Emmerik, H. & Van Riet, P. 2008. How job demands, resources, and burnout predict objective performance: A constructive replication. *Anxiety, Stress & Coping*, 21(3):309-324.

Beam, J. 2009. What is employee turnover? *WiseGEEK*, 12 November. https://bit.ly/39eikwO [Accessed October 2017.]

Bezuidenhout, A. & Cilliers, F.V.N. 2010. Burnout, work engagement and sense of coherence in female academics in higher education institutions in South Africa. *SA Journal of Industrial Psychology*, 36(1):1-10.

Bothma, F.C. & Roodt, G. 2012. Work-based identity and work engagement as potential antecedents of task performance and turnover intention: Unravelling a complex relationship. *SA Journal of Industrial Psychology*, 38(1):1-17.

Chimote, N.K. & Srivastava, V.N. 2013. Work-life balance benefits: From the perspective of organizations and employees. *IUP Journal of Management Research*, 12(1):62-73.

Du Plooy, J. & Roodt, G. 2010. Work engagement, burnout and related constructs as predictions of turnover intentions. *South African Journal of Industrial Psychology*, 36(1):1-13. https://doi.org/10.4102/sajip.v36i1.910

Durrheim, K. 2006. Research design. In: Terre Blanche, M., Durrheim, K. & Painter, D. (eds), *Research in practice: Applied methods for the social sciences* (2nd Edition), pp.33-59. Cape Town: University of Cape Town Press.

Defence Web. 2011. Scarce skills still bugging SANDF. 2 December 2011 Available at https://bit.ly/2WE4ukO

Engelbrecht, L. 2010. Fact File: 121 Infantry Battalion. *Fact Files*, 2 March. https://bit.ly/3dkBh4h [Accessed 26 September 2019]

Fox, S.R. & Fallon, B.J. 2003. Modelling the effect of work/life balance on job satisfaction and turnover intentions. Symposium paper presented at the 5th Australian Industrial and Organisational Psychology Conference, 26-29 July, Melbourne, Australia.

Glen, C. 2006. Key skills retention and motivation: The war for talent still rages and retention is the high ground. *Industrial and Commercial Training*, 38(1):37-45.

Global Security. 2012. SA Army Infantry Formation. Available at https://bit.ly/2UetPAq [Accessed 10 October 2019].

Goel, A.K., Gupta, N. & Rastogi, R. 2013. Measuring the level of employee engagement: A study from Indian automobile sector. *International Journal of Indian Culture and Business Management*, 6(1):5-21.

Griffeth, R.W., Hom, P.W. & Gaertner, S. 2000. A meta-analysis of antecedents and correlates of employee turnover: Update, moderator tests, and research implications for the next millennium. *Journal of Management*, 26(3):463-488.

Grundy, K. 1981. A Black Foreign Legion in South Africa? *African Affairs*, 80(318):101-114. Available at http://www.jstor.org/stable/721432

Hakanen, J.J., Perhoniemi, R. & Toppinen-Tanner, S. 2008. Positive gain spirals at work: From job resources to work engagement, personal initiative and work-unit innovativeness. *Journal of Vocational Behaviour*, 73(1):78-91.

Halbesleben, J.R.B. & Wheeler, A.R. 2008. The relative roles of engagement and embeddedness in predicting job performance and intention to leave. *Work & Stress: An International Journal of Work, Health & Organizations*, 22(3):242-256.

Heitman, H. 2009. SANDF personnel could be trimmed by ten thousand. Defence Web, 2 May 2019. Available at https://bit.ly/3dgoPm6

IBM Corp. Released 2015. IBM SPSS Statistics for Windows, Version 23.0. Armonk, NY: IBM Corp.

Jacobs, E.J. (2005). The development of a predictive model of turnover intentions of professional nurses. Unpublished DCom thesis, University of Johannesburg, Johannesburg.

Jacobs, E. & Roodt, G. 2008. Organisational culture of hospitals to predict turnover intentions of professional nurses. *Health SA*, 13(1):63-78. https://doi.org/10.4102/hsag.v13i1.258

Janssen, O. 2001. Fairness perceptions as a moderator in the curvilinear relationships between job demands, and job performance and job satisfaction. *Academy of Management Journal*, 44(5):1039-1050.

Kahn, W.A. 1990. Psychological conditions of personal engagement and disengagement at work. *Academy of Management Journal*, 33(4):692-724.

Kalliath, T.J. & Beck, A. 2001. Is the path to burnout and turnover paved by a lack of supervisory support? A structural equations test. *New Zealand Journal of Psychology*, 30(2):72-78.

Kennedy, S.A. 2006. Intention to leave and organizational commitment among child welfare workers. Doctoral dissertation, University of Tennessee, Knoxville. Available at https://bit.ly/2QCsMIj

Koyuncu, M., Burke, R.J. & Fiksenbaum, L. 2006. Work engagement among women managers and professionals in a Turkish bank: Potential antecedents and consequences. *Equal Opportunities International*, 25(4):299-310.

Kuean, W.L., Kaur, S. & Wong, E.S.K. 2010. The relationship between organizational commitment and intention to quit: The Malaysian companies perspectives. *Journal of Applied Sciences*,10(19):2251-2260. https://doi.org/10.3923/jas.2010.2251.2260.

Layne, C.M., Hohenshil, T.H. & Singh, K. 2004. The relationship of occupational stress, psychological strain, and coping resources to the turnover intentions of rehabilitation counsellors. *Rehabilitation Counselling Bulletin*, 48(1):19-30. https://doi.org/10.1177/00343552040480010301

Lehong, G. & Hongguang, D. 2012. Research on turnover intention and countermeasure of key employees in Xuzhou coal mining group. *Research Journal of Applied Sciences, Engineering and Technology*, 4(21):4438-4442.

Louw, G.J. & Martins, N. 2004. Exploring inertia in a typical state organisation. *SA Journal of Industrial Psychology*, 30(1):55-62.

Lunenburg, F.C. 2011. Motivating by enriching jobs to make them more interesting and challenging. *International Journal of Management, Business, and Administration*, 15(1):1-11

Macey, W.H. & Schneider, B. 2008. The meaning of employee engagement. *Industrial and Organizational Psychology*, 1(1):3-30: https://doi.org/10.1111/j.1754-9434.2007.0002.x

Martin, A. & Roodt, G. 2008. Perception of organisational commitment, job satisfaction and turnover intentions in a post-merger South African tertiary institution. *SA Journal of Industrial Psychology*, 34(1):23-31. https://doi.org/10.4102/sajip.v34i1.415

Martins, N. & Coetzee, M. 2011. Staff perceptions of organisational values in a large South African manufacturing company: Exploring socio-demographic differences. *SA Journal of Industrial Psychology*, 37(1): article 967 (11 pages). https://doi.org/10.4102/sajip.v37i1.967

Marvasti, A. 2004. *Qualitative Research in Sociology*. Thousand Oaks CA: Sage.

Maslach, C., Jackson, S.E. & Leiter, M.P. 1996. *Maslach Burnout Inventory manual* (3rd Edition). Palo Alto: Consulting Psychologists Press.

Meyer, J.P. & Gagné, M. 2008. Employee engagement from a self-determination theory perspective. *Industrial and Organizational Psychology*, 1:60-62. https://doi.org/10.1111/j.1754-9434.2007.00010.x

Mossholder, K.W., Settoon, R.P. & Henagan, S.C. 2005. A relational perspective on turnover: Examining structural, attitudinal, and behavioural predictors. *Academy of Management Journal*, 48(4):607-618.

Moshin. A. 2016. A Manual for selecting sampling techniques in research. Available at https://bit.ly/2UbSipX

Miller, J., Cabrita, J. & Vargas, O. (Oxford Research). 2011. *Social dialogue and working conditions. Eurofound* (European Foundation for the Improvement of Living and Working Conditions in Dublin). Dublin: Eurofound.

Perez, M. 2008. Turnover intent. Diploma thesis, University of Zürich, Zürich. Available at https://bit.ly/3abkYos

Pitts, D., Marvel, J. & Fernandez, S. 2011. So hard to say goodbye? Turnover intention among U.S. federal employees. *Public Administration Review*, 71(5):751-760. https://doi.org/10.1111/j.1540-6210.2011.02414.x

Quan, J. & Cha, H. 2010. IT certifications, outsourcing and information systems personnel turnover. *Information Technology & People*, 23(4):330-351.

Rahman, M.M. & Iqbal, M.F. 2013. A comprehensive relationship between job satisfaction and turnover intention of private commercial bank employees in Bangladesh. *International Journal of Science and Research*, 2(6):17-23.

Ramesar, S., Koortzen, P. & Oosthuizen, R. M. 2009. The relationship between emotional intelligence and stress management. *South African Journal of Industrial Psychology*, 35(1):1-10.

Regts, G. & Molleman, E. 2013. To leave or not to leave: When receiving interpersonal citizenship behavior influences an employee's turnover intention. *Human Relations*, 66(2):193-218. https://doi.org/10.1177/0018726712454311

Rhoades, L. & Eisenberger, R. 2002. Perceived organizational support: A review of the literature. *Journal of Applied Psychology*, 87(4):698-714.

Rich, B.L., Lepine, J.A. & Crawford, R.E. 2010. Job engagement: Antecedents and effects on job performance. *Academy of management journal*, 53(3):617-635. https://doi.org/10.5465/AMJ.2010.51468988

Roodt, G. 2004. Turnover intentions. Unpublished document, University of Johannesburg, Johannesburg, South Africa.

Rothmann, S. 2008. Job satisfaction, occupational stress, burnout and work engagement as components of work-related wellbeing. *South African Journal of Industrial Psychology*, 34(3):11-16. https://doi.org/10.4102/sajip.v34i3.424

Saks, A.M. 2006. Antecedents and consequences of employee engagement. *Journal of Managerial Psychology*, 21(7):600–619.

Schaufeli, W.B. & Bakker, A.B. 2004. Job demands, job resources, and their relationship with burnout and engagement: A multi-sample study. *Journal of Organizational Behavior*, 25(3):293-315.

Schaufeli, W.B. & Salanova, M. 2008. Enhancing work engagement through the management of human resources. In: Näswall, K., Hellgren, J. & Sverke, M. (eds), *The individual in the changing working life*, pp.380-402. Cambridge: Cambridge University Press.

Schaufeli, W.B., Salanova, M., González-Romá, V. & Bakker, A.B. 2002. The measurement of engagement and burnout: A two sample confirmatory factor analytic approach. *Journal of Happiness Studies*, 3(1):71-92.

Schreuder, A.M.G. & Coetzee, M. 2009. *Careers: An organisational perspective* (3rd Edition). Cape Town: Juta.

Schreuder, D. & Coetzee, M. 2010. An overview of industrial and organisational psychology research in South Africa: A preliminary study. *SA Journal of Industrial Psychology*, 36(1):1-11. https://doi.org/10.4102/sajip.v36i1.903

Taris, T.W. & Kompier, M.A.J. 2006. Games researchers play: Extreme-groups analysis and mediation analysis in longitudinal occupational health research. *Scandinavian Journal of Work, Environment and Health*, 32(6):463-472.

Tett, R.P. & Meyer, J.P. 1993. Job satisfaction, organizational commitment, turnover intention, and turnover: path analyses based on meta-analytic findings. *Personnel Psychology*, 46(2):259-293.

Wu, X. & Polsaram, P. 2012. Factors influencing employee turnover intention: The case of retail industry in Bangkok, Thailand. *Journal of Finance, Investment, Marketing, Business Management*, 3(3):127-142. Available at https://bit.ly/2Ud5hry

11

Posttraumatic Growth: New Opportunities for the South African Military

Ngoako Mashatola
Petrus Bester

Soldiers face occupational hazards, such as trauma-related to life-threatening situations, injuries and death, active fighting and factors of human error. It is, therefore, no surprise that members of the South African National Defence Force (SANDF) are at risk for exposure to trauma. Recent incidents serve to highlight the nature of exposure South African soldiers may face: in March 2013, 200 South African soldiers took part in intensive warfare in 'the battle of Bangui' (Mphofu & Van Dyk, 2016); and in South Sudan in November 2018 a platoon (led by the first South African female commander) engaged in battle with heavily armed rebel militia (Martin, 2019); within South Africa, in August 2019, the SANDF were deployed in the Western Cape (Van Diemen, 2019), to support the South African Police Service in curbing gang violence and crime. In the last instance, the potential trauma may present differently: military action against one's 'own people' can be deeply disturbing for soldiers trained to act with force against a military opponent.

Dhladla and Van Dyk (2016) record several studies that describe a high prevalence of posttraumatic stress disorder (PTSD) among military veterans in Africa. These studies show that PTSD rates are affected by various personal or pre-service risk factors, such as a family history of psychopathology, gender, childhood trauma and others. Such risk factors are not restricted to Africa, as a recent study on American soldiers indicates that 15% of soldiers could not be deployed overseas because they had medical problems, of which PTSD was the most common. Their PTSD rendered them incapable of handling combat stress (StrategyPage, 2019). It was noted that appropriate screening interventions during recruitment, selection and training could have prevented many of these cases.

The alarming incidence of reported cases of PTSD in the military reflects ineffective posttraumatic growth (PTG) response models. From a positive psychology perspective (see key concepts in Figure 11.1), PTG refers to the positive changes or growth that trauma survivors experience in the post-trauma adjustment period (Tedeschi & Calhoun, 1995, 2004; Webb, 2013), although the outcomes after trauma can vary greatly (Aflakseir, Nowroozi, Mollazadeh & Goodarzi, 2016). It is important to note that one can refer to posttraumatic growth only in response to a traumatic event (Peterson, Craw, Park & Erwin, 2011). Growth is demonstrated when the sufferer begins to experience fewer psychological problems and less severe PTSD symptoms (Frazier, Conlon & Glaser, 2001). The task, from a military psychology perspective, is to identify how individuals can navigate their psychological challenges and gain something positive despite the effects of an adverse event (the experience of adversity can be discrete or chronic, specific or diffuse, and controllable versus uncontrollable).

Military psychology seeks to address mental health challenges experienced by military personnel through applying the findings, principles and methods of psychological research. The objective is to improve the behavioural capability of the forces and to counter the potentially diminishing effects on them of the opponent's actions (Bester, 2016).

PTG in the SANDF is a relatively new area of research for South African military psychologists. The notion that individuals can be changed in radically good ways through their struggle with trauma is not new. However, there is a need for research into PTG for the South African military context, particularly in terms of modifying the training philosophy and adjusting selection processes to be more relevant and consistent with new findings in the field. A useful posttraumatic growth response model would operationalise PTG within the military by framing necessary preventative and corrective interventions in the processes of recruitment, selection, training and education.

Current studies indicate that a more systematic approach needs to be taken in terms of setting up effective screening procedures to identify risk factors for the development of PTSD on exposure to trauma, and also to determine what protective factors are at play for those less likely to develop PTSD (Carlson, Palmieri & Spain, 2017). The current focus on soldiers' physical combat readiness is not enough: the evidence of increasing PTSD supports the rationale for developing and implementing a conceptual PTG framework or model for the SANDF to help soldiers develop psychological strength that can act as an 'emergency kit' when initial coping responses fail.

CONTEXTUALISING A PTG MODEL FOR THE SANDF

Existing research on combatant and veteran PTG in the military is of interest to this study, in terms of both the theoretical and empirical frameworks developed for preventative interventions and holistic trauma management. The objective of the study was to investigate existing conceptual models of PTG, the process, factors, related constructs and domains, and to propose a contextualised PTG model for implementation in the SANDF that would facilitate an increase in effective PTG initiatives in the military. At the least, the study's findings may help create a knowledge base for effective practice to reduce the occurrence of PTSD and to increase PTG, good mental health, and the optimal mental functioning of soldiers.

In this study, certain definitions and concepts relating to PTG have general currency, and these are listed in Figure 11.1, with an effort to contextualise them in military terms.

FIGURE 11.1 Definition of Key Concepts Related to PTG
Growth The condition where one does better after an adverse event than before it.[a] The experience of growth is demonstrated by fewer psychological problems and less severe PTSD symptoms.[b]
Hardiness Also referred to as dispositional resilience; a "generalized mode of functioning that incorporates commitment (conviction that life is interesting and worth living), control (belief one can control or influence outcomes), and challenge (adventurous, exploring approach to living)."[c]
Mental toughness "The ability to achieve personal goals in the face of pressure from a wide range of different stressors."[d]
Optimism An individual's expectations of positive outcomes in response to a traumatic crisis. Optimism is associated with finding meaning in life, self-efficacy as well as PTG in the aftermath of a traumatic crisis.[e]
Positive Psychology The application of psychological principles to real-life issues, aiming to understand the causes and consequences of optimal human functioning to promote effectiveness in the workplace, to deliver better and more compassionate health care, and to provide effective and engaging education in ways that optimise achievement, wellbeing, and the development of community.[f]
Psychological Spare Wheel An emergency kit – a variety of mental resources, with particular focus on MT, hardiness and resilience – that the soldier can use after being exposed to trauma. Like the spare wheel in a car, one must maintain this set of resources by mental exercise, and periodic review to ensure that it remains relevant for use when required.[g]
PTG Posttraumatic Growth, a cognitive processing model developed by Tedeschi and Calhoun, describes the positive psychological change individuals experience as a result of adversity, suffering or trauma. It refers to the ability of an individual to rise above the levels of functioning experienced before adversity. PTG is the cornerstone of success in surviving trauma, and it is key to mental health.[h]
PTSD Posttraumatic Stress Disorder describes a condition in which the individual fails to recover after experiencing or witnessing a terrifying event, or protracted exposure to circumstances of extreme violence, destruction and/or emotional stress.[i]
Resilience The ability to maintain a state of psychological balance and continue to function normally with few mental problems despite exposure to traumatic or potentially life-threatening events.[j]
Sense of coherence A person's ability to perceive that resources are available to help him or her confront and find meaning in adverse situations. It describes a soldier's ability to cope, manage and find meaning in exposure to traumatic combat experiences that can include growth. It is sometimes regarded as part of resilience.[k]
Trauma Emotional and psychological response to an adverse event that exceeds "the individual's capacity to meet the demands of the situation, and [disrupts their] frame of reference or other psychological needs."[l] Occurrence in a given subject may result from several risk factors that include pre-traumatic factors, peri-traumatic factors and posttraumatic factors.
Sources: (a) Brooks, 2018; Peterson et al. 2011; Tedeschi & Calhoun, 2004; (b) Frazier et al. 2001; (c) Bartone & Hystad, 2010, p.261; Escolas, Pitts, Safer & Bartone, 2013; Sandvik et al. 2019; (d) Arthur et al. 2015, p.15; Gucciardi et al. 2014; Lin, Mutz, Clough & Papageorgiou, 2017; (e) Helgeson, Reynolds & Tomich, 2006; Peterson et al. 2011; (f) Joseph, 2015; (g) authors' construct, as discussed; (h) Tedeschi & Calhoun, 1995, 2004; Brooks, 2018; (i) Dhladhla & Van Dyk, 2007; (j) Tedeschi & Calhoun, 2004, p.88; Hornby, 2015; (k) Antonovsky, 1987; Tedeschi & Calhoun, 1995; (l) Brooks, 2018, pp.13-14; APA, 2013.

PTG refers to the positive changes that trauma survivors experience in the post-trauma adaptation period (Peterson et al., 2011; Tedeschi & Calhoun, 2004). These changes are more than a return to prior functioning after a period of loss; they are viewed as actual gains beyond the level of functioning, pre-trauma (Zalta et al., 2017). However, the possibility of PTG after a traumatic event is not a way to eliminate the distressing effect of trauma (Brooks, 2018; Looney, 2017), although the individual may have perceptions of profound changes in life after the occurrence of a traumatic crisis (Zoellner & Maercker, 2006). Research quoted by Peterson et al. (2011) found demonstrations of growth in character strengths such as religiousness, gratitude, kindness, hope and bravery. Areas of growth are multidimensional, and not everyone will grow in the same domains (social, personal, spiritual) after a traumatic event (Brooks, 2018). These studies all arrive at definitions of PTG similar to that of Dekel and Nuttman-Schwartz as the "subjective experience of positive psychological change reported by an individual as a result of a struggle with trauma" (Dekel & Nuttman-Schwartz, 2009).

According to the American Psychiatric Association (APA, 2013), trauma is an emotional and psychological response to a traumatic event. A traumatic event creates psychological trauma when it overwhelms the individual's ability to cope and results in diminished hope. In the PTG literature (for instance, Brooks, 2018; Tedeschi & Calhoun, 1995; 2004), the word trauma is often used interchangeably with terms such as 'highly stressful event' and 'crisis'. Brooks (2018) prefers to work with the concept of 'adverse events' as not all negative events are traumatic. This chapter will, however, focus on the traumatic, and related constructs, per Dhladhla and Van Dyk and numerous other researchers, who concur in defining PTSD as a reaction to "a psychologically traumatic event that is extremely distressing in a manner that is beyond the range of normal human experience" (Dhladhla & Van Dyk, 2016, p.198).

Psychological constructs that promote PTG

Tedeschi and Calhoun (1995) acknowledge the role of personality and its related constructs in coping with trauma. Personality-related constructs identified in PTG literature include resilience, sense of coherence, optimism, hardiness and mental toughness (MT) (summarised in Figure 11.1). Integrating these constructs may help develop a PTG model relevant to SANDF soldiers in that they indicate processes that may lead to the effective facilitation of PTG in trauma survivors (Aflakseir et al., 2016; Kampman, Hefferon, Wilson & Beale, 2015; McFarland & Alvaro, 2000). It is beyond the scope of this chapter to explore the differences between these concepts, but they represent some key terminology associated with PTG and contribute to an understanding of growth in the context of psychotherapy.

Resilience

Tedeschi and Calhoun (2004, p.88) describe resilience as "a person's ability to maintain a state of psychological balance, to be stable with few mental problems despite traumatic exposure or potentially life-threatening events." Cacioppo, Reis and Zautra (2011) suggest a relationship between social resilience and PTG when they state that social resilience leads to growth through enhancing relationships, meaning-making, social engagement and coordinated social response to challenging situations. Cacioppo et al. (2011) indicate other aspects of resilience, such as emotional and spiritual, as being interrelated. Hornby (2015) confirms that resilience is a term with multiple definitions and connotations. The significance of spiritual resilience in strengthening and preserving does indicate a role for the chaplaincy in the development of initiatives to promote PTG, assisting soldiers in persisting with life following combat trauma.

Hardiness

Although closely associated with resilience, hardiness has come to be seen as a soldier's tendencies toward a constellation of three attributes of commitment (to life and others), control (over the events of one's life), and being able to embrace challenges (seeing them as opportunities rather than threats), in responding to combat trauma (Bartone, 2000; Bartone & Hystad, 2010; Brooks, 2018; Escolas et al., 2013; Kobasa, 1979; Peterson et al., 2011). Bartone, with Escolas, and others who worked with them in ongoing research into PTSD, were in search of a 'protective factor' which lends itself to training and found that psychological hardiness is "a trainable resilience resource, that leads those in stressful occupations to cognitively appraise stressors more positively, thereby negating some of the detrimental health effects of stress" (Escolas et al., 2013, p.116; Bartone & Hystad, 2010). Similarly, Eschleman, as cited by Sandvik et al. (2019), concludes that hardiness is an important and unique stress-resiliency resource, while Bonanno, as mentioned in Hornby (2015), locates resilience as a form of hardiness, confirming the interrelatedness of these concepts. The evidence gathered in these, and similar studies indicates that training interventions to improve hardiness can reduce the effect of trauma on an individual.

Optimism and hope

Pak and Ai (quoted in Aflakseir et al., 2016) suggest a positive correlation between PTG and optimism and hope. Helgeson, Reynolds and Tomich (2006) define optimism as an individual's expectations of positive outcomes in response to a traumatic crisis. Optimism is associated with finding meaning in life, and with self-efficacy and PTG in the aftermath of adversity. Peterson et al. (2011) indicate that it foreshadows resiliency.

Sense of coherence

Sense of coherence refers to a person's ability to perceive that resources are available to help them confront and find meaning in adverse situations, and which Antonovsky (1987) believed was the key factor in overcoming stress and maintaining health. A sense of coherence enables a soldier to cope, manage and make sense of traumatic combat experiences and can be a predictor of PTG.

Mental toughness (MT)

The construct of mental toughness (MT) has been shaped principally in the context of sports endurance (Arthur, Fitzwater, Hardy, Beattie & Bell, 2015; Gucciardi et al., 2014; Fitzwater, Arthur & Hardy, 2018), and is also associated with resilience and grit. However, it is equally relevant to describe the dispositional traits that are activated or shaped by trauma in combat. MT is the ability to adapt under stress to perform optimally in a given time and space (Arthur et al., 2015); it allows individuals to proactively seek out opportunities for personal growth (Lin, Mutz, Clough & Papageorgiou, 2017) and facilitates coping with a highly stressful or traumatic environment, inclining the individual towards PTG (Fitzwater et al., 2018). Zaccaro, Weis, Hilton, and Jefferies (2011) observe that MT and hardiness are often viewed as stable individual attributes. In a military operational environment, MT may mitigate the adverse effects associated with trauma, enabling one to persevere beyond physiological and psychological hardships.

Psychological spare wheel

Also, based on the above definitions related to PTG, we conceptualise 'psychological spare wheel' as an emergency kit that the soldier can use after being exposed to trauma. An emergency kit – a variety of mental resources, with particular focus on MT, hardiness and resilience – that the soldier can use after being exposed to trauma. Like the spare wheel in a car, one must maintain this set of resources by mental exercise, and periodic review to ensure that it remains relevant for use when required (authors' construct, as discussed).

Growth in the context of psychotherapy

In conventional psychotherapy domains, the psychological growth of trauma survivors has not been explicitly fostered as an intervention. The traditional focus of psychotherapy has been on the negative or the 'dark side' of the human psyche (Tedeschi & Calhoun, 2004). Trauma survivors were regarded as patients rather than survivors (as in constructivist self-development theory, Cohen & Collens, 2013). The traditional clinically orientated model of treatment is concerned with clinical symptoms and diagnosis, focused on giving therapeutic help for negative conditions, which are manifested in interpersonal, social and work-related problems.

The main goal of traditional psychotherapy is to help 'patients' return to their 'normal' functional state. This approach has been shown to be inadequate in helping trauma survivors in the military to regain positive mental health. PTG, which represents more than a 'return' to 'normal', requires a more positive trauma survivor-oriented framework to supplement the current clinical models.

Understanding trauma in the military

The battlefield, as described by Van Dyk (2016), is a chaotic, intense, complex and highly destructive theatre of events. Events occurring on the battlefield are generally stressful and traumatic, and tend to be sudden, unexpected, and unusual (McFarland & Alvaro, 2000; Tedeschi & Calhoun, 2004). Soldiers may typically experience the elements of battle as being out of their control and yet there is commonly a sense of blame. Van Dyk (2016) submits that, if not managed holistically, a trauma in previous combat has the potential to hinder soldiers' combat readiness and morale going forward. By its nature, war is a traumatic and stressful event that affects soldiers' emotional, cognitive and behavioural functioning (Kasujja & Van Dyk, 2013).

Trauma outcomes

In referring to adverse events (including trauma), Brooks (2018) describes four possible outcomes. First, the affected individual may succumb to the event with irreparable psychological damage. Second, the individual may survive with impairment and never recover to the pre-event state. Third, the person may act with resilience and return to the same level of functioning (baseline) as before the event. Finally, they may go beyond recovery and reach an improved level of functioning that is beyond pre-event levels. The first two outcomes refer to a deteriorated level of functioning, while the latter two are ameliorative.

Such outcomes are expressed in classified psychological disorders in which exposure to a traumatic or stressful event is listed explicitly as a diagnostic criterion. They include reactive attachment disorder, disinhibited social engagement disorder, PTSD, acute stress disorder, and various adjustment disorders (APA, 2013). These were observed after the deployment of SANDF soldiers to the Central African Republic (CAR), where they were exposed to intensive and unpredictable combat trauma in the battle of Bangui (Kasujja & Van Dyk, 2013). Post-combat trauma outcomes experienced by soldiers may vary depending on trauma risk management. Based on the findings of the studies consulted, that PTG can be both an outcome and a coping strategy (Brooks, 2018), the authors suggest that developing PTG in CAR trauma survivors is likely to result in more resilient, mentally tough, optimistic and hardy soldiers for future operations.

Some SANDF soldiers who survived the battle of Bangui exhibited a phenotype (a set of observable characteristics of a trauma-surviving soldier) resulting from their engagement interactions, the most prominent clinical features being anhedonic and dysphoric symptoms, externalised anger and aggressive symptoms, or dissociative symptoms (APA, 2013). The battle of Bangui thus offers a relevant case study in analysing trauma, its outcomes and PTG in the SANDF. We recommend awareness training for military instructors focusing on trauma outcomes, early identification and holistic trauma management. Sensitising and equipping instructors with the knowledge to identify and support soldiers experiencing these symptoms would not turn the instructors into therapists, or replace the role of psychologists, but would help sensitise military instructors to understand and respond appropriately when various trauma dimensions manifest in their subordinates.

Trauma dimensions comprise: (a) affect, characterised by mood swings, depression, suicidal tendencies and general irritability; (b) impaired impulse control, resulting in risk-taking behaviour; and (c) frequent somatisation, characterised by dissociation and intra-psychic conflict (Park & Helgeson, 2006). We assert that military psychologists and commanders require psycho-education. Further, not only instructors, soldiers should be made aware of early trauma identification, (self) referral, risk management and holistic trauma management. Knowledge of holistic trauma management will facilitate PTG, post-deployment. During pre-deployment, it will develop soldiers' psychological capital – the positive state of development characterised by self-efficacy, optimism, hope, and resilience (Grundlingh, 2016).

Trauma risk factors

Military psychologists and instructors must be educated on the nature of risk factors influencing the occurrence of trauma. According to the APA (2013), trauma risk factors include pre-traumatic factors, peritraumatic factors and posttraumatic factors as indicated in Table 11.1.

TABLE 11.1 Trauma Risk Factors

	Temperamental	*Environmental*	*Genetic & physiological*
PRE-TRAUMATIC FACTORS	• Childhood emotional problems encountered before age six[a,b] • Prior traumatic exposure, externalised anger and anxiety problems[a,b] • Prior mental disorders such as panic disorder, depressive disorder, PTSD, and obsessive-compulsive disorder[a,b]	• Socioeconomic status: lower education, exposure to prior trauma, childhood adversity, economic deprivation, family dysfunction and cultural characteristics[a,b] • Minority racial, ethnic status and family psychiatric history[a,b]	• Vulnerability of female soldiers[b] • Protective genotype or with increased risk for PTSD[a]

Sources:
a - APA, 2013
b - Van Dyk, 2016
c - Dhladhla & Van Dyk, 2007
d - Tedeschi & Calhoun, 2004
e - Joseph, Murphy & Regel, 2012
f - Linley & Joseph, 2004

TABLE 11.1 Trauma Risk Factors

PERI-TRAUMATIC FACTORS		• Severity of trauma: perceived threat to life, personal injury, interpersonal violence[a,b] including being a perpetrator, witnessing atrocities or killing the enemy[a,b] • Dissociation during trauma[a,b] • The higher the magnitude of combat the greater the likelihood of soldiers developing PTSD[c]	
POSTTRAUMATIC FACTORS	• Inflate risk of trauma: soldiers' negative appraisals, inappropriate coping strategies and development of acute stress disorder[c] • Individual coping style after a traumatic crisis correlates positively with cognitive processing[e,f]	• Subsequent exposure to repeated upsetting reminders, adverse life events and financial or trauma-related losses[a,b,d]	

Sources:
a - APA, 2013
b - Van Dyk, 2016
c - Dhladhla & Van Dyk, 2007
d - Tedeschi & Calhoun, 2004
e - Joseph, Murphy & Regel, 2012
f - Linley & Joseph, 2004

From the analysis of Table 11.1, the authors propose that a PTG model for the SANDF must give priority to screening for pre-service trauma-related risk factors and pre-existing generic and physiological factors. Furthermore, research findings indicate that soldiers' perception of social support from the family and unit before trauma exposure has a protective function and leads to growth (PTG). In this respect, proper person-environment fit and person-job fit should be given earnest attention during selection and placement. In the proposed PTG model for the SANDF, the focus should be on early trauma identification, risk management and holistic trauma management.

When considering peritraumatic factors, commanders must receive psycho-education. Also of prime importance is the detachment of a multidisciplinary, or multi-professional, team (MDT). The MDT comprises health care practitioners from different disciplines, such as nursing, medicine, psychology and social work, who can make clinical diagnoses. From time to time, a chaplain can be co-opted to the team, when a patient requires spiritual support or guidance. When agents of non-medical disciplines – commanders and instructors – are included, the role of the MDT changes to that of a multi-integrated team with less focus on the purely medical aspects.

In developing the PTG of soldiers, the proposed model will also consider posttraumatic factors, which would include provision for psycho-education on positive coping strategies among soldiers at all levels, as well as intense psychological debriefing measures and creation of unit awareness of trauma survivors.

Cross-cultural dynamics in trauma and recovery

Although the relation of culture to trauma does not form part of the scope of this chapter, it is useful to briefly highlight some typical cross-cultural dynamics in the experience of and recovery from trauma, since members of the SANDF respectively represent numerous cultures, as well as differences in ways of experiencing trauma and implementing recovery mechanisms. Yet the existence of adaptive mechanisms, and conventional wisdom in dealing with trauma is attested to across cultures throughout human evolution (Moodley & West, 2005; Wilson, 2005). Hence, it cannot be blindly assumed that only well-documented Western psychotherapies for trauma, including PTSD, are universally applicable, especially in non-Western cultures. In light of individual genetic and cultural differences, there is reasonably a broad range of individual responses to trauma.

Given this, it is possible that Western conceptualisation of trauma or PTSD is foreign and not readily comprehensible across cultures not accustomed to clinical psychological explanations for maladaptive human behaviour. To avoid undesirable misconceptions and misapplications of therapeutic initiatives, trauma and processes of recovery should be meaningfully defined by cultural norms and expectations about what is 'normal' and 'abnormal' behaviour (Moodley & West, 2005). Such considerations pave the way for an appropriate PTG model for the SANDF's culturally diverse workforce, in which assessment, diagnosis, and treatment are explored within a sensitive cultural framework that reflects knowledge and understanding of PTG. Although beyond the scope of this chapter, it should be acknowledged that how different cultural groups deal with the psychological consequences of trauma does raise an important issue: that of the availability of an appropriate range of therapeutic modalities of healing and recovery.

A PTG MODEL FOR THE SANDF

An existing theoretical model

In the preceding sections, an effort was made to define PTG and to establish how it might relate to associated concepts. In broad terms, it is a multidimensional construct that encompasses changes in the domain of interpersonal relationships, self-perception and philosophy of life (Taku, Cann, Calhoun & Tedeschi, 2008). The experiences of trauma survivors indicate that many of them undergo changes that they regard as highly positive, a construct termed 'posttraumatic growth'.

An overview of existing research on PTG (Brooks, 2018; Tedeschi & Calhoun, 1995, 2004) produced several models, of which Tedeschi and Calhoun's (1995) model of growth demonstrated excellent utility for this study. It illustrates how trauma survivors cope with trauma, from initial to secondary responses, initial and further growth. Tedeschi and Calhoun (2004) emphasise that the experience of a highly stressful or traumatic life event is a precondition for the perception of growth, as

PTG is inextricably part of the struggle with coping and processing of the traumatic experience and its impact.

Need for a posttraumatic growth model in the SANDF

As shown in the preceding discussion, the multiple benefits of a PTG approach or orientation for the functioning of the SANDF strongly indicate the development of a model appropriate to the SANDF. In models tested in other environments, with implementation of some months' duration, the initial trauma experienced may be fully integrated into soldiers' current adjustment profile and both positive and negative effects may be attenuated (Kunz, Joseph, Geyh & Peter, 2018, 2019), manifesting in enhanced emotional and psychological functioning (Calhoun, Cann & Tedeschi, 2012; Kunz et al., 2018). Soldiers who perceive benefits or growth following combat trauma report changes in their intrapersonal and interpersonal relationships. Such self-reported changes may relate to soldiers' having learnt new coping skills and developing a strengthened social support network, which may further result in reordered priorities and life goals for them. The changes constitute an increase in their available psychosocial resources and coping repertoires, necessary for effective current and future functioning. The prospect of future functioning facilitates resolution and enables surviving soldiers to frame new meaning.

A formalised PTG model would provide fertile ground for soldiers' adjustment if applied by a multi-integrated team (MIT), consisting of the MDT and military instructors at the tactical level, implementing measures to ensure current and future combat readiness and adjustment. Moreover, it would enable health care practitioners (HCPs) and commanders to make the most of the positive relationship between PTG and ameliorative change during military operations (Kunz et al., 2018, p.19; Tedeschi, 2011) and post-deployment phases (De Soir, 2017). This is likely to contribute to the crucial outcome of growth, which – whether perceived or real – in turn, leads to enhanced functioning in personal, family and work life.

An overview of PTG literature supports the notion that perceived growth correlates positively with adjustment (Cacioppo et al., 2011; Lee et al., 2010; Looney, 2017; Mawji, 2016; Mitchell et al., 2013; Tedeschi, 2011; Tedeschi & Calhoun, 2004; Zalta et al., 2017). Thus, both growth and adjustment are correlates of the underlying variable associated with personality functioning and coping. Both growth and adjustment are prerequisites for the enhanced functioning and effective combat readiness that can be facilitated through a PTG model.

Perceiving growth facilitates resolution for survivors, and gives new meaning to their lives, leading to enhanced functioning (Adams & Sutker, 2002; Morris, Shakespeare-Finch, Rieck & Newberry, 2005). Though soldiers did not choose to endure combat trauma, they come to perceive it as an important life event. Traumatic combat events, reframed favourably, potentially lose their perceived harshness, thus resulting in decreased symptomatology and the development of broader adjustment traits and effective coping styles.

We emphasise both the necessity and utility of a PTG model for the SANDF. An appropriate PTG model will enable MIT to support soldiers to cope better, sometimes as a traumatic event is unfolding (Adams & Sutker, 2002), and in the post-combat life (Tedeschi, 2011; Friedman, 2006), facilitating soldiers' recursive needs for renewed psychological resources, coping attempts and adjustment outcomes (Calhoun & Tedeschi, 2006), and broaden the scope of trauma therapeutic responses for trauma survivors (Tedeschi & Calhoun, 2004). Besides supplementing existing models, it will help to dispel the notion that one is 'sick' when reporting that he or she is affected by trauma.

It would also play a preventative role in involving both commanders and HCPs (MDT) at all levels in screening initiatives, and particularly in PTG training on the tactical level, where the most significant impact can be made. It would involve the chain of command (platoon commanders, platoon sergeants and section leaders) by training them to help trauma survivors to understand 'how, why and what next' in combat trauma and PTG. Commanders – whose attitudes influence not only the afflicted soldier but also the response of other soldiers in the unit (Inbar, Solomon, Spiro & Aviram, 1989) – thus fulfil the role of gatekeeper through early identification and treatment of combat-related stress to prevent the development of PTSD. In their direct and indirect role in fostering hardiness in soldiers (Peterson et al., 2011), commanders and instructors will be empowered with knowledge about traumatic stress and be more sensitive to survivors' needs (McFarland & Alvaro, 2000). The organisation would also focus on risk identification and holistic trauma management, PTSD and fostering PTG resilience, hardiness and a state of optimism in survivors as proposed by Van Dyk (2016).

The process of posttraumatic growth

In generic terms, the process of PTG is commonly set in motion by a major life crisis that severely contradicts and shatters the individual's assumptive world (McFarland & Alvaro, 2000; Walsh et al., 2018) – that is, the assumptions he or she holds about identity, safety and a future world based on benevolence, predictability and controllability (Friedman, 2006; Tedeschi, 2011).

For example, a mid-deployment crisis involving uncertainty and fear of death can typically occur among SANDF soldiers engaged in high-risk external deployments. At the point of crisis, certain individual personality traits (many of which can be developed through training) come into play immediately, for example, resilience, hardiness, optimism, growth potential, openness to experience and extraversion, contributing to PTG (Kampman et al., 2015; McFarland & Alvaro, 2000; Tedeschi & Calhoun, 2004; Aflakseir et al., 2016). The individual demonstrates an initial and secondary response to trauma. Significant levels of psychological distress in the initial response to trauma, necessitate a degree of PTG on the soldier's side (Walsh et al., 2018). The secondary response to trauma initiates as soon as the primary control fails (Tedeschi & Calhoun, 1995). Successful implementation of response skills during secondary response would ultimately result in initial growth, also referred to as coping success, and over time, secondary growth also referred to as wisdom. The level of intensity of cognitive engagement in response to trauma is fundamental to the process of PTG, especially in terms of initial growth through coping success where the initial unmanageable distress is experienced as manageable, initially incomprehensible schemas become comprehensible after revision, and new goals that are experienced as manageable are set when primary controls fail (Tedeschi & Calhoun, 1995).

This process of resistance and growth is dependent on specific personality traits, such as hardiness and resilience that become evident during deployment, where combat stress is high. Failure to cope with trauma results in psychological casualties (Kasujja & Van Dyk, 2013; Van Dyk, 2016), and indicates the importance of recruiting and selecting personnel with suitable psychological make-up. In this sense, embracing the PTG process in the military means focusing on proper screening in the pre-employment stage of recruitment.

A vital new training focus for the SANDF is (re)building cognitive skills to achieve coping success and wisdom, the precondition for PTG. A proposed conceptual PTG model for the SANDF should thus cover a soldier's career in terms of pre-employment, pre-, mid- and post-military deployments.

Domains of posttraumatic growth

Identifying the domains one should focus on to achieve PTG is crucial. The research revealed that the most significant PTG is experienced after a traumatic experience (loss of a spouse, physical disability, combat trauma, and even exposure to posttraumatic events). Taku et al. (2008) refer to changes in the broad domains of interpersonal relationships, self-perception and the philosophy of life, while others (Brooks, 2018; Helgeson et al., 2006; Lee, Luxton, Reger & Gahm, 2010; Mitchell, Gallaway, Millikan & Bell, 2013; Pak, 2007; Tedeschi & Calhoun, 2004; Tedeschi, Calhoun & Groleau, 2015; Webb, 2013) indicate five domains, and it is suggested that the proposed PTG model for the SANDF should be tailored to effect positive changes in at least the following five domains:

- *Relationships* – relating to others through greater connections and deeper compassion for others;
- *New possibilities* – outlook on life resulting in taking a new path in life;
- *Personal strength* – perceptions of themselves where they believe that since they survived trauma, they will be able to survive anything;
- *Spiritual change* – spiritual beliefs and developing a greater interest in the philosophical questions of life; and
- *Appreciation of life* – no longer taking small details in life for granted.

Many trauma survivors report positive changes in all or some of these five domains of their lives (Mitchell et al., 2013). Personality differences and demographic variables will decide what domains of PTG are perceived as priorities: for instance, a surviving soldier who witnessed the death of a comrade would have an appreciation for life, indicating increased existential awareness (Lindstrom, Cann, Calhoun & Tedeschi, 2013). One should, however, take cognisance of Tedeschi et al. (2015, p.505), who emphasise that "people who experience significant levels of PTG will not necessarily experience a commensurate decrease in their levels of distress nor an increase in their level of happiness." PTG will thus not necessarily resolve distress, but the sufferer can gain something positive in the aftermath of trauma.

Accordingly, in developing a PTG model, the SANDF should focus on recruitment and selection tailored to select people who fit the profile of a mentally tough soldier (Dodd, 2016), and on training instructors and commanders to the same purpose. The selected soldier's resilience, hardiness and MT will be enhanced by tailored hardiness and resilience training, thus fostering positive growth from as early as basic military training and through all phases of deployment. The main focus should become that of a mental shift from harmful degeneration to positive psychological growth concerned with positive characteristics that lead to optimal functioning (Keyes, Fredrickson & Park, 2012), thus a shift from 'victim' to 'survivor' mentality. This positive mental shift is incorporated in psycho-education and training (on resilience and hardiness, MT, developing self-efficacy, existential courage), and a holistic approach to trauma (Van Dyk, 2016). Peterson et al. (2011) also suggest introducing soldiers to the concept of learned helplessness.

PSYCHOLOGICAL GROWTH IN EACH PHASE OF DEPLOYMENT

Loss of control over one's immediate fate and feelings of helplessness and panic are only the first of many distressing psychological experiences that challenge the soldier's capacity to cope (Adler, Castro & Britt, 2006). Fostering PTG is thus seen to be very important before, during and after military deployments. Part of ensuring that the process is effective, according to Van Dyk (2016) is to incorporate psychological debriefing (PD) into the new PTG framework for the SANDF. Although a growing body of literature doubts the efficacy of PD (Leaman, Kearns & Rothbaum, 2013; Lilienfeld, 2007; Perry, 2014), it remains part of the SANDF's standard response to traumatic incidents, with particular reference to Critical Incident Stress Debriefing. (For further discussion see Perry (2014), with reference to an SANDF document, *Protocol: Post-traumatic Stress Disorder*, which guides the health care practitioner (HCP) on what to do after a traumatic incident.) Although the arguments of Perry and others are relevant and of interest, the current discussion is based on SANDF governance, which assumes that individuals who receive PD are at lower risk for developing PTSD. Furthermore, as discussed previously, the authors suggest that besides PD after an event, the focus on PTG should begin as early as pre-employment and continue throughout all deployment phases, involving military instructors and health professionals as part of an MIT.

Pre-deployment preparedness

The language of health prevention and wellness includes combat stress control activities, combat trauma management and a holistic trauma approach focusing on primary and secondary prevention (Van Dyk, 2016). Primary prevention interventions are designed to prevent the development of illness (PTSD in this instance) before actual exposure. Conversely, secondary prevention seeks to reduce the development of long-term disability by providing services at the earliest sign of illness (Friedman, 2006). Psycho-education can be considered for inclusion as a preventative measure. This encompasses a system for positive development at the mobilisation centres by HCPs and military instructors as part of the MIT.

Mobilisation is a critical stage during preparation for operations, whether within or beyond the borders of the country. The time spent at the mobilisation centre should be used to the maximum benefit of the soldier about to go on the mission (Friedman, 2006). Training should focus not only on tactics and battle drills but also on the resilience and hardiness of SANDF soldiers to ensure enhanced functioning (growth). Psycho-education should be proactively focused, based on holistic trauma management principles to create early awareness and develop a psychological 'spare wheel' in soldiers (Van Dyk, 2016). Looney (2017) refers to Polusny et al.'s, (2011) finding that the soldier's perceptions of inadequate preparation for deployment are linked to behavioural health concerns.

Primary preventative efforts promote the credibility of the supported command and provide leaders with specific guidance to prevent and reduce the number of combat operational trauma and psychological casualties (Peterson et al., 2011; Van Dyk, 2016). Taku et al. (2008) believe that resilience, hardiness and cognitive rebuilding are the key elements of PTG. A new PTG model will consequently have to focus on a mental shift from addressing negative consequences to fostering positive psychological growth. The military's urgent efforts to develop facilitation of this positive psychological growth would help develop a 'psychological spare wheel' in soldiers. This will ensure hardy, gritty and resilient soldiers who are combat-ready.

The fostering of positive psychological growth should begin early as a preventative measure before military deployments. This could be achieved through a concerted effort by the multidisciplinary team (MDT) to develop methods of delivering the psychological interventions that would lead to PTG in soldiers. The authors thus suggest a more focused approach aimed at developing MT in soldiers. This will have to be achieved through MT training, hardiness and resilience training, as well as psycho-educational military programmes before and after deployments (Adler et al., 2006; Dhladhla & Van Dyk, 2007).

The MDT may foster psychological growth through psycho-education at the unit level, focusing on trauma risk identification, coping skills and holistic trauma management. This may help develop resilient, hardy and gritty soldiers and organisational wellbeing, as described by Adler et al. (2006). Also, providing psycho-education to equip military commanders and military instructors with knowledge of the PD process is essential to early trauma identification, risk management and referrals of deployed soldiers affected by combat trauma, and to ensure that they view themselves as survivors rather than victims of the incident.

Training of multidisciplinary teams and subordinates

It has been found that team development of an educational training model, contributing on both the individual and collective level, is effective in shaping the desired profile of a soldier prepared for combat (Bester, 2016). Looney (2017) emphasises that helping soldiers understand the negative aspects of trauma, such as shattered beliefs about self/others/future, leaders and caregivers, can lay the foundation for PTG in the future. Military instructors and the MDT should form a multi-integrated team (MIT) and undergo orientation training to be fully informed about PTG. Adler et al. (2006) found that not all soldiers experience combat stress reactions of such severity that these make them incapable of performing their duties, and this is another pointer to teamwork. Those who are not affected should be able to assist and support those who are affected (Deahl et al., 2000). To develop the 'psychological spare wheel' in mentally tough soldiers, hardiness and resilience training is essential. Further deliberation on the benefits of hardiness, resilience and MT training is, however beyond the scope of this paper.

Psychological growth during the deployment phase

A new PTG model should focus on enhancing and sustaining the psychological growth of the deployed soldier through a system of early intervention by tactical commanders and the MDT as part of the MIT. The aim would be to facilitate secondary prevention and sustain psychological growth. In this instance, secondary prevention would encompass early combat trauma stress identification. During the operation/deployment, the MDT continuously assesses every soldier's resilience and hardiness level in relation to physical and psychological functioning. This will assist the military psychologist in noting any leading symptoms or change in behaviour in relation to combat trauma (Van Dyk, 2016; Zoellner & Maercker, 2006). It is thus important to have a psychological support structure in the field during conventional operations. For the SANDF, Bester (2016) emphasises that the force structure must be coordinated from a central command-and-control structure, which in the case of the SANDF would be the Directorate Psychology.

Platoon commanders, platoon sergeants and section leaders play a critical role on especially the tactical level for traumatic stress risk management. They assist in early identification and referrals to the MDT, thus facilitating early risk and holistic trauma management. Knowledge of holistic trauma management and skills for both the military psychologist and commanders is important. It is essential in sustaining the soldier's cognitive functioning and ensuring that a 'psychological spare wheel' is intact (Van Dyk, 2016). On the home front, the authors suggest psychological growth and support should be extended to the families of the members deployed. With a PTG approach, soldiers will experience growth relating to a greater appreciation of life and changed priorities during military deployment.

Greater appreciation of life and changing priorities

The battlefield is characterised by a high degree of complexity, and therefore, growth becomes essential in sustaining a soldier's physical and cognitive functioning while continuously confronted with complexity (Bester, 2016). Upon confrontation with combat trauma, cognitive reconstruction is required as soldiers experience a sense of individual vulnerability, as their assumptive world becomes contradictory and shattered. These soldiers consciously recognise the fragility of life, which challenges how priorities are set, and will then alter previous degrees of priority ascribed to specific events (Tedeschi & Calhoun, 2004). They begin to value small things, for example, their weapons, for safety (Van Dyk, 2016). Other factors that were previously more valued, such as finances and family, are deprioritised in the heat of the moment. They then begin to appreciate life and significant others more (Lindstrom et al., 2013). Depending on the degree of trauma experienced, providing psychological debriefing (PD) to soldiers throughout the deployment phase and especially after a critical incident such as the death or severe injury of a fellow combatant, is likely to contribute to PTG. Post-deployment PD can focus the individual's gains at both the individual and group level (as platoon, unit or even as part of the SANDF) from deployment. Family and friends become a priority in the posttraumatic deployment phase. Deployment of the MDT and holistic trauma management become essential in facilitating PTG.

Posttraumatic growth and the post-deployment phase

Positive changes leading to survivors' behavioural changes encompass positive growth. Therefore, proper demobilisation and readjustment during the post-deployment phase are essential (Bester, 2016). Surviving a traumatic crisis enhances soldiers' appreciation of their vulnerability, sensitivity and emotional experience (Tedeschi, 2011). Although soldiers' appreciation of vulnerability may be perceived as a negative outcome of combat trauma, positive changes resulting from it lead to behavioural adjustments essential for coping, as discussed earlier. Positive growth includes changes in the domains of interpersonal relationships, self-perceptions, personal strength and philosophy of life, and also the discovery of new possibilities (Taku et al., 2008). To effectively put this in place requires a multidisciplinary approach by the MDT with a system of care aimed at holistic trauma management (Van Dyk, 2016), PD, and trauma treatment and healing: this assists returning soldiers with socialisation and reintegration into society.

Relating to others (interpersonal strength)

During the post-deployment phase, a soldier tends to seek warmer, supportive and intimate relationships with significant others for social support. Tedeschi and Calhoun (2004) emphasise that after exposure to combat trauma, a soldier engages in cognitive reconstruction to understand traumatic situations. In response, cognitive rebuilding is achieved through social support after combat trauma and the related environmental stressors (Bester, 2016). Social support from a soldier's unit, family and close friends serves as a critical adjustment and coping resource after trauma. The SANDF through SAMHS provides social support for the soldier and the family. Van Dyk (2016) points out that social support becomes quite essential in buffering posttraumatic stress and other related effects of PTSD.

A greater sense of intrapersonal strength

After deployment-related combat trauma, soldiers derive – in varying degrees – either a sense of intrapersonal strength or psychological distress (a common symptom of PTSD) (Van Dyk, 2016). A soldier's perception of a sense of intrapersonal strength correlates positively with PTG (Lindstrom et al., 2013). According to Tedeschi and Calhoun (2004), a greater sense of intrapersonal strength helps surviving soldiers to cope with the prospect of repeated future combat trauma and other life crises. Soldiers with a greater sense of intrapersonal strength tend to have an internal locus of control, permitting them to change situations that need to be changed (Aldwin & Levenson, 2004). Through sensitising soldiers on how to use coping skills effectively, some soldiers may emerge with greater coping skills than others.

Spiritual development

In some individuals, spiritual development may serve as a source of strength. As part of individual strength and source of meaning, trauma survivors experience a perception of growth of faith in the spiritual realm (Lindstrom et al., 2013; Webb, 2013). Belief in a higher spiritual being or power has the potential to lead to PTG and to serve as a coping resource (Calhoun & Tedeschi, 2006; Lindstrom et al., 2013). The impact of spiritual development may vary between individuals and their experience of faith; hence, the chaplain, as part of the MIT, is also a resource in terms of facilitating spiritual development of soldiers.

New possibilities

Lindstrom et al. (2013) indicate that PTG provides trauma survivors with reflexive thinking and cognitive reconstruction, which is necessary for facilitating soldiers' role integration and re-establishment of family and interpersonal relationships. If the development of PTG accompanies post-combat trauma, it necessitates a new life path for soldiers. Soldiers who have developed PTG and new possibilities in life can thrive in difficult, stressful and traumatic situations (Ford, Tennen & Albert, 2008). Resilience and hardiness training and psycho-education programmes aimed at developing the 'psychological spare wheel' are required interventions: training and psycho-education are essential to help trauma survivors to derive hope and discover new possibilities in life.

CONCEPTUAL SANDF PTG MODEL

After analysing the relevant literature, a conceptual model for applying PTG in the SANDF is proposed and is represented graphically in Figure 11.2 below. The model assumes that PTG is a life-long process and consists broadly of three components. The first component deals with the different phases of employment/deployment in the SANDF, which are viewed as relevant to PTG. The second deals with various systems that can be applied to foster PTG and the last component is about the role players, and about following a progressive approach that is developmental.

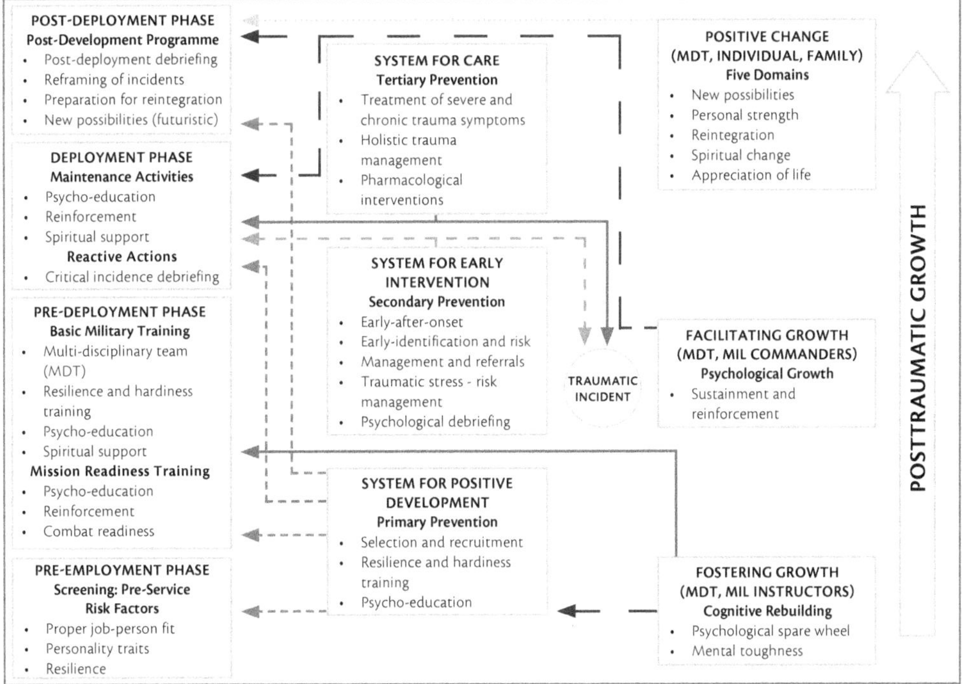

Figure 11.2 Conceptual SANDF Posttraumatic growth (PTG) model

(Compiled by N.J. Mashatola & P.C. Bester)

The first component starts with the pre-employment phase, dealing with recruitment and selection of prospective employees, where screening should be done for what is referred to as pre-service risk factors. During this phase, it is essential to ensure proper person-job fit based on the soldier's basic profile as provided through psychometric and related tests. The SANDF's recruits should thus satisfy the physical and mental resilience requirements from the start. In recruitment, the selection process will focus on specific personality and related traits that will predict a predisposition to PTG. Military psychologists, as part of the MDT, will play a vital role in the selection process.

Once individuals with a predisposition towards PTG are selected, then PTG begins to be fostered in the pre-deployment phase. This includes basic military training and mission readiness training. The pre-deployment phase already involves the MIT, consisting of various health care practitioners, the chaplain and the military instructors. During basic military training, the focus will be on resilience and hardiness training, psycho-education by military psychologists and spiritual support by the chaplain. The second component of the model becomes relevant, referred to as a system of positive development. The aim here is primary prevention, which began at recruitment and selection, and is then developed through resilience and hardiness training and psycho-education. Before deployment, the various military units will also undertake combat readiness training, but one of the focus areas will be mission readiness training directly before deployment to a specific mission area. During training, the focus will be on the reinforcement of preceding PTG-promoting activities, as well as tailored psycho-education targeting newly identified mission-specific needs, if these were left unaddressed previously.

Primary prevention still takes place in the mission area or during what is referred to as the deployment phase. The focus here is on maintenance activities such as reinforcement, psycho-education and spiritual support for deployed soldiers. It is during the deployment phase that a traumatic incident is most likely to occur, although in general, it can occur at any time in a person's life. This necessitates reactive action and where early intervention systems become relevant. In terms of the possible development of PTSD, it is here that secondary prevention initiatives become essential, with early-after-onset actions such as PD or critical incident debriefing. This process identifies any risk or susceptibility to PTSD with referrals being managed as part of traumatic stress risk management.

During the post-deployment phase, the system for positive development continues, as there is always the likelihood of future deployments. The system of care related to tertiary prevention starts in reaction to a critical incident, whether during the deployment phase or whenever it takes place after the early intervention when the soldier has been referred for follow-up treatment. This is usually for soldiers presenting with severe and chronic trauma symptoms and will require holistic trauma management and even pharmacological interventions by a psychiatrist or medical officer. It is important to emphasise again that a traumatic incident can occur at any time during a soldier's working life.

The progressive component refers to a process of growth consisting of three elements, namely fostering growth, facilitating growth and finally positive change. The fostering of growth is primarily facilitated by the MDT and the military instructors as part of the MIT during the pre-deployment phase, is used for maintenance during deployment and post-deployment and is part of the system of positive development. This may include the use of cognitive rebuilding to establish the notion of being a survivor rather than a victim after trauma. In this way, an individual develops the metaphorical 'psychological spare wheel' that can be used after exposure to trauma to ensure coping.

Facilitating growth takes place after the initial fostering of growth and involves the MDT and the military commanders. Military commanders can play an important role during communication periods and the day-to-day command of the unit. These two role players (military commanders and the MDT) are thus responsible for sustaining and reinforcement of a PTG orientation. This takes place during the deployment and post-deployment phase and is part of the system for positive development.

The final part of the growth/development component deals with positive change. This deals with the post-deployment phase where the MDT, the individual personally and the family play a role, specifically with respect to the five domains identified by Taku et al. (2008). This also relates directly to the period after a traumatic incident, when the emphasis would be on the positive change as part of PTG. The post-deployment programme must contain elements of PTG, and MDTs should include it in their post-deployment debriefings to, among other things, reframe incidents and to prepare the soldiers for reintegration with their families, society and other unit members who did not deploy with them. The emphasis is on positive change, and they will look at new possibilities that can be reaped from their experience, whether it was positive or negative.

The model can be extended to the support of veterans after retirement, but in the present volume, it must be treated as beyond the scope of this discussion. Furthermore, it is important to note that these recommendations do not suggest that this model should replace the existing processes of dealing with traumatic incidents: it is intended that the model should instead be viewed as complementary to the current processes of the SANDF's South African Military Health Service (SAMHS).

CONCLUSIONS AND RECOMMENDATIONS

Based on the reviewed literature, there is a need to redefine a conceptual PTG model and develop a multi-contextual standard PTG model for the military in general and more specifically for the SANDF. This study contributes to the literature and research community in developing and proposing a PTG model for the SANDF, which optimises positive changes that can occur after adversity. The proposed practically orientated PTG model, focusing on the positive side of trauma, may have high practical value for the military, as it can contribute, among other things, to reducing the attrition rate after exposure to trauma, as well as to maintaining individual combat-readiness. The development of the proposed PTG model for the SANDF has crucial implications for preventative interventions based on a positive psychology approach. Further development and refinement of this model may contribute to positioning PTG as a key element of military psychology, focusing as it does on improved behavioural capability.

The SANDF can attain new standards of effectiveness and efficiency by improving the psychological wellbeing of its workforce through implementation of the proposed PTG model, and by considering the following recommendations:

- Foster a positive psychology approach through psycho-education to educate commanders about the dimensions of trauma, early trauma identification and psychological risk management.
- Develop tailored professional selection processes focusing on screening military applicants for pre-service and service-related risk factors.
- Educate commanders and train military health care personnel in traumatic stress risk assessment, focusing on early trauma identification and referral.
- Offer resilience, hardiness and MT training to promoting physical and mental health on an ongoing basis.
- Deliver and promote psychosocial resilience (social capital) training through the SAMHS and its MDT.
- Provide a safe social environment through PD to afford soldiers opportunities for safe emotional expression pre-, mid-, and post-deployment.
- Put theory into practice by including formulation of PTG in the SANDF doctrine and policies and reflect it in the standing operational orders and standing work procedures related to operational deployment.

Concerning ongoing research in this field, it would be worthwhile to expand the theory and operationalise the model postulated in this research. The model can be expanded to include military veterans after retirement and the families of soldiers. Additionally, future research can explore the notion of MT training and investigate how it affects, or can dovetail with, PTG. Given what we hope to achieve through PTG, we end this chapter with the famous words of the philosopher Friedrich Nietzsche: "That which does not kill us makes us stronger."

REFERENCES

Adams, H.E. & Sutker, P.B. 2002. *Comprehensive handbook of psychopathology.* (3rd Edition). Boston NY: Kluwer Academic Publishers.

Adler, A.B., Castro, A. & Britt, T.W. 2006. *Military life: The psychology of serving in peace and combat.* New York: Praeger Security International.

Aflakseir, A., Nowroozi, S., Mollazadeh, J. & Goodarzi, M.A. 2016. The Role of Psychological Hardiness and Marital Satisfaction in Predicting Posttraumatic Growth in a Sample of Women With Breast Cancer in Isfahan. *International Journal of Cancer Management*, 9(4). Advance online publication. https://doi.org/10.17795/ijcp-4080

Aldwin, C.M. & Levenson, M.R. 2004. Posttraumatic growth: A developmental perspective. *Psychological Inquiry*, 15(1):19-92.

American Psychiatric Association [APA]. 2013. *Diagnostic and statistical manual of mental disorders (DSM-5).* (5th Edition). Washington DC: American Psychiatric Association.

Antonovsky, A. 1987. *Unraveling the mystery of health: How people manage stress and stay well.* San Francisco CA: Jossey-Bass.

Arthur, C.A., Fitzwater, J., Hardy, L., Beattie, S.J. & Bell, J. 2015. Development and validation of a military training mental toughness inventory. *Military Psychology*, 27(4):232-241. https://doi.org/10.1037/mil0000074

Bartone, P.T. & Hystad, S.W. 2010. Increasing mental hardiness for stress resilience in operational settings. In: Bartone, P.T., Johnsen, B.H., Eid, J., Violanti, J. & Laberg, J.C. (eds), *Enhancing human performance in security operations*, pp.257-274. Springfield, IL: Charles C. Thomas.

Bartone, P.T. 2000. Hardiness as a resiliency factor for United States forces in the Gulf War. In: Violanti, J.M., Paton, D. & Dunning, C. (eds), Posttraumatic stress intervention: *Challenges, issues, and perspectives*, pp.115-133. Springfield IL: C. Thomas.

Bester, P. 2016. Military psychology for conventional operations in Africa. In: Van Dyk, G.A.J. (ed.), *Military psychology for Africa*, pp.1-37. Stellenbosch: African sun Media.

Brooks, M. 2018. Rethinking post-traumatic growth: Psychological processes, outcomes and individual differences between survivors of multiple types of adverse events. Doctoral dissertation, University of Central Lancashire, UK. Available at http://clok.uclan.ac.uk/25394/.

Cacioppo, J.T., Reis, H.T. & Zautra, A.J. 2011. Social resilience: The value of social fitness with an application to the military. *American Psychologist*, 66(1):43-51.

Calhoun, L.G. & Tedeschi, R.G. (eds). 2006. *Handbook of posttraumatic growth: Research and practice.* New York: Routledge.

Calhoun, L.G., Cann, A. & Tedeschi, R.G. 2012. The posttraumatic growth model: Socio-cultural considerations. In: Weiss, T. & Berger, R. (eds), *Posttraumatic growth and culturally competent practice: Lessons learned from around the globe* (eBook), pp.1-14. Hoboken NJ: Wiley.

Carlson, E.B., Palmieri, P.A. & Spain, D.A. 2017. Development and preliminary performance of a risk factor screen to predict posttraumatic psychological disorder after trauma exposure. *General Hospital Psychiatry*, 46:25-31.

Cohen, K. & Collens, P. 2013. The impact of trauma work on trauma workers: A metasynthesis on vicarious trauma and vicarious posttraumatic growth. *Psychological Trauma: Theory, Research, Practice, and Policy*, 5(6):570-580.

De Soir, E. 2017. Psychological adjustment after military operations: The utility of postdeployment decompression for supporting health readjustment. In: Bowles, S.V. & Bartone, P.T. (eds), *Handbook of military psychology: Clinical and organizational practice*, pp.89-103. New York: Springer.

Deahl, M.P., Srinivasan, M., Jones, N., Thomas, J., Neblett, C. & Jolly, A. 2000. Preventing psychological trauma in soldiers: The role of operational stress training and psychological debriefing. *British Journal of Medical Psychology*, 73(1):77-85.

Dhladhla, T.J. & Van Dyk, G.A.J. 2007. *Management of stress and post-traumatic stress in the South African National Defence Force: A model for discussion.* 1st Bi-Annual Conference of the School for Defence and Resource: Deployment Challenges of Peacekeeping Operations in Africa Management (South African Military Academy), 10-12 September 2007, Saldanha Bay, South Africa.

Dodd, N. 2016. Selection of soldiers and military personnel. In: Van Dyk, G.A.J. (ed.), *Military psychology for Africa*, pp.87-128. Stellenbosch: African Sun Media.

Escolas, S.M., Pitts, B.L., Safer, M.A. & Bartone, P.T. 2013. The protective value of hardiness on military posttraumatic stress symptoms. *Military Psychology*, 25(2):116-123. https://doi.org/10.1037/h0094953

Fitzwater, J., Arthur, C. & Hardy, L. 2018. 'The tough get tougher': Mental skills training with elite military recruits. *Sport, Exercise and Performance Psychology*, 7(1):93-107. https://doi.org/10.1037/spy0000101

Ford, J., Tennen, H. & Albert, D. 2008. A contrarian view of growth following adversity. In: Joseph, S. & Linley, P.A. (eds), *Trauma, recovery and growth: Positive psychological perspectives on posttraumatic stress*, pp.297-324. Hoboken NJ: Wiley.

Frazier, P.A., Conlon, A. & Glaser, T. 2001. Positive and negative life changes following sexual assault. *Journal of Consulting and Clinical Psychology*, 69(6):1048-1055.

Friedman, M.J. 2006. Posttraumatic stress disorder among military returnees from Afghanistan and Iraq. *American Journal of Psychiatry*, 163(4):586-593.

Grundlingh, A. 2016. New military leaders for new wars in Africa. In: Van Dyk, G.A.J. (ed.), *Military psychology for Africa*, pp.323-347. Stellenbosch: African Sun Media.

Gucciardi, D.F. Hanton, S., Gordon, S., Mallett, C.J., Temby, P. 2014. The concept of mental toughness: Tests of dimensionality, nomological network, and traitness. *Journal of Personality*, 83(1):26-44. https://doi.org/10.1111/jopy.12079

Helgeson, V.S., Reynolds, K.A. & Tomich, P.L. 2006. A meta-analytic review of benefit finding and growth. *Journal of Consulting and Clinical Psychology*, 74(5):797-816.

Hornby, S.J. 2015. *Heroes and hooligans: Men's experiences of resilience and belonging in posttraumatic stress disorder recovery*. Master's dissertation, University of Prince Edward Island, Charlottetown, Canada. Available at https://bit.ly/2wt04CS

Inbar, D., Solomon, Z., Spiro, S. & Aviram, U. 1989. Commanders' attitude toward the nature, causality, and severity of combat stress reaction. *Military Psychology*, 1(4):215-233.

Joseph, S. 2015. Preface. In: S. Joseph (ed.), *Positive psychology in practice: Promoting human flourishing in work, health, education, and everyday life* (2nd Edition), pp.xi-xiii. Hoboken NJ: Wiley.

Joseph, S., Murphy, D. & Regel, S. 2012. An affective-cognitive processing model of post-traumatic growth. *Clinical Psychology & Psychotherapy*, 19(4):316-325. https://doi.org/10.1002/cpp.1798

Kampman, H., Hefferon, K., Wilson, M. & Beale, J. 2015. "I can do things now that people thought were impossible, actually, things that I thought were impossible": A meta-synthesis of the qualitative findings on posttraumatic growth and severe physical injury. *Canadian Psychology*, 56(3):283-294.

Kasujja, R.S. & Van Dyk, G.A.J. 2013. *A psychological evaluation of war affected families in Uganda*. Saarbrücken, Germany: Lambert Academic Publishing.

Keyes, C.L.M., Fredrickson, B.L. & Park, N. 2012. Positive psychology and the quality of life. In: Land, K.C., Michalos, A.C. & Sirgy, M.J. (eds), *Handbook of social indicators and quality of life research*, pp.99-112. New York: Springer.

Kobasa, S. C. (1979). Stressful life events, personality, and health: An inquiry into hardiness. *Journal of Personality and Social Psychology*, 37(1):1-11.

Kunz, S., Joseph, S., Geyh, S. & Peter, C. 2018. Coping and posttraumatic growth: A longitudinal comparison of two alternative views. *Rehabilitation Psychology*, 63(2):240-249. https://doi.org/10.1037/rep0000205

Kunz, S., Joseph, S., Geyh, S. & Peter, C. 2019. Perceived posttraumatic growth and depreciation after spinal cord injury: Actual or illusory? *Health Psychology*, 38(1):53-62. https://doi.org/10.1037/hea0000676

Leaman, S.C., Kearns, M.C. & Rothbaum, B.O. 2013. Prevention and early intervention: PTSD following traumatic events. *Focus*, 11(3):321-327. https://doi.org/10.1176/appi.focus.11.3.321

Lee, J.A., Luxton, D.D., Reger, G.M. & Gahm, G.A. 2010. Confirmatory factor analysis of posttraumatic growth inventory with a sample of soldiers previously deployed in support of the Iraq and Afghanistan Wars. *Journal of Clinical Psychology*, 66(7):813-819. https://doi.org/10.1002/jclp.20692

Lilienfeld, S.O. 2007. Psychological treatments that cause harm. *Perspectives on Psychological Science*, 2(1):53-70. https://doi.org/10.1111/j.1745-6916.2007.00029.x

Lin, Y., Mutz, J., Clough, P.J. & Papageorgiou, K.A. 2017. Mental toughness and individual differences in learning, educational and work performance, psychological wellbeing, and personality: A systematic review. *Frontiers in Psychology*, 8: article 1345 (15 pages). https://doi.org/10.3389/fpsyg.2017.01345

Lindstrom, C.M., Cann, A., Calhoun, L.G. & Tedeschi, R.G. 2013. The relationship of core belief challenge, rumination, disclosure, and sociocultural elements of posttraumatic growth. *Psychological Trauma:Theory, Research, Practice, and Policy*, 5(1):50-55. https://doi.org/10.1037/a0022030

Linley, P.A., Joseph, S., Cooper, R., Harris, S. & Meyer, C. 2003. Positive and negative changes following vicarious exposure to the September 11 terrorist attacks. *Journal of Traumatic Stress*, 16(5):481-485.

Linley, P.A. & Joseph, S. 2004. Positive change following trauma and adversity: A review. *Journal of Traumatic Stress*, 17(1):11-21.

Looney, J.D. 2017. Darkest before the dawn: Post-traumatic growth in the military. In: Macintyre, A., Lagacé-Roy, D. & Lindsay, D.R. (eds), *Global views on military stress and resilience*, pp.191-206. Kingston: Canadian Defence Academy Press.

Martin, G. 2019. Female SANDF commander leads combat engagement in Sudan. DefenceWeb, 16 January. Available at http://bit.ly/2UjSphN

Mawji, N. 2016. Post-traumatic growth and terrorism, Doctoral thesis, University of Leicester. Available at https://lra.le.ac.uk/handle/2381/39348.

McFarland, C. & Alvaro, C. 2000. The impact of motivation on temporal comparisons: Coping with traumatic events by perceiving personal growth. *Journal of Personality and Social Psychology*, 79(3):327-343.

Mitchell, M.M., Gallaway, M.S., Millikan, A.M. & Bell, M.R. 2013. Combat exposure, unit cohesion, and demographic characteristics of soldiers reporting posttraumatic growth. *Journal of Loss and Trauma*, 18(5):383-395.

Moodley, R. & West, W. 2005. *Integrating traditional healing practice into counseling and psychotherapy*. Thousand Oaks CA: Sage.

Morris, B.A., Shakespeare-Finch, J., Rieck, M. & Newbery, J. 2005. Multidimensional nature of posttraumatic growth in an Australian population. *Journal of Traumatic Stress*, 18(5):575-585.

Mphofu, R. & Van Dyk, G.A.J. 2016. A model to apply military psychology in Africa: The case of Bangui. In: Van Dyk, G.A.J. (ed.), *Military psychology for Africa*, pp.401-423. Stellenbosch: African Sun Media.

Pak, C. 2007. Transcendence in resilient American POWs: A narrative analysis. Doctoral dissertation, The Catholic University of America, Washington DC. Available at https://cuislandora.wrlc.org

Park, C.L. & Helgeson, V.S. 2006. Introduction to the special section: Growth following highly stressful life events – current status and future directions. *Journal of Consulting and Clinical Psychology*, (74)5:791-796. https://doi.org/10.1037/0022-006X.74.5.791

Perry, M. J. 2014. A staff paper for the Director Psychology on the efficacy of psychological debriefing. Port Elizabeth: Area Military Health Unit, Eastern Cape Headquarters, 10 September.

Peterson, C., Craw, M.J., Park, N. & Erwin, M.S. 2011. Resilience and leadership in dangerous contexts. In: Sweeney, P.J., Matthews, M.D. & Lester, P.B. (eds), *Leadership in dangerous situations: A handbook for the armed forces, emergency services, and first responders*, pp.78-96. Annapolis MD: Naval Institute Press.

Sandvik, A.M., Gjevestad, E., Aabrekk, E., Øhman, P., Kjendlie, P., Hystad, S.W., Bartone, P., Hansen, A.L. & Johnsen, B.J. 2019. Physical fitness and psychological hardiness as predictors of parasympathetic control in response to stress: A Norwegian police simulator training study. *Journal of Police and Criminal Psychology*. https://doi.org/10.1007/s11896-019-09323-8

StrategyPage. 2019. Morale: The hidden costs of war and peace. Morale, 13 April, *Strategy Page: The news as history*. Available at https://bit.ly/33L8Loj

Taku, K., Cann, A., Calhoun, L.G. & Tedeschi, R.G. 2008. The factor structure of the Posttraumatic Growth Inventory: A comparison of five models using confirmatory factor analysis. *Journal of Traumatic Stress*, 21(2):158-164. https://doi.org/10.1002/jts.20305

Tedeschi, R.G. 2011. Posttraumatic growth in combat veterans. *Journal of Clinical Psychology in Medical Settings*, 18(2):137-144. https://doi.org/10.1007/s10880-011-9255-2

Tedeschi, R.G. & Calhoun, L.G. 1995. *Trauma and transformation: Growing in the aftermath of suffering*. Thousand Oaks CA: Sage.

Tedeschi, R.G. & Calhoun, L.G. 2004. Posttraumatic growth: Conceptual foundations and empirical evidence. *Psychological Inquiry*, 15:1-18. https://doi.org/10.1207/s15327965pli1501_01

Tedeschi, R.G., Calhoun, L.G. & Groleau, J.M. 2015. Clinical applications of posttraumatic growth. In: Joseph, S. (ed.), *Positive psychology in practice: Promoting human flourishing in work, health, education, and everyday life* (2nd Edition), pp.503-518. Hoboken NJ: Wiley.

Van Diemen. E. 2019. SANDF's Cape Flats deployment a 'success', but boots, barrels and bullets won't end gangsterism, says Defence Minister. *News 24*, 27 August. Available at https://bit.ly/2vRiywu

Van Dyk, G.A.J. 2016. Trauma management: A holistic approach. In: Van Dyk, G.A.J. (ed.), *Military psychology for Africa*, pp.129-147. Stellenbosch: African Sun Media.

Walsh, D.M.W., Morrison, T.G., Conway, R.J., Rogers, E., Sullivan, F.J. & Groarke, A. 2018. A model to predict psychological and health related adjustment in men with prostate cancer: The role of posttraumatic growth, physical posttraumatic growth, resilience and mindfulness. *Frontiers in Psychology*, 9: article 136 (12 pages). https://doi.org/10.3389/fpsyg.2018.00136.

Webb, K.C. 2013. Effects of religiosity and combat exposure to predict combat service member posttraumatic growth. Doctoral dissertation, George Fox University, Newberg OR. Available at http://digitalcommons.georgefox.edu/psyd/120.

Wilson, J.P. (ed.). 2005. *The posttraumatic self: Restoring meaning and wholeness to personality*. New York: Routledge.

Zaccaro, S.J., Weis, E.J., Hilton, R.M. & Jefferies, J. 2011. Building resilient teams. In: Sweeney, P.J., Matthews, M.D. & Lester, P.B. (eds.), *Leadership in dangerous situations: A handbook for the armed forces, emergency services, and first responders*, pp.182-201. Annapolis MD: Naval Institute Press.

Zalta, A.K., Gerhart, J., Hall, B., Rajan, K.B., Vechiu, C., Canetti, D. & Hobfoll, S.E. 2017. Self-reported posttraumatic growth predicts greater subsequent posttraumatic stress amidst war and terrorism. *Anxiety, Stress, and Coping*, 30(2):176-187. https://doi.org/10.1080/10615806.2016.1229467

Zoellner, T. & Maercker, A. 2006. Posttraumatic growth in clinical psychology – A critical review and introduction of a two component model. *Clinical Psychology Review*, 26(5):626-653. https://doi.org/10.1016/j.cpr.2006.01.008

12

Conclusion

Nicole Dodd
Justin van der Merwe
Petrus Bester

The preceding chapters presented a snapshot of various aspects of military psychology in the South African context. They set out to provide insight into the psychological 'climate' in selected units, into the processes of cognition and personality of SANDF members, as well as looking at new opportunities for an expanded scope of practice in the field. Here, we gather together some of the resultant recommendations for future research, and also some practical recommendations for enhancing the performance of the SANDF.

Military psychology is tasked with two separate forms of optimisation. The first is the optimal utilisation by the SANDF of the soldier as a resource. The second aspect relates to the optimisation of the soldier's wellbeing. All of this is done with the aim of achieving what the current Deputy Surgeon General (Ndhlovu, 2019 p.19) refers to as: "mental and cognitive superiority over our opponents". As military psychologists the Directorate Psychology serves both the organisation and the member and must seek to reconcile these two tasks in a way that maximises the likelihood of a positive outcome for both parties. With this aim in mind, the military psychologist must manage the relationship between the SANDF and its members not only during their time in the forces, but in the time before (recruitment and selection) and the time after (separation).

In this volume we have touched on some of the predictors of efficiency in the SANDF, opening up opportunities for future research into their use in the SANDF's recruitment, selection and utilisation practices to select those individuals who will require minimum additional interventions in future. Related to this matter is the issue of how to optimise the fit between the soldier and his or her mustering. In this regard the employment relationship plays a vital role.

Once the employment relationship is established, education, training and development are essential tools for optimising force utilisation. Accordingly, many of the chapters dealt with the activities of the South African Military Academy. The Academy's activities merited attention because of the role the institution plays in laying the foundation for future utilisation and in developing the SANDF's future leaders.

Because of the cost involved in military education (students are employees and earn a monthly salary) students must be selected carefully for education, training and development opportunities in the military. The selection process has to go beyond the assessment of fitness and basic ability to assess other determinants of academic success. The SANDF's student body is conscientious, emotionally stable, agreeable, extraverted and resilient to a far greater extent than the civilian population and in comparison with international norms; and the naval population also displays high levels of resilience and mental toughness), indicating that the SANDF possesses a deep talent pool that needs only to be unlocked through appropriate and active management and development. The SANDF's potential students are, however, under-prepared for higher education. This is a national problem, not only that of the SANDF (Mungal & Cloete, 2016). Yet despite their lack of formal preparation for higher education, the students of SAMA demonstrate better memory and understanding than the national norm and the Academy continues to maintain high throughput levels despite the challenges faced.

The findings reflected in this book highlight how the contribution of military psychology – in terms of positive participation in the work, studies and family domains of people's lives – can have a beneficial effect on the other domains. In light of this, the SANDF should consider ways of facilitating more effective functioning in soldiers' studies and family lives, to improve their performance as soldiers. Achieving appropriate balance in their studies and their participation in family life can energise soldiers and motivate them to work harder for the SANDF. Investing in education, training and development is wasted if the organisation constrains the students' capacity for achievement through unsupported practices. Thus, students' circumstances must be considered, including their family, financial and cultural obligations. Military students are likely to experience negative spillover between work, family and study domains if they are incorrectly selected and then inadequately supported. The findings laid out in the book point to the need to understand and accommodate soldiers' circumstances in order to maximise their effectiveness during their employment as military personnel. Consequently, military student support presents itself as an area in need of further consideration, both in practical terms and in investigative research.

The notion that there should be individualised consideration is a departure from the traditional standard practice of encouraging the soldier to adapt to the demands of the SANDF; but the need for individualised consideration is a recurring theme in the chapters. Drawing on research and findings in the wider society, it has been shown that every employee has needs that might differ from his or her counterparts. Future research could explore transformational leadership and the potential for individualised consideration from the organisation's perspective in the SANDF. This would entail linking every employee's priorities with the organisation's.

Personal differences aside, cultural differences exist among the members of the SANDF. These differences suggest that there is a need for a critical conversation around decolonisation in the SANDF. Is the SANDF accommodating its multicultural workforce effectively? South Africa is a melting pot of cultures, and each places its expectations on its own members. Work–family interface and cultural demands look different for different members of the SANDF. Linked to this is the economic burden faced by a large proportion of members because of the large number of dependents who rely on them for financial support. There are no 'uniform' culturally related needs in the SANDF.

Although there is a need to be cognisant of South Africa's unique cultural and socioeconomic context, and to accept the demands this places on the SANDF's members, it is also vital that one begins to benchmark against international practices, particularly in the field of Military Psychology. This will mean more international research cooperation in our research projects, going forward.

The contributions in this book point towards the SANDF's need to innovate and adapt, owing to changing environmental conditions and because of the profile of the SANDF's workforce. This is illustrated by shortcomings in the psychological assessments that are highlighted in this book. Many of the instruments of measurement at the SANDF's disposal do not 'speak to' the SANDF's multicultural population. Military Psychologists must therefore begin to develop and adapt instruments that meet the needs of the population that they are serving and can better serve the needs of the organisation in a changing environment. All eleven of the country's official languages are represented among SANDF employees, and this means that test development and adaptation should receive significant research attention. The attention is clearly warranted because (despite their shortcomings) variables such as resilience have demonstrated incredible utility for selection, utilisation and development in the SANDF, but as predictors must be measured using instruments that are valid, reliable and fair across cultural differences. Further research into variables such as hardiness, mental toughness, posttraumatic growth and conscientiousness will enable the SANDF to develop the capacity to 'inoculate' its members against the strains they face.

The chapters signal the need for a broad shift towards positive psychology and proactivity in the management of wellness in the South African military context. In keeping with this, the mandate of SANDF military psychologists, in relation to soldiers' actual or potential exposure to trauma, will have to shift from treatment of negative symptoms to fostering resilience and growth. This shift will include devising new and creative ways of contending with post-traumatic stress disorder and facilitating posttraumatic growth and mental toughness. It will be a shift away from 'pathogenesis' towards the creation of innovative, local practices that promote 'fortigenesis' and 'salutogenesis'; in other words, practices that generate strength and wellness. A paradigm shift like this provides an opportunity to decolonise military psychology in South Africa and to accommodate the country's rich cultural profile into its practices.

This volume presented three areas of focus that merit further empirical investigation. First, Mashatola, Dodd and Van Zyl's 'work-study-family interface' merits further investigation with a broader sample. Arendse's 'psychosocial wellbeing model' should also be expanded and empirically tested. Finally, Mashatola and Bester's 'posttraumatic growth model' could be applied and tested in a clinical setting.

A further pressure towards innovative thinking and practice lies in the circumstance that the SANDF has to do more with fewer resources every year. South Africa's defence budget has declined over the past five years (Husseini, 2019), and the economic outlook suggests that military spending is unlikely to be prioritised soon. The SANDF will have to be frugal. The output of every soldier must therefore be maximised. This calls for innovative human resources management practices that prioritise intrinsic rather than extrinsic motivators of performance.

South Africa's currently distressed economy can result in dissatisfied soldiers remaining with the organisation because they have few opportunities for employment outside the organisation; they might thus be demotivated and plateaued, and this could have an adverse effect on morale. The SANDF must, therefore, motivate people who have very different reasons for enlisting and remaining with the organisation: people who will engage wholeheartedly in the organisation.

That said, relationships in the SANDF are not purely transactional. Instead, organisational commitment is based on relationships and kept promises. Satisfied, educated members of the SANDF are more likely to be engaged than those who are dissatisfied. Engaged employees are, in turn, more likely to remain with the organisation. This then also places a burden of responsibility on the SANDF as the employing organisation.

In order to achieve a return on the investment in developing skilled staff, the SANDF has to prioritise their retention. It is recommended that leadership should follow a proactive approach by taking cognisance of factors leading to turnover intention, and to adapt styles of leadership to dissuade staff from leaving the SANDF. Fortunately, the risk of turnover seems to be low. For example, the students at the South African Military Academy appear to have high levels of affective commitment and show limited experience of psychological contract breach and violation, pointing to the substantial likelihood of retaining these talented junior officers.

This volume fell short of addressing issues that affect the periods during and after soldiers' separation from the SANDF. South Africa has had a violent past, and although the present democratic dispensation has been peaceful, many veterans saw major combat during their time in service. This area merits careful research as there is most likely residual trauma, and unresolved issues may stem from veterans' military experiences. There are several areas where more research could be useful when it comes to staff separations. Research could be conducted into the effective management of career transitions, for example, for those who are retiring, and those whose contracts are not renewed. Both groups are still relatively young when they separate from the SANDF and must make the transition to civilian working life. This separation period can be a stressful time in that soldiers' identities are often strongly linked to their work; more can be done to facilitate a smooth career transition.

Many of the chapters in this volume employed cross-sectional survey research and as a result, provided a snapshot of the circumstances faced by the SANDF at present. Future volumes could focus less on 'what is happening' and more on practitioner-led solutions related to 'what should be done next.' From the above it is clear that there is still a great deal of research to do, within the domain of military psychology in general, and more specifically within the SANDF. We would like to believe that this volume will serve as a platform for the launching of noteworthy ongoing research.

REFERENCES

Husseini, T. 2019. South African military spending: what does the future hold? *Army Technology: Analysis*, 3 May. Available at https://bit.ly/2y2lohz

Mungal, A. & Cloete, M. 2016. Preparing underprepared students for higher education and beyond: The development and implementation of an integrated project. *Accounting Education*, 25(3):203-222. https://doi.org/10.1080/09639284.2016.1157760

Ndhlovu, N. 2019. Discussion paper on enabling the South African Military Health Service to deliver an affordable and best-quality military healthcare service, 7 January, Pretoria.

www.ingramcontent.com/pod-product-compliance
Lightning Source LLC
LaVergne TN
LVHW080330110826
845155LV00024B/140